YOUNG ADULT LITERATURE IN ACTION

A Librarian's Guide

Rosemary Chance

Library and Information Science Text Series

LIBRARIES

UNLIMITED

A Member of the Greenwood Publishing Group

Westport, Connecticut • London

Library of Congress Cataloging-in-Publication Data

Chance, Rosemary.
    Young adult literature in action : a librarian's guide / Rosemary Chance.
        p. cm. — (Library and information science text series)
    Includes bibliographical references and index.
    ISBN: 978–1–59158–558–9 (alk. paper)
    ISBN: 978–1–59158–555–8 (pbk. : alk. paper)
    1. Teenagers—Books and reading—United States—Bibliography. 2. Young
adults—Books and reading—United States—Bibliography. 3. Young adult
literature—Bibliography.   4. Young adult literature, American—Bibliography.
5. High school libraries—United States—Book lists. I. Title.
    Z1037.C446 2008
    028.1'625—dc22   2008027090

British Library Cataloguing in Publication Data is available.

Library of Congress Catalog Card Number: 2008027090
ISBN: 978–1–59158–558–9
        978–1–59158–555–8 (pbk.)

First published in 2008

Libraries Unlimited, 88 Post Road West, Westport, CT 06881
A Member of the Greenwood Publishing Group, Inc.
www.lu.com

Printed in the United States of America

The paper used in this book complies with the
Permanent Paper Standard issued by the National
Information Standards Organization (Z39.48–1984).

10 9 8 7 6 5 4 3 2 1

Contents

Acknowledgments

To Blanche Woolls, who invited me to undertake this project and who kept encouraging me. To Sylvia Vardell, who collaborated with me on the title and on fleshing out Blanche's concept for this book.

To Charles Chance, my beloved husband, who didn't complain about the time I spent at the computer instead of traveling in our RV.

Thanks to each of you! What an experience this has been!

Introduction

I am a cheerleader for young adult books! From my first Nancy Drew book, read almost 50 years ago, through Richard Peck's novels, Harry Potter fantasies, and Michael Printz Award winners, I have recommended authors and their books to anyone who would listen. My first job as a librarian was to work alongside another librarian, who was the cheerleader sponsor for Wunsche Middle School in Spring, Texas. During football season it was usual to have cheerleaders practicing in the library next to a traditional card catalog housed in a massive wooden cabinet. Initially, it was disconcerting to hear girls cheering loudly in the library. I grimaced as the quiet of the library was shattered with their enthusiasm. The old wooden floors vibrated. But gradually, I began to understand that all this spirit and energy was good. I envisioned it waking up the characters in the books and began to wonder if they were listening and that suddenly Ponyboy (and others from S. E. Hinton's *The Outsiders*) might leap from the pages and cheer and jump around in the dark after we had left for the evening.

Young adult books, both fiction and nonfiction, that made me laugh or cry, that surprised me or tantalized me, those are the books I shared with friends, family, and with middle school and high school students. Those are the books I still love to share. If nothing happens in a book to intrigue me, if no character wins my heart, if the style is annoying, then I don't want to talk about those books.

The purpose of this textbook is to provide an activity-oriented survey of young adult literature for undergraduate and graduate students seeking licensure and degrees leading to careers working with young adults in school and public libraries. This textbook is intended to acquaint college students with classic and current literature published for young adults. Although young adult literature can refer to anything that young adults read, for the purposes of this textbook I'll focus primarily on books published for young adults, using the definition agreed upon by the Young Adult Library Services Association (YALSA), a division of the American Library Association. YALSA defines young adults as ages 12 through 18. This textbook will focus on the books specifically published for those ages, with a few exceptions. One exception relates to format—literary graphic novels and manga. Interest in graphic novels is expanding rapidly, and many are published for adults or without an age recommendation. A second exception is the recognition of young adults' interest in books published for adults. Two YALSA award lists—the Alex Award and Outstanding Books for the College Bound—contain adult titles of interest to young adults.

The goal of the textbook is two-fold: (1) to provide an overview of young adult literature with recommended titles and (2) to suggest activities for promoting and using literature with young adults in middle schools, high schools, and public libraries. I hope that future school librarians and public librarians will find the information useful as they begin working with young adults.

The first chapter—An Introduction to Young Adults and Their Literature—describes young adults and their literature and provides lists of awards, review sources, and professional organizations and resources. Subsequent chapters describe young adult literature according to genres, using award-winning titles, titles popular with young adults, and titles that I particularly admire. Chapter 2: Quick Reads includes comic books, graphic novels, series books, magazines, short stories, and poetry. Chapter 3: Realistic Fiction focuses on both the lighter side and the more serious side of modern realistic fiction, including historical fiction at the end of the chapter. Humor, mysteries, wilderness adventure/survival stories, and sports stories make up the lighter side; stories of violence, substance abuse, and death make up the darker side. And last, historical fiction about war and specific historical periods conclude the chapter. Chapter 4: Fantastic Fiction presents fantasy, horror, supernatural, and science fiction. Chapter 5: Informational Books includes biographies, autobiographies, memoirs, and other informational books. Chapter 6: Cultural Diversity shares literature of many cultures, both ethnic and international. Finally, Chapter 7: The Freedom to Read defines intellectual freedom and provides scenarios to help understand the role of a librarian who faces complaints and challenges in school and public libraries.

Each chapter includes specific activities for promoting and discussing specific genres and titles and suggested activities to be used when promoting any young adult literature. Embedded in the text are history in action, books in action, authors in action, librarians in action, literature in action, assignments in action, and recommended professional resources, among other features, to help librarians who work with young adults.

After studying young adult literature, you will feel confident in recommending books to young adults, either singly or in groups. When the first teen asks you about a good book on the Vietnam war, you'll recommend Walter Dean Myers's *Fallen Angels*. For an intriguing fantasy, other than Harry Potter books, you'll recommend Philip Pullman's *The Golden Compass*. For a laugh-out-loud book you'll know to recommend Richard Peck's *A Long Way from Chicago* and Louise Rennison's *Angus, Thongs, and Full-Frontal Snogging*. You'll know why each of these books (and many more) are important reads for teens because you read and studied them in your young adult literature class, and you were just waiting for the right teens to recommend them to. Your cheerleading career will have begun!

Chapter 1

An Introduction to Young Adults and Their Literature

The trouble is, grownups write about teen-agers from their own memories, or else write about teen-agers from a stand-off, I'm-a-little-scared-to-get-close-they're-hairy view. Teen-agers today want to read about teen-agers today. The world is changing, yet the authors of books for teen-agers are still 15 years behind the times.

From "Teen-Agers Are for Real" by Susan Hinton (1967, 26)

At the beginning of the twenty-first century the world is changing even more rapidly than it was in the 1960s when S. E. Hinton wrote *The Outsiders*, effectively revolutionizing young adult fiction. Fortunately for young adults today, the 15-year lag between the real life of teens and the literature of teens is gone. Authors are writing about issues and concerns important to young adults. The taboos of the twentieth century have disappeared from poetry, fiction, and informational books, helping to open up literary possibilities. In this chapter young adults will be defined by age, as individuals, through reading interests, by type of reader, and through developmental tasks. Young adult literature will begin to be defined historically and through the viewpoints of award criteria. Chapters that follow will focus on the variety and specifics of genres.

DEFINING YOUNG ADULTS

Until the mid-twentieth century there wasn't a clear designation for young adult literature. Once children grew out of juvenile books, they read adult classics. Sometimes teenagers fell into the juvenile category. Today the term "juvenile" suffers from negative connotations, such as childish and immature.

The publication of J. D. Salinger's *Catcher in the Rye* in 1951 and other coming-of-age novels marked the beginning of so-called adolescent literature. The term "adolescent" became popular and continues to be used today although it has an outdated feel to it. Today's preferred term is "young adult," although in recent years experts in the field of young adult services and literature have suggested alternative terms. In his *Booklist* column Michael Cart (2005) proposed three categories: "middle school" for ages 10–14; "teen" for ages 13–19 (or 12–18); and "young adult" for those 18–25 (or 16–24).

The truth is that it's difficult to find one term that's appropriate for this special group of people. It's impossible to draw a sharp line between children and teens. Puberty may emerge with little prior notice, and a child becomes a preteen or a teen. Still, adults struggle to label this ever-changing population. The Young Adult Library Services Association (YALSA) of the American Library Association (ALA) defines young adults as youth aged 12 through 18. This textbook will focus on materials published specifically for these ages, although some picture books and adult books that have young adult appeal will be described.

Defining Young Adults as Individuals

It's tempting to try to define a typical young adult. If we know what a typical young adult is like, then we will know which materials to select and purchase and promote. Of course, that's not the way it works. There isn't a typical young adult. They are defined by their heritage, environment, and individuality, just as adults are. Today's young adults live in cities, suburbs, and rural settings. They are valedictorians, athletes, chess players, musicians, and sometimes all of those at once. They are defined by what they read, what they watch, and what they purchase. Their parents may be Asian, African, Jewish, Italian, Mexican, or any of numerous cultural and ethnic groups. Young adults are popular at school; they are also bullied and invisible. They are religious or not. They take drugs and drink alcohol; they are healthy. They are sexually active or not. They perform community services. They go to prison. They are kind, and they are violent. They are obese; they are thin. The challenge for librarians is to find the right books for such a diverse population and the right book for the individual.

Defining Young Adults through Reading Preferences, Interests, and Choices

It's relatively simple to determine which books young adults want to read. Two of the best ways to make that determination is by asking the young adults you serve and by observing what they check out and read.

Reading Surveys

Reading surveys give you insight into the reading preferences, interests, and choices of young adults. Through reading surveys you can determine what individual readers are already reading and what they want to read. By collating the data on the surveys, you can determine what the majority of readers want to read. For results a librarian can use to better understand the reading interests of young adults, questions should be both open-ended and specific. For a quick survey, ask a dozen or fewer questions. Answering these questions shouldn't feel like a homework task to teens. Ask for specific titles of books, movies, and magazines they have enjoyed. These choices will give you clues to similar titles. Ask what topics they're interested in reading about. It may be the first time anyone has ever asked them. Ask about favorite authors. Prepare to be surprised at the range of authors, including authors of children's and adult books. Ask if they prefer novels to informational books. Ask what types of fiction and nonfiction they like to read.

Reading Survey Questions

1. What is the title of the last book you read for pleasure?
2. What is the title of the last movie you watched and enjoyed?
3. If you have a choice between a really good novel and a really good informational book on a topic you're interested in, which would you choose?
4. What are some topics you would like to read about?
5. Would you rather read a novel or an informational book about those topics?
6. What's the title of the best book you ever read?
7. What's the title of the best movie you ever saw?
8. Who's your favorite author (or authors)?
9. Which magazines do you like to read?
10. What do you read on the Internet?

In schools, surveys can be distributed through reading or English classes to reach every student, or they can be available in the library at the circulation desk or as part of a book display. In public libraries, librarians can distribute surveys to young adult volunteers, to members of advisory groups, and to young adults as they check out books at the circulation desk or when they attend library programs. As a thank you, offer a special bookmark or a cookie to those who complete the survey and return it to you by a specific date. Share the results of the survey with teachers, parents, and other librarians in your community. It will be tempting to rely on circulation records to help you get to know the reading tastes of your young adult population. Circulation records will tell you what students are checking out, but the data won't tell you if they read and liked the books.

good point!

Young Adult Reading Choices

Besides conducting local survey information about reading preferences, interests, and choices, you can examine a national list of books chosen by young adults. Young Adults' Choices, a project of the International Reading Association, is ideal for this examination. The 30 books on the annual list are selected by students in grades 7–12 with little adult interference. Middle school and high school students throughout five designated regions of the United States have access to approximately 250 new titles. Students are invited to read any of the books and submit a ballot for each book they read. Books with the most favorable ballots are placed on the annual list. For the 2007 Young Adults' Choices list, more than 11,000 ballots were submitted, making this the largest national reading project of its kind (Young Adults' Choices for 2007).

Characteristics of Popular Young Adult Fiction

From a study of books on the Young Adults' Choices lists we can learn about the characteristics of the books that young adults are choosing. In 2006, predominant book characteristics included the following:

1. Overwhelmingly, young adults chose more modern realistic fiction than fantastic or historical fiction.
2. There were almost twice as many girl protagonists as boy protagonists in the chosen books.
3. There were four times as many high school age protagonists as middle school protagonists.
4. More than half of the books were recommended for grades 11–12.
5. A fourth of the books were more than 277 pages in length.

From these characteristics we can make a few assumptions: Modern realistic fiction is more popular than historical or fantastic fiction. More girls are reading novels than are boys. Young adults are reading books with protagonists older than they are. Some young adults are reading lengthy books. In later chapters, titles from the 2006 Young Adults' Choices list will be used as examples of fiction popular with young adults today.

Using surveys and making assumptions about reading preferences, interests, and choices from a large project like Young Adults' Choices can help you make selections for your library's young adult students and patrons

Defining Young Adults as Types of Readers

Although we want to understand readers as individuals, it is also useful to understand young adults as types of readers. General guidelines can be useful when selecting and recommending books. Three special types of readers that deserve attention are reluctant readers, boy readers, and girl readers.

Reluctant Readers

Reluctant readers can read, but they will be quick to tell you that they don't like to read. Librarians want everyone to enjoy reading and to be able to read well. Bring together young adults who don't like to read and librarians who have strategies to entice them to read, and nonreaders can be changed into readers. Librarians use the following strategies to encourage reluctant readers to read:

1. Maintain an updated collection of high-interest print materials. These include short story collections, graphic novels, picture books for older

readers, illustrated informational books, short novels, and magazines covering a wide range of topics.

2. Give reluctant readers choices. Display high interest materials and let them choose. Forcing nonreaders to select a biography or a particular kind of book is counterproductive.

3. Incorporate book-related activities. Library programming should include booktalking (see chapter 3), storytelling, offering contests, bringing in authors, reading aloud, and providing time to read.

4. Get help from professional resources. Choose *Connecting with Reluctant Teen Readers: Tips, Titles, and Tools*, by Patrick Jones, Maureen L. Hartman, and Patricia Taylor, or *Reaching Reluctant Young Adult Readers: A Handbook for Librarians and Teachers*, by Edward T. Sullivan.

Boy Readers and Girl Readers

From the larger percentage of girl protagonists in the 2006 Young Adults' Choices project, we can assume that most of the readers of these books are girls. From G. Robert Carlsen, a professor and authority in YA literature, we learned that girls prefer to read about girls (Carlsen 1980). From a 1991 study (Monson and Sebesta 1991) we learned that seventh- and eighth-grade girls enjoy reading stories of mystery, romance, animals, religion, careers, comedy, and biography. From the same study we learned that boys enjoy science fiction, mystery, adventure, biography, history, and animal and sports stories. While these reading interests have changed some, they indicate that there are differences in what young adult males and females like to read. In recent years there has been a focus on what boys like to read, the perception being that not as many boys as girls like to read.

To help librarians select books that boys will read, one man took action. Jon Scieszka, author of the popular *The True Story of the 3 Little Pigs by A. Wolf*, founded the Guys Read initiative to encourage boys of all ages to keep reading and to help them find books to enjoy. For titles that boys will read visit Scieszka's Guys Read Web site at www.guysread.com. To further support his initiative, he edited a collection of writings by boys' favorite authors, titled *Guys Write for Guys Read*. Ninety-two authors and illustrators share humorous and heartfelt stories of growing up. The result is a collection to be used as brief read-alouds to introduce authors to young adults in an entertaining way.

Defining Young Adults through Developmental Tasks

Traditionally, a set of developmental tasks of young adults ages 12 through 18 are credited to the work of Robert Havighurst, based on concepts developed in the 1930s and 1940s. Havighurst defined a developmental task as "midway between an individual need and a societal demand" (1971, vi). Young adults move through many tasks on their way from childhood to adulthood. Novels can help young adults better understand and vicariously experience these critical tasks. The following questions represent physical, social, emotional, intellectual, and moral (Havighurst 1971) developmental areas.

Can I accept the way my body looks?

How do boys behave? How do girls behave?

Am I acting more mature socially?

Am I beginning to understand sexuality, marriage, and parenthood?

Can I Accept the Way My Body Looks?

Sally Nemeth's *The Heights, the Depths, and Everything in Between* presents an extreme challenge of accepting one's physique. Lucy is 5 feet 10 inches tall by seventh grade, and her best friend is a dwarf. They unrealistically expect to go unnoticed at the junior high. Of course, things change between them and around them as they grow up. Still, they remain friends.

How Do Boys Behave? How Do Girls Behave?

In Catherine Gilbert Murdock's *Dairy Queen*, D. J. Schwenk is 15 years old and does all the heavy work at her family's Wisconsin dairy farm. Once she begins training Brian Nelson, a cute quarterback from a rival team, she realizes how much she loves football. Her older brothers passed along their knowledge and love of the game. Much to the dismay of Brian, she joins her school football team. D. J. isn't afraid to be who she is.

Am I Acting More Mature Socially?

In *Here Lies the Librarian*, Richard Peck dedicates the novel to "living librarians everywhere" and proceeds to tell about Peewee (Eleanor) McGrath, a tomboy who becomes an aspiring librarian. When the town library closes after the death of the librarian, four women library science students apply for the job and are hired to share the position. Peewee puts on a dress and learns how to act at a formal library tea.

Am I Beginning to Understand Sexuality, Marriage, and Parenthood?

In *Make Lemonade* readers are privileged to an up-close view of a young single mother who struggles to support her two children. Jolly is 17 years old, poor, uneducated, and living in squalor. After advertising for a babysitter, she finds 14-year-old Verna who helps her with the children, becomes her friend, and inspires her to pursue an education.

Am I aware of other community groups outside my own?

Can I function emotionally without depending on my parents and other adults?

Do I know what career I want to pursue? Have I begun preparing for it?

What do I believe in? Do I know how to behave ethically?

Am I Aware of Other Community Groups Outside My Own?

Jordan Sonnenblick's *Notes from the Midnight Driver* shows 16-year-old Alex forced to do community service at a nursing home after getting drunk and trying to drive a car. Disgusted with the old man he's assigned to help, Alex tries to get the judge to change his assignment. Stuck with Mr. Solomon, Alex gradually becomes fond of him and learns from him. Humorous exchanges between Alex and Mr. Solomon are interwoven.

Can I Function Emotionally Without Depending On My Parents and Other Adults?

Sometimes young adults are forced to separate from their parents or other supportive adults through tragedy. In *Firestorm: Book One of the Caretaker Trilogy* by David Klass, 17-year-old Jack discovers during one dramatic evening that he's adopted and shortly afterwards his adopted parents are killed. Bewildered and bereft, Jack is completely on his own as he tries to make sense of a dog that speaks to him telepathically, a ninja babe who tries to kill him, and continuing messages that he's the only one who can save the planet.

Do I Know What Career I Want to Pursue? Have I Begun Preparing for It?

Chew on This: Everything You Don't Want to Know about Fast Food, by Eric Schlosser and Charles Wilson, is a revealing history of the fast food industry that may inspire readers to join Schlosser's mission or may simply disgust them. Verbal tours of feedlots in Greeley, Colorado, and a tour of a poultry farm in West Virginia that supplies McDonald's with chicken may have readers thinking more carefully about choosing to work at a fast food place. Information is carefully documented.

What Do I Believe in? Do I Know How to Behave Ethically?

Han Nolan's *A Summer of Kings* illustrates the awakening of 14-year-old Esther as she comes to understand racism through her friendship with King-Ray, an 18-year-old African American boy who's staying with her wealthy family during one summer. Esther's studying and exposure to King-Ray's passion about civil rights leads her to persuade her family to join her in the 1963 March on Washington.

DEFINING YOUNG ADULT LITERATURE

Flux is a major trait of young adult literature. It changes and grows as quickly as the life of a teenaged boy or girl. In the last several years, new types of literature have become established, extending the range of young adult fiction through the verse novel, the graphic novel, the crossover novel, chick lit, and dark realism. Before examining current young adult literature, it's worthwhile to view the beginnings of this literature to better understand its development into the vital literary field of today.

History in Action: Early Adult Books Read by Young People

Before books were specifically written and published for them, young adults were reading adventure stories written for adults. John Bunyan's *Pilgrim's Progress* (1678) and Daniel Defoe's *Robinson Crusoe* (1719) were read for the excitement of the story rather than for religious and didactic themes. Imitators of *Robinson Crusoe* are known as robinsonades, stories such as Johann Wyss's *Swiss Family Robinson* (1812) and Gary Paulsen's *Hatchet* (1987). Upon the republication of Anne Stephens's *Malaeksa: Indian Wife of a White Hunter* (1860), dime novels captured the attention of males seeking adventure. Featuring action and overwritten prose, dime novels, originally costing a dime and usually set in Colorado and farther west, became wildly popular for their thrilling plots (Nilsen and Donelson 2000).

Other adult adventure books avidly read by young people and considered among today's classics are Jonathan Swift's *Gulliver's Travels* (1726), Jules Verne's *Twenty Thousand Leagues Under the Sea* (1870), Robert Louis Stevenson's *Treasure Island* (1883) and *Kidnapped* (1886), Howard Pyle's *The Merry Adventures of Robin Hood* (1883), and Mark Twain's *The Adventures of Huckleberry Finn* (1884). These are some of the best-known and most popular books to capture the attention of teenagers. They continue to be in print and to appeal to an audience as classic literature.

If dime novels were satisfying reading for males, domestic novels were the answer to reading selections for females. The first domestic novel, *Wide, Wide World* (1850), was written by Elizabeth Wetherell under the pen name of Susan Warner. Her novel remained popular for forty years. Domestic novels such as Warner's featured an orphaned girl who meets a handsome man in need of redemption. Charlotte Yonge's *The Daisy Chain* (1856), a story about a large family, reflects the Christian ethic of the Victorian period. These adventures for women included moral lessons that were conspicuously absent from dime novels (Nilsen and Donelson 2000).

More History in Action: First Books Written for Young Adults

Louisa May Alcott's *Little Women* is sometimes referred to as the first young adult novel, although there was no such designation in 1868 when it was published. Unlike previous novels for women, Alcott's story more closely depicted real life with its joys and sadness but devoid of extreme sentimentality. Today *Little Women* shines as a readable and enjoyable classic story.

Published in the same year as *Little Women, Ragged Dick; or, Street Life in New York* by Horatio Alger, Jr. was the first book of a popular series for young people. Dick leaves home to find a more affluent life and through luck, goodness, and a little work, he is transformed into a respectable young man. Unlike

Alcott's timeless book, Alger's books are seldom read for pleasure because of their stilted language, unrealistic plots, and stereotypical characters. Other popular books for boys in the last half of the 1800s include "bad boy" books and adventure novels. Thomas Bailey Aldrich's *The Story of a Bad Boy* (1870) set in Portsmouth, New Hampshire, treats readers to the charming and humorous adventures of mischievous Tom (Meigs et al. 1969). Based on his boyhood recollections in Missouri, Mark Twain's *The Adventures of Tom Sawyer* (1876), like his adult book, *The Adventures of Huckleberry Finn* (1884), "combine adventure, imagination, realism, humor, and human nature to a degree which makes them—especially *Huckleberry Finn*—great books and books that are essentially American" (Meigs et al. 1969, 243). These few books mark the beginning of a flood of young adult books. Other historical books will be discussed in subsequent chapters as they relate to specific genres.

Authors in Action: Paul Zindel

Paul Zindel's lifetime contribution to young adult literature began in 1968 with the publication of *The Pigman*, a classic realistic novel. Zindel began his professional life as a high school chemistry teacher, but fortunately for us, he quit in 1969 after six years and devoted his life to writing. In 1971 he won a Pulitzer Prize for his play with the bizarre title of *The Effects of Gamma Rays on Man-in-the-Moon Marigolds: A Drama in Two Acts*. The play opened in Houston, Texas, Off Broadway in 1970, and then moved to Broadway. In an interview for *School Library Journal*, Zindel admitted that his most fearful character was Beatrice from the play. "Her character really conveys my mother and the house I lived in. Like my mother, Beatrice was a scorned woman whose husband had left her, and who was left to raise two kids who were like a stone around her neck. She felt that the world was lurking out there to ridicule her clothes, and to attack her with unkindness" (Scales 2002, 54). The play may have special appeal to young adults as it's the story of an abusive mother's psychological effect on her two teenaged daughters.

It's no surprise to librarians who work with teens that Zindel won the 2002 Margaret A. Edwards Award for his lifetime of writing for young adults. In addition to *The Pigman* and *The Effects of Gamma Rays on Man-in-the-Moon Marigolds*, the Edwards Award committee chose to honor *The Pigman's Legacy*, a long-awaited sequel to *The Pigman; The Pigman and Me*, an autobiography; and *My Darling, My Hamburger* (1969), a story with an approach to sexuality and friendship that was somewhat shocking at the time. Sadly, Paul Zindel died of cancer in 2003 at the age of 66.

Contemporary Young Adult Literature

Loosely defined, contemporary young adult literature is anything that young adults read: magazines, newspapers, graphic novels, manga, comic books, novels, short story collections, poetry, folktales, informational books, biographies, and even picture books and adult books. If young adults are reading it, it can be considered young adult literature.

manga— Japanese genre of cartoons, comic books

In most cases, novels published for young adults have certain characteristics in common. To illustrate these commonly held characteristics, here is a synopsis of *Dairy Queen: A Novel* by Catherine Gilbert Murdock, selected as a 2007 Best Books for Young Adults. In this novel D. J. Schwenk is the Dairy Queen for one major reason: At 15 she does all the heavy work at her family's Wisconsin dairy farm. It isn't because she loves milking cows but because her father broke his hip, and her two older brothers have left for college. D. J.'s mom doesn't help much around the farm since she's a teacher and part-time middle school principal. The story picks up speed when Brian Nelson, a cute quarterback from a rival school, reluctantly begins helping out at the dairy farm. At first Brian is scornful of D. J. "Don't you see how you live? You do all the work they expect you to do, and you don't even mind. It's like you're a cow. And one day in about fifty years they're going to put you in a truck and take you away to die and you're not even going to mind that either" (Murdock 2006, 25).

Having Brian around makes D. J. nervous as she falls in love with him. At this point, the whole story seems like the usual romantic comedy: boy and girl are thrown together and fall in love despite some ups and downs in their relationship. The unexpected twist to this story is football. D. J. trains Brian during the summer. He's reluctant about this, too. After all, she's a girl. What can she possibly know about football? But, her brothers were captains of the football team, and they knew plenty about football. D. J. learned from them and loved it. Then D. J. decides to try out for the football team, and she makes it. Now there's going to be trouble when D. J. faces Brian on the field.

Characteristics of Young Adult Novels

Keeping *Dairy Queen* in mind as an example, the following characteristics are usual in a realistic young adult novel:

1. The protagonist is a teenager and the narrator of the story. Parents and other adults fade into the background as the young people control events.

2. Sometimes the setting is relatively unimportant. It might be a familiar backdrop, such as a school. Other times the setting is integral to the story with details of the place and time period.

3. The style of writing has lots of dialog, some humor, and avoids long descriptions.

4. The plot is straightforward with few or no subplots.

5. There's a message for readers but it's an integral part of the story.

6. The ending is optimistic and hopeful, even if there are tragic events. Not all novels today are light-hearted like *Dairy Queen*. Some novels tackle societal issues.

7. Most novels have fewer pages than adult books. *Dairy Queen* is 275 pages in length. There are exceptions, of course. Stephenie Meyer's sensual fantasy trilogy consists of weighty volumes: *Twilight*—498 pages; *New Moon*—563 pages; and *Eclipse*—629 pages.

Classic Young Adult Titles

Classic titles for young adults are those that have not only remained in print for at least 20 years (well beyond the age of a young adult), but they are also titles that have appeal to teens. Young adult classics may be well written and have great style. They may be disturbing and have meaningful themes. Whatever the specifics, classic titles touch young adult readers generation after generation. A sampling of classics for young adults:

Little Women by Louisa May Alcott (1868)
Seventeenth Summer by Maureen Daly (1942)
Lord of the Flies by William Golding (1951)
The Chosen by Chaim Potok (1967)
The Outsiders by S. E. Hinton (1967)
The Pigman by Paul Zindel (1968)
The Chocolate War by Robert Cormier (1974)
Beauty: A Retelling of the Story of Beauty and the Beast by Robin McKinley (1978)
Jacob Have I Loved by Katherine Paterson (1980)
Annie on My Mind by Nancy Garden (1982)
The Blue Sword by Robin McKinley (1982)
Running Loose by Chris Crutcher (1983)

One Book in Action: *The Outsiders* by S. E. Hinton

When *The Outsiders* was published in 1967, Susan Hinton was 19 years old. In an article in the *New York Times Book Review*, Hinton states, "The teenage years are a bad time. You're idealistic. You can see what should be. Unfortunately, you see what is, too. You're disillusioned, but only a few take it as a personal attack" (1967, 26). Forty years later, young adults still identify with characters in the story. After they read *The Outsiders*, it would be interesting to ask today's teen readers the following questions:

1. What has changed for teens during the forty years since *The Outsiders* was published?
2. Do you agree with Hinton's statement above?
3. Why do you think *The Outsiders* continues to be in print and popular with teens?

SELECTING BOOKS FOR YOUNG ADULTS

What's the best way to approach selecting books for young adults? Hundreds of books are published each year for ages 12 through 18. As a librarian, it's your job to sort through those books and select the best ones for the young adults who frequent your library. If you could purchase everything appropriate for the age levels you serve, your job would be really easy. Available funding for books forces you to be carefully selective when choosing books for a young adult collection. Library books must meet one of two major needs for young adults: help with school work and entertainment. Conducting reading surveys, observing teens, and talking with them about books are excellent ways to gain insight into reading preferences. Consulting curriculum guides, book award lists, and book reviews enable librarians to approach selecting books in a professional manner.

Literature in Action: Awards and Award Lists

The list of awards for young adult books and authors is growing each year. These lists can help you decide which books to read, order, and recommend to young adults. The trick is to understand what each award is given for. In this section ten major young adult literature awards will be highlighted: Best Books for Young Adults, Young Adults' Choices, Margaret A. Edwards Award, Quick Picks for Reluctant Young Adult Readers, Michael L. Printz Award, Popular Paperbacks for Young Adults, Outstanding Books for the College Bound, Alex Awards, Odyssey Award for Excellence in Audiobook Production, and Amazing Audiobooks for Young Adults. Nonfiction book awards and other specialty awards will be discussed in later chapters. Still other awards that include both children and young adults will be discussed as appropriate. Young adult literature awards provide a representative selection of the best in young adult literature, including quality of writing and appeal to teens.

Best Books for Young Adults

The award list with the most history is Best Books for Young Adults (BBYA), currently sponsored by the Young Adult Library Services Association (YALSA), a division of the American Library Association (ALA). The idea of a recommended list for young adults began in 1930 and was called "Books for Young People." The list has since evolved from 30 titles to approximately 100 titles, and the committee has evolved from 3 members to 15 (Carter 1991). According to the Web site, the purpose of BBYA has remained the same: "It is a general list of fiction and nonfiction titles selected for their proven or potential appeal to the personal reading tastes of the young adult. Such titles should incorporate acceptable literary quality and effectiveness of presentation" (BBYA Policies and Procedures) Each year the committee gathers to discuss current quality books for young adults, including nonfiction and fiction and books published for young adults and for adults with appeal to young adults. These best of the best books showcase the quality and diversity of books published for young adults during one year. For a sampling of the range of titles, BBYA 2005 includes *The Race to Save the Lord God Bird* by Phillip Hoose, an adventure to track the decline of the Ivory-billed Woodpecker in the United States and a reflection on the plight of endangered species. Kenneth Oppel's *Airborn* is an adventure of another sort, providing exotic creatures, a love interest, and smooth writing in a suspenseful airship story. *So B. It: A Novel* by Sarah Weeks chronicles the unusual life of a teenager living with a mentally challenged mother. Winning titles like these are announced each January after the Midwinter Meeting of ALA and are available on the association's Web site at www.ala.org/yalsa/booklists/bbya.

Young Adults' Choices

A much younger list, and a list that differs from BBYA in its purpose and procedures, is Young Adults' Choices (YAC), sponsored by the International Reading Association (IRA), and begun in 1987.

> The goals of the project are to encourage young people to read; to make teens, teachers, librarians, and parents aware of new literature for young adults; and to provide middle and secondary school students an opportunity to voice their opinions about books being written for them. (Young Adults' Choices for 2006, 223)

According to the guidelines of the YAC program, each year, trade books published during the previous calendar year are requested from over 50 publishers. Each book submitted by publishers has to receive two favorable reviews from recognized reviewing sources, such as *Booklist*, *The Horn Book*, *School Library Journal*, *Journal of Adolescent & Adult Literacy*, or *Voice of Youth Advocates*, to be eligible for the field test. The IRA uses the term "field test" for the process of placing books in schools, giving students the opportunities to choose freely and to read them, and having students rate each book they read. Five team leaders in five separate regions of the United States coordinate the project.

Between September and February, one year following the publication date of the books, team leaders conduct field testing. Books provided by publishers are expected to be widely available to students in school libraries or classrooms. After a student has read one of the books being field tested, he or she marks a ballot either "I like the book," "It was okay," or "I didn't like the book." An annotated list of the approximately 30 books that receive the highest votes from students in grades 7 through 12 is published in the November issue of *Journal of Adolescent & Adult Literacy*. Winners are announced each spring at the IRA Annual Conference.

Publishers may submit books from all genres, although providing balance among types of books is not a mandate. Overwhelmingly, fiction titles appear on the final list each year. In 2006, for example, over 11,000 ballots were counted for the 30 books submitted for the year's list. Twenty-seven of the 30 titles that made the list are fiction; only three titles are nonfiction. These ballots are cast each year by approximately 4,500 students (Young Adults' Choices for 2006).

Because of the large scope of the project, YAC is unique among book award lists. The number of books, the geographical areas included, the number of teachers and librarians involved, and the number of students participating add up to an enormous cooperative effort. These procedures indicate that YAC has the least interference from adults between books and youth. Titles chosen for YAC are the ones that young adults chose, read, and liked the best. Fiction titles for 2006 include mostly realistic fiction with a few titles of fantasy and paranormal stories. *Emako Blue* by Brenda Woods shocks readers with the death of

Emako, a beautiful African American girl with a beautiful singing voice, who is killed in a drive-by shooting. Julia DeVillers' novel, *How My Private, Personal Journal Became a Bestseller* is frivolous and funny compared to Woods' novel. *The Dragon's Son* by Margaret Weiss provides a fantasy with plenty of action, suspense, and surprises. For more information about Young Adults' Choices visit www.reading.org/resources/tools/choices_young_adults.html.

Margaret A. Edwards Award

Imagine that your task is to choose the single best young adult author in the United States? Who would you choose? There's good and bad news: Both the good news and the bad news is that some great authors have already been chosen for the Edwards award. This is good news because Richard Peck, Gary Paulsen, Paul Zindel, and 17 other authors have already been honored, so you don't have to struggle with choosing between Chris Crutcher and S. E. Hinton, for instance. The good and the bad news? Some of your favorite authors have already been selected. And more good news, it means there are still many young adult authors to choose from. New authors are being recognized every year, such as John Green, the 2006 Printz Award winner for *Looking for Alaska*, a novel about growing up and feeling indestructible. In other news, neither good nor bad, to be eligible for the award, the authors must have been published at least five years before nominations to allow time for young adults and librarians to read and recognize their work. Actually, all of this is good news. The Edwards Award is all about annually honoring an excellent young adult author and one or more of his or her books. Clear guidelines come from YALSA, the administrating organization. The winner must be a living author chosen by a five-member committee of YALSA. According to criteria for the award listed on the YALSA Web site,

> The committee making its selection of nominees must be aware of the entire range of books for young adults and will take into account the following:
>
> 1. Does the book(s) help adolescents to become aware of themselves and to answer their questions about their role and importance in relationships, society and in the world?
> 2. Is the book(s) of acceptable literary quality?
> 3. Does the book(s) satisfy the curiosity of young adults and yet help them thoughtfully to build a philosophy of life?
> 4. Is the book(s) currently popular with a wide range of young adults in many different parts of the country?
> 5. Does the book(s) serve as a "window to the world" for young adults? (Margaret A. Edwards Award Policies and Procedures)

The award honors Margaret A. Edwards, an early champion of young adult literature and services. According to the Web site, Edwards was a librarian and "administrator of young adult programs at Enoch Pratt Free Library in Baltimore for over 30 years" (Carter 1992, 45). She is the author of *The Fair*

Garden and the Swarm of Beasts: The Library and the Young Adult, a must-read for public and school librarians who work with young adults. Edwards's dedication to young adults and their literature, outreach services to young adults, and training programs for librarians beginning to work with young adults continues to inspire librarians today.

Also according to the Web site, the Margaret Edwards Award gives "recognition to those authors whose book or books have provided young adults with a window through which they can view their world and which will help them to grow and to understand themselves and their role in society" (Margaret A. Edwards Award Policies and Procedures). For more information about the Edwards award winners and for promotional ideas, visit www.ala.org/yalsa/edwards.

Quick Picks for Reluctant Young Adult Readers

Commonly known as "Quick Picks," the titles in this list try to entice reluctant young adult readers to read. Titles are chosen by a YALSA committee of 11 members. Books selected for the list are intended for leisure reading and are evaluated by "subject, cover art, readability, format, and style," according to the Web site (Quick Picks for Reluctant Young Adult Readers Policies and Procedures).

Vegan Virgin Valentine by Carolyn Mackler is representative of a novel for reluctant readers. In a clear writing style using simple vocabulary, Mara Valentine's first-person viewpoint quickly draws the reader into the story with an enticing hook. "The first thing V did upon arriving in Brockport was fool around with my ex-boyfriend" (Mackler 2004, 1). After that opening line, the novel fulfills all the desirable criteria of fiction writing for reluctant YA readers. It's no wonder that Mara Valentine and her same-age niece, Vivian Vail Valentine, don't get along. Mara is a vegan, a virgin, an overachiever, and a possible valedictorian; V smokes, drinks, and uses the F-word. In short, it's easy to distinguish between the two young women. Mara is conventional; V is outrageous. There's plenty of dialog, sometimes humorous, sometimes sarcastic. In the kitchen one night Mara is making vegetarian chili and defending her vegan diet to V. "'I just don't like to eat anything that comes out of a cow's udder or chicken's butt.' 'Eggs don't come out of a chicken's butt,'" V said. 'They come out of a chicken's ___'" (Mackler 2004, 48). Then Mara is teased for avoiding saying the word, "vagina." The plot is believable and has enough suspense to keep readers interested in Mara and V's relationship and their individual lives. The thematic idea of taking responsibility for one's own life is evident as Mara realizes that at her age she doesn't have to accept being repressed and controlled by her parents, an idea that young adults can easily identify with.

Besides fiction, the Quick Picks list includes a large variety of nonfiction. For instance, on the 2008 lists three titles are indications of the range of offerings. John Grandits's _Blue Lipstick: Concrete Poems_ is an oversize, thin paperback edition with humorous poems, such as "Bad Hair Day," "All My Important Thinking Gets Done in the Shower," and "How I Taught My Cat to Love Poetry." All the poems are from the viewpoint of Jessie, a teenaged girl, who interacts with her parents, her younger brother, and her best friend Lisa. A second book that will appeal to girls is _Breathe: Yoga for Teens_ by Mary Kaye Chryssicas. Brightly colored pages, limited text, and photographs of teen girls demonstrating positions and exercises combine into an attractive and useful package. *A Practical Guide to Monsters* by Nina Hess is likely to appeal to fantasy fans and to teens who enjoy horror. A large format hardback edition with vivid, lively illustrations of monsters and limited text includes familiar and not-so-familiar types of monsters: creepy crawlers, flying fiends, viperous villains, sneaky shape shifters, gruesome goblinoids, mammoth monsters, unsightly dead, and otherworldly outsiders. Access lists and more information about Quick Picks by going to www.ala.org/yalsa/quickpicks.

Michael L. Printz Award

Most parents, teachers, and librarians have heard of the John Newbery Medal, awarded to the most distinguished book for children of those published during one calendar year. In 1999 the YALSA board decided to honor a YA book that exemplifies literary excellence. At last, YA librarians have an award comparable to the Newbery Medal for older readers. In 2000 *Monster* by Walter Dean Myers was the first winner of the Michael L. Printz Award. *Monster* was a ground-breaking title. On trial for felony murder, Steve Harmon, 16 years old, tells his story through a pretend screenplay and journal entries detailing his time in prison. As an accessory to murder, but not the one who pulled the trigger that shot and killed a grocery store owner, Steve disturbs readers with his possible verdict. Each year one winner and up to four honor books may be chosen for ages 12 through 18.

The Printz Award is named for a longtime active member of YALSA, Michael L. Printz, a school librarian at Topeka High School in Kansas. A nine-member YALSA committee chooses the winning books for this annual award. Unlike the Newbery Medal, which honors a book published by a U.S. author, Printz awards have been given to British, Canadian, and Australian authors. Two British authors were winners in 2001 and 2003: David Almond for *Kit's Wilderness* and Aidan Chambers for *Postcards from No Man's Land*. For easy access to lists of winners and other information about the Michael L. Printz Award go to www.ala.org/yalsa/printz.

Popular Paperbacks for Young Adults

For great book lists with variety in genres, topics, themes, and age range, Popular Paperbacks for Young Adults delivers both wacky and practical lists with appeal to teens. The purpose of the lists is to encourage pleasure reading available in paperback from classic to current titles. A 15-member YALSA committee creates one to five annotated lists of 10 to 25 recommended paperback titles. Just reading the committee's lists is enough to whet a teen's appetite. List titles for 2008 are: *Sex is...*, *What Makes a Family?*, *Magic in the Real World*, and *Anyone Can Play*. Other years have produced such provocative titles as: *I'm Not Making This Up* (2007), *Books That Don't Make You Blush: No Dirty Laundry Here* (2006), *Read 'Em & Weep* (2005), *Guess Again: Mystery and Suspense* (2004); *Lock It, Lick It, Click It: Diaries, Letters and Email* (2003), *Graphic Novels: Superheroes and Beyond* (2002), *Paranormal* (2001), and *Page Turners* (2000). Visit www.ala.org/yalsa/booklists/poppaper for all lists and titles from 1997 to the current year.

Outstanding Books for the College Bound

Designed for students planning on continuing their education beyond high school, this list provides reading recommendations in up to five categories. Traditional categories are the arts, biography, fiction, nonfiction, and poetry. Begun in 1992 as a YALSA committee, 15 members revise the list once every five years and include both young adult and adult titles. The major strengths of the lists are quality writing and variety in style and topic. The latest list is 2004 and includes the following academic disciplines: history, humanities, literature and language arts, science and technology, and social sciences. Each committee has freedom to focus on specific criteria within the general framework of the lists. According to the Web site, the 2004 committee selected works with the following criteria: "readability, cultural and ethnic diversity, balance of view points, and variety of genres and title availability, with a focus on titles that have been published over the past five years" (Outstanding Books for the College Bound Introduction). These annotated lists would typically be promoted among high school students. Example titles from the 2004 Humanities list include Tracy Chevalier's *Girl with a Pearl Earring*, Chris Crutcher's *Whale Talk*, Myra Goldberg's *Bee Season*, and Susan Vreeland's *The Passion of Artemesia*. For more information about the lists and for annotated lists, go to www.ala.org/yalsa/booklists/obcb/.

Alex Awards

Although this textbook focuses on books published specifically for young adults, ages 12–18, we know that teens read adult books. You will not be surprised to know that YALSA also has an award list specifically for adult books with special appeal to teens. The first Alex Awards were given in 1998 by a taskforce charged with selecting 10 adult titles, and in 2002 the award was approved as an official ALA award governed by a committee of nine members. Further details of the award and award lists are available at www.ala. org/yalsa/alex. Books chosen for the award can be fiction or nonfiction, but the majority of the titles are fiction. The following two titles are examples from the 2007 and 2008 lists, respectively: In Lisa Lutz's *The Spellman Files*, 28-year-old Izzy Spellman loves being a private investigator in her family's business. Izzy is a hard-edged Nancy Drew trying to balance the stress of her job with the stress of her unusual family in this humorous story. Young adults will appreciate the humor, the mystery, and Izzy's frustration with her parents and siblings. In Sara Gruen's *Water for Elephants*, Jacob, a young veterinary student, is suddenly homeless and runs away from his former life. He connects with a circus in need of a veterinarian and for seven years works with the circus, finding danger, love, and an elephant named Rosie. This historical novel will fascinate older teens as Jacob struggles to find his place in the world.

Audiobooks

Audiobooks are increasing in popularity with teachers, librarians, parents, and most importantly, with young adults. Audiobooks are being welcomed into young adult literature as another format for reading pleasure and for information. This is good news. Listening to audiobooks mimics the benefits of reading aloud that children should experience early in their lives, but listening to audiobooks has the advantage of literally placing control of the medium into the hands of young adults. They can stop the recording when they want to and listen again to sections they didn't understand or want to hear again for the pleasure of it. MP3s, iPods, and Playways ensure portability of audiobooks and have great appeal to teens. The benefits of listening to audiobooks include an impressive list of desirable and potentially favorable reading behaviors. Recordings "can model reading, teach critical listening, build on prior knowledge, improve vocabulary, encourage oral language usage, and increase comprehension" (Wolfson 2008, 106). Of course, the real key to an appealing audiobook is the skill of the reader. Jim Dale has gained a reputation as an excellent reader for his performances of all seven of the Harry Potter books. For reluctant readers or poor readers audiobooks can generate enthusiasm for reading and for books.

Librarians are taking note of the growing trend to offer audiobooks to teens in both public and school libraries. Review journals, award lists, and Web sites offer help to librarians who are ready to begin acquiring a collection of audiobooks. Two journals, *Booklist* and *Voice of Youth Advocates*, offer columns on audiobooks in each issue. Two award lists, the Odyssey Award for Excellence in Audiobook Production and Amazing Audiobooks for Young Adults, offer excellent starting places for building a new collection. For locating audiobooks online visit Web sites such as:

Audible.com (http://www.audible.com)

Full Cast Audio (http://www.fullcastaudio.com)

LibriVox (http://librivox.org)

Listening Library (http://listeninglib.com)

Recorded Books (http://recordedbooks.com)

Odyssey Award for Excellence in Audiobook Production

The Odyssey Award is a new award administered jointly by the Association of Library Services to Children and Young Adult Library Services Association and is sponsored by *Booklist*. Six winners may be chosen each year: one award and up to five honor audiobooks. Only audiobooks produced in English and distributed in the United States are eligible for an award. According to the Odyssey Award Web site, the following production qualities must be met.

Narration

Does the reader (or readers) have good voice quality, diction, and timing? Is the reader (or readers) believable and convincing?

Does the reader (or readers) distinguish between characters by changing pitch, tone, and inflection? Are accents or dialects used and if so, are they handled authentically and consistently?

Are all words, including proper nouns, locales, foreign terms, character names, and others pronounced correctly and consistently?

Does the reader (or readers) avoid condescending vocal mannerisms and style and is the reading believable and convincing?

Is the performance dynamic and does it reflect the expressive nature of the text?

Sound Quality

Is the sound sharp and clear with no obvious humming, distortion, or electronic interference?

Does the sound quality remain consistent throughout the recording?

Background Music and Sound Effects

If music and sound effects are used, do they enhance the text and support the vocal performance?

Does the music represent the emotional and structural content of the text? (Odyssey Award Policies and Procedures)

The year 2008 is the first time the award has been given, and each of the winners met the production qualities listed here. *Jazz*, produced by Live Oak Media is the 2008 winner. Four of the five 2008 Honor Audiobooks are appropriate for young adults.

Bloody Jack: Being an Account of the Curious Adventures of Mary "Jacky" Faber, Ship's Boy, produced by Listen & Live Audio

Harry Potter and the Deathly Hallows, produced by Listening Library

Skulduggery Pleasant, produced by HarperChildren's Audio

Treasure Island, produced by Listening Library

For continuing information about the Odyssey Award, visit http://www.ala.org/ala/yalsa/booklistsawards/odyssey/odyssey.cfm.

Amazing Audiobooks for Young Adults

First presented in 1999, Amazing Audiobooks is a list of recommended audiobooks administered and sponsored by Young Adult Library Services Association. According to the award's Web site,

The final list of recommended titles numbers between 25 and 30 and addresses the wide scope of interests and concerns of listeners between 12 and 18. No one title need address the interests of all listeners in this range, but the list as a whole must offer a balance of developmental levels, intellectual concerns, and experiential backgrounds. (Amazing Audiobooks Policies and Procedures)

Of the 21 titles on the 2008 list, 20 are fiction and one is nonfiction. The list includes five winners of the Odyssey Award. Visit Amazing Audiobooks at http://ala.org/ala/yalsa/booklistsawards/selectedaudio/audiobooks.cfm.

Book Review Sources

Professional reviews of young adult books are the best source for selecting books that will fit your teen population. The best reviews include a brief summary of the book and critical comments to help librarians decide if the book is worth purchasing. Most reviews will also include the most appropriate grades or age range for its readers. For the best reviews of young adult books, consult these respected journals:

Booklist is published twice monthly September through June and monthly in July and August by the American Library Association. Reviewers are professional, and only recommended books, video, DVD, and audio are reviewed. Materials reviewed are for adults and youth, including professional reading. Subscriptions are available for both print and online editions. Visit www.BooklistOnline.com.

The Horn Book Magazine is published six times a year in January, March, May, July, September, and November. Like *Booklist*, reviewers are professional, and only recommended books are reviewed. Unlike *Booklist*, reviews are focused on materials for youth only. Visit their Web site at www.hbook.com.

School Library Journal is published monthly and includes reviews of books for children and young adults plus reference and professional books. Visit www.slj.com.

VOYA—Voice of Youth Advocates is published bimonthly, April through February, by Scarecrow Press. Reviews focus on fiction, science fiction/fantasy/horror, nonfiction, series nonfiction, reference, and professional books. A unique and popular feature of their book reviews is the book review code, which rates each book on a scale of 1–5 for quality and popularity. This journal is a must-have for high school and public libraries. For more information visit www.voya.com.

Professional Resources for Selecting Books

Books containing lists of recommended books for school and public libraries are a valuable resource for selecting books for young adults. A useful source of other professional titles can be found in annual lists from *VOYA*, beginning with the 1997 October issue.

Barber, Raymond W., and Patrice Bartell (eds.). *Senior High Core Collection: A Selection Guide.*
Beers, Kylene, and Teri Lesesne (eds.). *Books for You: An Annotated Booklist for Senior High.* 14th ed.
Brown, Jean E., and Elaine C. Stephens. *Your Reading: An Annotated Booklist for Middle School and Junior High.* 11th ed.

Herald, Diana Tixier. *Teen Genreflecting: A Guide to Reading Interests.*
Jones, Patrick, Maureen L. Hartman, and Patricia Taylor. *A Core Collection for Young Adults.*
Price, Anne (ed.). *Middle and Junior High Core Collection: A Selection Guide.* 9th ed.

LIBRARIANS IN ACTION: CELEBRATING TEEN READ WEEK

Teen Read Week is a national, annual celebration sponsored by YALSA.

Here's a possible scenario: It's your second year as a high school librarian/ media specialist, and you've heard about Teen Read Week. A friend at another high school in the same school district said, "It's a great way to promote reading!" It's always the third week in October, and you decide to try it. The generic-themed slogan is "Read for the Fun of It!" You can download the free logo from the "Teen Reading" Web page or you can use a themed logo, such as "Get Real! at Your Library" (2005), "Get Active! at Your Library" (2006), "LOL @ your library" (2007), or "Books with Bite @ your library" (2008). Visit "Teen Reading" at www.ala.org/ala/yalsa/teenreading/teenreading.cfm to register for free. You can explore the wiki, download a toolkit, and find many promotional ideas. From now on, the third week of October will be on your calendar for celebrating teen literature and involving your students in fun activities!

Professional Organizations

YALSA is a division of the ALA. Join it and participate or be left behind! This is the most dynamic, fastest-growing division in ALA. To explore the benefits to you, go to www.ala.org/yalsa.

The National Council of Teachers of English (NCTE) features the Assembly on Literature for Adolescents (ALAN), an independent assembly. ALAN publishes *The ALAN Review* three times a year, and it can be subscribed to independently of membership in NCTE. For more details about the journal and the assembly go to www.alan-ya.org.

The IRA offers a Special Interest Group (SIG) for a Network on Adolescent Literacy. The SIG offers programs and a journal devoted to the study of adolescent literature and ways of teaching it. Author interviews, presentations, and reviews are featured. For information about receiving the journal, visit www.reading.org/association/about/sigs_network.html.

A NOTE FROM PAM SPENCER, PAST PRESIDENT OF YALSA

What is that mouthful of words—Young Adult Library Services Association? Well, first of all, it's usually referred to as YALSA (replace the "Y" with an "S" and it sounds the same as salsa), which is much quicker and easier to say, and it refers to the liveliest, fastest-growing division within the ALA.

Though referring to YALSA's Web site will give you the official mission, vision statement, and goals, it's easiest to remember that YALSA is the division whose primary purpose is to ensure that teens are receiving the best in library services.

YALSA is the division of choice for teen librarians, but it's also the division to which library professors and educators belong. It's the division for public library administrators who want to stay current with the changing teen population, for publishers, and of course for school librarians. It's the one spot where everyone who not only enjoys, but also interacts, with teens is able to be with like-minded people. It's also the division where teens have some involvement, whether it's helping select the Teens Top Ten during Teen Read Week or being part of a group that attends conferences and shares their opinions on various books. There are times when teens are part of programs, serving as panelists or even being on the program committee itself.

Just as teens often feel alienated from parents, friends, or school personnel, so too do teen librarians often feel out of the mainstream of their library. When you need to share concerns about teen programs, decide on which books to order, learn how video games are circulated in a library, find ways to encourage teens to participate in library programs, or learn how to explain the need for teen spaces, YALSA is the place to find the answers. A variety of listservs are available for member usage, including yalsa-bk, where a multitude of book discussions take place; ya-yaac, where program ideas are shared; yalsa-l, which serves as the official news source for the division; and ya-urban, which is intended for librarians working in large systems.

For those librarians who are able to attend conferences, there are opportunities to serve on YALSA committees, select from a variety of programs offered at the annual conference, meet other YALSA members at the Midwinter Membership reception, learn more about the division by attending the YALSA 101 hour-long program offered each Friday afternoon at the annual conference, or attend the all-committee meeting on Saturday morning to learn more about YALSA's nearly 40 committees. Member volunteers are always welcome on these committees, some of which are even virtual, which is perfect for those YALSA folks unable to attend the conference. Attending the conference is often difficult, but as more YALSA attendees are podcasting or blogging during the conference, it's easy for someone to follow conference events from their own home or workplace.

YALSA is a welcoming, supportive division—joining them is your first step to becoming a great teen librarian.

CONCLUSION

As librarians, the more you know and understand about young adults, the better prepared you will be to serve this special population. It's crucial to understand their needs related to age and developmental tasks, and it's crucial to provide an up-to-date, diverse book collection to help satisfy their reading needs, for curricular assignments and for leisure reading. The library profession provides necessary assistance through the ALA Web site and through professional publications.

PROFESSIONAL RESOURCES FOR READING PROMOTION AND SERVICES

Alessio, Amy J., and Kimberly A. Patton. *A Year of Programs for Teens.*

Anderson, Sheila B. (ed.). *Extreme Teens: Library Services to Nontraditional Young Adults.*

Anderson, Sheila B. (ed.). *Serving Older Teens.*

Anderson, Sheila B. (ed.). *Serving Young Teens and 'Tweens.*

Brehm-Heeger, Paula. *Serving Urban Teens.*

Chelton, Mary K. (ed.). *Excellence in Library Services to Young Adults.*

Dresang, Eliza T., Melissa Gross, and Leslie Edmonds Holt. *Dynamic Youth Services through Outcome-Based Planning and Evaluation.*

Follos, Allison M. G. *Reviving Reading: School Library Programming, Author Visits and Books That Rock!*

Honnold, RoseMary. *The Teen Reader's Advisor.*

Jones, Patrick, Maureen L. Hartman, and Patricia Taylor. *Connecting with Reluctant Teen Readers: Tips, Titles, and Tools.*

Kan, Katherine L. *Sizzling Summer Reading Programs for Young Adults*, 2nd ed.

Krashen, Stephen D. *The Power of Reading: Insights from the Research*, 2nd ed.

Kunzel, Bonnie, and Constance Hardesty. *The Teen-Centered Book Club: Readers into Leaders.*

Langemack, Chapple. *The Author Event Primer.*

Leslie, Roger, and Patricia Potter Wilson. *Igniting the Spark: Library Programs That Inspire High School Patrons.*

Nichols, Mary Anne. *Merchandising Library Materials to Young Adults.*

O'Dell, Katie. *Library Materials and Services for Teen Girls.*

Ott, Valerie A. *Teen Programs with Punch: A Month-by-Month Guide.*

Sullivan, Edward T. *Reaching Reluctant Young Adult Readers.*

Trelease, Jim *The Read-Aloud Handbook*, 6th ed.

Vaillancourt, Renee J. *Bare Bones Young Adult Services: Tips for Public Library Generalists.*

Welch, Rollie James. *The Guy-Friendly Teen Library.*

ASSIGNMENTS IN ACTION: YOUNG ADULTS AND THEIR LITERATURE

1. Interview a young adult about his or her reading interests.

2. Observe a group of young adults at a mall or another gathering place. Pretend you are an anthropologist describing a group of people you did not know existed. Describe their behavior. How have young adults changed since you were a teen? How have they remained the same?

3. Explore the YALSA Web site. What features can help you as a university student? What features will help you as a teacher and librarian?

Chapter 2

Quick Reads

So there she was, leaning against the wall, when all of a sudden Tennessee shot from the playground crowd like a meteor, his blond hair blazing in the sun, his blue jeans jacket steaming behind him. Faster than the speed of light, he blew by her, paused only long enough to kiss her right on the mouth, then zoomed back into orbit.

From *Kissing Tennessee* by Kathi Appelt (2000, 82)

Librarians recognize that young adults make reading choices that are as individualized as young adults themselves. This chapter focuses on "quick reads," print materials that are usually briefer than traditional novels and informational books. Most of these selections can be read in a short amount of time but appeal to young adults for a variety of reasons other than their brevity. "Quick reads" appeal to both proficient and less skillful readers. Don't mistake "quick reads" as only suitable for reluctant readers. Teens of all ages and reading abilities are drawn to comic books, graphic novels, series books, short stories, magazines, and poetry. Comic books, graphic novels, series books, and magazines reflect current reading interests and popular culture, while short stories and poetry represent more traditional literary forms. Also termed "light reading," popular culture selections may serve as conduits to more complex reading (Krashen 2004).

COMIC BOOKS

Superman, Batman, Wonder Woman, and Archie—three superheroes and a teenager who enthralled young adult readers in the Golden Age of comic books (1937 to 1955)—are being "discovered" by new generations of readers. The Silver Age of comic books (1961 to the present) began with the publication of Marvel Comics' *Fantastic Four* and the introduction of *Spider-Man* in 1962

(Krashen 2004). These comic book heroes and many more still flourish today because of their devoted readers, both children and adults. The establishment of comic book stores and the incorporation of comic books into library collections, especially in public libraries, are evidence that this format answers a need among young adults: quick reading for sheer pleasure.

For librarians, it's important to consider the benefits of offering comic books to young adults:

1. Reading comic books can help with language development. For example, in a sampling of comic books, a researcher found that *The Amazing Spiderman* #187 had reading levels of 7.4, 3.0, and 2.8 for an average of 4.4. *Superman* #329 revealed reading levels of 7.3, 8.3, and 3.5 for an average of 6.4 (Wright 1979, in Krashen 2004).

2. The combination of text, primarily dialog, with illustration may help reluctant and second language readers become more proficient in reading.

3. For visual learners, comic books offer clues to the text and can aid readers in their understanding of the story.

4. Comic books may be "conduits" to other types of reading (Krashen 2004). A natural transition from the adventures of superheroes is fantasy with its focus on good versus evil.

5. Comic books serve as a transition to more ambitious and more sophisticated graphic novels.

6. Comic books can function as lures to attract young adults to the library. A high school librarian in Kentucky decided to offer comics and graphic novels as a way to inspire students to read more. "Now, she says, 'I can't keep these books in the library. I can hardly check them in before they're checked out. The kids just devour them'" (Grillo 2005, 26).

7. Offering comic books in the library may increase circulation of other materials. In a junior high library, researchers found that after comic books were made available for reading in the library, circulation of noncomic materials increased by 30 percent (Dorrell and Carroll 1981).

8. The format of comic books makes them accessible. Comic books measure about 6¾" by 10¼" and are stapled, usually 32 pages in length with a shiny paper cover. They are inexpensive to buy and are easy to carry around.

9. Comic books have special appeal to boys for the fast action, the superheroes, and the visuals combined with narrative. Thus, boys are more inclined to read comic books than girls are (Smith and Wilhelm 2002).

Superheroes and Cartoon Characters

Today's comic book titles include historically favorite superheroes and cartoon characters as well as new additions. Superheroes appeal across age levels, while cartoon characters are usually limited to children and to younger teens. Comics that seem geared to teens because of titles and teen characters are mostly read by younger teens, such as *Teen Titans Go!* and *Archie*. The *Archie* series celebrates its 65th anniversary in 2007, and, except for minor updating in style and adding technology, it retains the fun and angst of a group of teens. In the early 1990s, *Bone* by Jeff Smith became popular with all ages of comic book fans and is recommended for any comic book collection. Bone, a character who looks like a cross between Casper the Ghost and Pogo, takes readers on fanciful adventures with humor, simply drawn black and white illustrations, and a storyline carried completely in dialog (Rothschild 1995).

Archick for project

GRAPHIC NOVELS

The most distinctive trend in today's literature for young adults is the increasing publication of and fascination with graphic novels. Will Eisner coined the term "graphic novel" in 1978 with the publication of *Contract with God* (Weiner 2003). This break-through story was published for adults and because of mature content is not recommended for young adults. As with any novels published today, some are appropriate for young adults and some are intended for adults. Librarians must be especially aware of maturity levels and rely on reviews and recommended lists for selecting suitable titles for young adults. Only in the last few years have public and school libraries begun to embrace this popular format and extend their collections and activities to include it. To understand the composition of a graphic novel, think of the marriage of text and illustration. Graphic novels have emerged from traditional comic books, and the term refers to its format, not to content. Unlike comics, which are published as a series, graphic novels are self-contained stories. A graphic novel may be fiction or nonfiction. Usually, graphic novels have sophisticated illustrations and are printed on high quality paper. Illustrations are either in color or black and white. In graphic novels there is a continuing conversation between text and illustration, like what occurs in reading comic books. One without the other would not work as a story. Although it may take little time to read a graphic novel, they are meant to be savored and re-read.

Francisca Goldsmith, author of *Graphic Novels Now: Building, Managing, and Marketing a Dynamic Collection*, concisely sums up the attributes of graphic novels: "Unlike the cartoon, comic strip, or comic book, the graphic novel is complete within itself and provides a beginning, a middle, and an end to the story or information it places before the reader. However, it shares the earmarks of sequential art that comic books incorporate: image and word are bound together in order for the narrative to unfold" (Goldsmith 2005, 25). As a format, graphic novels consist of three basic types: literary graphic novels, comic book series and collections, and manga. The literary graphic novel is designed with slick covers, either paperback or hardback, high quality paper, and rendered in color or black and white. Format size varies from small (5½″ x 7″), the size of *Babymouse: Our Hero* by Jennifer L. Holm and Matthew Holm, to enormous (10″ x 14½″), the size of Art Spiegelman's *In the Shadow of No Towers.*

1) literary graphic novel
2) comic book series + collections
3) manga

Literary Graphic Novels

Literary graphic novels, distinguished from comic book collections and manga, are more complex, with more mature themes than in comic books. One way to understand the scope of literary graphic novels is to divide them into fictional and informational books, much as we would any books in a library. Fictional graphic novels typically include fantasy, stories of superheroes, alternate histories, realistic stories, and mysteries. Informational graphic novels focus on true stories of real people and histories. The best way to find a reliable sampling of excellent graphic novels is to consult the Great Graphic Novels for Teens award list, first announced in January 2007. This new award list is sponsored by YALSA and reflects the current popularity of graphic novels. Committee members read graphic novels published within a 16-month period. Recommended graphic novels chosen for the list meet the following criteria:

Criteria

1. Integration of images and words.
2. Clarity of visual flow on the page.
3. Ability of images to convey necessary meaning.
4. Outstanding quality of the artwork's reproduction.
5. Narrative enhanced by the artwork.
6. Narrative dominated by sequential art component.

For further details of the selection process and an annotated list of winning titles visit www.ala.org/ala/yalsa/booklistawards/greatgraphicnovelsforteens.

Fictional Literary Graphic Novels

A close look at several recommended titles will provide a better sense of this emerging genre. The winner of the 2007 Michael Printz Award is *American Born Chinese* by Gene Luen Yang. This is the first graphic novel to win a Printz Award, giving it special significance. Illustrated in color, Yang merges the tales of three characters into one coming-of-age story. To his dismay, Jin Wang discovers he's the only Chinese-American in his new school. To complicate his life further, he's bullied, and he falls in love with an American girl. The second character swings into the story from a Chinese folktale as the Monkey King who doesn't want to be a monkey. The third and final character, Chin-Kee, is a negative stereotype of a Chinese boy, who is ruining his cousin Danny's life with his obnoxious behavior. The ending satisfies with a surprising twist while encompassing topics of friendship, racism, and Chinese fables and legends.

Also on the 2007 Graphic Novels for Teens list is a stunning story of Baghdad, inspired by a true story. *Pride of Baghdad*, written by Brian K. Vaughan and illustrated by Niko Henrichon, is a heartbreaking tale of a pride of lions who escaped the Baghdad Zoo during a 2003 American bombing raid. Readers view destruction and chaos through the eyes of four lions: two females, a male, and a cub. Anthropomorphic animals try to understand what is happening and why. Through the viewpoint of lions and other animals, Vaughan examines the meaning of freedom. Henrichon's earth tones, heavily accented with shades of orange, reflect the pride's anger and frustration and the destructive forces of war.

Three more titles demonstrate humor, fantasy, realism, and romance. *Plastic Man: On the Lam!* a series by Kyle Baker features a silly, stretchy, superhero with a clever and irreverent personality. Fans will root for Plastic Man as he tries to avoid capture for a crime he didn't commit. Vividly illustrated in primary colors, text and artwork combine for laugh-out-loud humor. *Flight,* Volume One, by Image Comics is a fascinating collection of stories and artwork on the topic of flying. There's a home-made helicopter flown by a boy and his dog, a flying whale, kite flying, a flying penguin, and much more. Some stories are humorous, some are depressing, but all will help the reader view the world in different ways. *The Summer of Love* by Debbie Drechsler features teen characters caught in dilemmas about love and friendship and appeals more to girls than to boys.

Informational Literary Graphic Novels

Real people and history figure in the majority of informational literary graphic novels. Art Spiegelman won the 1992 Pulitzer Prize for *Maus: A Survivor's Tale. Part I: My Father Bleeds History.* This story of the Holocaust seen through the eyes of Art's father, Vladick, alternates between Poland and New York, as terrible periods of their lives unfold. Older young adults are fascinated with this real and despairing account of a survivor and his son. A second volume completes the tale: *Maus: A Survivor's Tale. Part II: And Here My Troubles Began.* Two other notable graphic novels feature the stories of real people: *Pedro and Me: Friendship, Loss, and What I Learned* by Judd Winick and *Persepolis: The Story of a Childhood* by Marjane Satrapi. *Pedro and Me* recounts the life of HIV-positive AIDS educator Pedro Zamora who appeared on MTV's *The Real World: San Francisco.* His story is told by Pedro's roommate and cartoonist, Judd Winick. Captivating in its honesty, this candid account of Pedro's last days is heartbreaking. *Persepolis* is yet another heart-breaking memoir, this one of a young girl living in Iran. *9–11: Emergency Relief* focuses on the attack on the World Trade Center Towers with many views of the tragedy and how it affected people. These three books show older young adults pieces of a bleak world existing outside their own. Appropriately, all three books are illustrated in black and white. Light-hearted, colorful illustrations would not provide a suitable depiction of these stories.

Manga

Manga is the Japanese word for comics. Japanese manga have a distinctively different appearance from literary graphic novels. The consistent digest size (5″ x 7½″), the coarse paper, the reading orientation of the book from right to left, and the series approach quickly sets manga apart from American comic books and literary graphic novels. Additionally, the art work has distinctive features, such as stylized characters with large eyes and girls wearing short skirts, and story and visuals are embedded with Japanese culture. Translated manga available in the United States are published for specific age groups, usually rated for ages 13+ and ages 16+. For example, *Fruits Basket* by Natsuki Takaya is a popular series in both Japan and America and is intended for teens, ages 13+. The first one in the series is the story of Tohru Honda, an orphaned girl, who is rescued by the Sohmas, a mysterious family with a secret. Tohru learns their secret when she hugs one of the Sohma boys, turning him into a Chinese zodiac animal.

Japanese manga most likely began in the late 1940s and early 1950s and has become increasingly popular with both adults and young adults in Japan. In the United States, manga began to be popular in the 1990s. Manga is included with literary graphic novels in YALSA's Great Graphic Novels for Teens award list. For example, one title on the 2007 list is *Cantarella*, a story of Renaissance Italy and the intrigues of the Borgia family.

Librarians in Action: A Manga Club

With an interested teacher, form a manga club. Meet once a week or as often as possible. Let the teens decide what they would like to do: read the same manga and discuss them or read different ones and share what they read. For one activity, show an anime (a movie version of a manga) of *Howl's Moving Castle* by Diane Wynne Jones, a fantasy adventure novel. After seeing the movie, students read the novel and at least one book in the graphic novel series. Does the art change viewers' minds about the novel? Which format do they prefer? Why? Shelve manga and other graphic novels in a prominent location for easy access. Members of the club produce lists of their favorite manga and vote on their favorites, even giving an annual award to the one with the most votes.

Potential Benefits of Graphic Novels

Literary graphic novels and manga offer potential benefits similar to those offered by comic books:

1. Visual learners may be able to connect better to the combination of text and sequential art than to books with text only.
2. The visual clues and simple sentences may help readers who are learning English become more comfortable with the language.
3. Graphic novels are another medium for enjoying reading (Gorman 2003).
4. Displaying graphic novels may entice readers into the library.
5. Graphic novels may attract reluctant readers, particularly boys, for the visuals, dialog, and fast-paced action.

For further resources on graphic novels, consult "Graphic Novel Resources," a list of useful Web sites, magazines, books, and other sources that provide reviews, history, lists, library and classroom uses, management of a collection, and more available on YALSA's Web site.

One concern of librarians is the shelving of graphic novels. There are several choices: fiction and nonfiction can be shelved in appropriate Dewey numbers;

all can be shelved in 741.5 for cartoons; or special sections can be created for manga and for literary graphic novels. With the rising popularity of these formats, I recommend shelving them separately and prominently with lively signage and displays in both school and public libraries. Research shows us that comics, graphic novels, and manga can act as magnets to young adults. For instance, at West Junior High School in Columbia, Missouri the addition of comic books improved the library's image, increased circulation of noncomic book materials by 30 percent, and increased library traffic by 82 percent (Dorrell and Carroll 1981).

Professional Resources for Graphic Novels and Comic Books

Booklist: Spotlight on Graphic Novels 101, no. 14 (March 15, 2005).
Booklist: Spotlight on Graphic Novels 103, no. 14 (March 15, 2007).
Brenner, Robin E. 2007. *Understanding Manga and Anime.* Westport, CT: Libraries Unlimited.
Goldsmith, Francisca. 2005. *Graphic Novels Now: Building, Managing, and Marketing a Dynamic Collection.* Chicago, IL: American Library Association.
Kan, Katherine. Graphically Speaking. *Voice of Youth Advocates.* Column each issue.
Lyga, Allyson A. W. 2004. *Graphic Novels in Your Media Center: A Definitive Guide.* Westport, CT: Libraries Unlimited.
McCloud, Scott. 1994 (reprint). *Understanding Comics: The Invisible Art.* New York: HarperPerennial. (Suitable for high school students.)
McCloud, Scott. 2006. *Making Comics: Storytelling Secrets of Comics, Manga and Graphic Novels.* New York: Harper. (Suitable for high school students.)
Rothschild, D. Aviva. 1995. *Graphic Novels: A Bibliographic Guide to Book-length Comics.* Englewood, CO: Libraries Unlimited.
Weiner, Stephen. 2003. *Faster Than a Speeding Bullet: The Rise of the Graphic Novel.* New York: NBM.
Young Adult Library Service Association. http://www.ala.org/yalsa
Young Adult Library Services: Get Graphic @ Your Library 1, no. 1 (Fall 2002).
Young Adult Library Services: Graphic Novel Issue 3, no. 4 (Summer 2005).

Recommended Literary Graphic Novels

The Arrival by Shaun Tan. Relying on sepia-colored illustrations only, Tan tells the story of a man, his wife, and daughter immigrating to an exotic country, where they struggle to build a new life for themselves. Great Graphic Novels for Teens, 2008.
Fagin the Jew by Will Eisner. Based on the character of Fagin in Charles Dickens's *Oliver Twist*, Eisner tackles prejudice against Jews.
Babymouse: Our Hero by Jennifer L. Holm and Matthew Holm. Illustrated in black and white and pink, this second humorous adventure of Babymouse shows her dread of dodge ball in the hands of Felicia Furrypaws, the school bully. Great Graphic Novels for Teens, 2007.
Clan Apis by Jay Hosler. Black and white art help tell the story of the metamorphosis of a bee while integrating educational lessons about bee anatomy, behavior, and ecology.

Castle Waiting by Linda Medley. This extension of the Sleeping Beauty story offers universal themes of kindness and community and the power of storytelling. Illustrated in black and white, yet characters are colorful and every one of the book's 457 pages is magical. Great Graphic Novels for Teens 2007.

Romeo and Juliet by William Shakespeare, illustrated by Sonia Leong. This American series, originally published in England, is one of a series titled Manga Shakespeare. Since it isn't translated from Japanese, it reads from left to right. The story is set in Tokyo, which is somewhat distracting and incongruous with the Shakespeare dialog. Great Graphic Novels for Teens 2008.

To Dance: A Ballerina's Graphic Novel by S. C. Siegel. Beautifully told and illustrated in color, this memoir of a young girl's ambition to become a ballerina shows the thrill and deep emotion of dancing.

The Tale of One Bad Rat by Bryan Talbot. Helen, a lover of Beatrix Potter stories, molested by her father and hated by her mother, runs away and finally comes to terms with her mistreatment.

The Wall: Growing Up Behind the Iron Curtain by Peter Sis. Told in pictures and memories, this is the story of Sis's childhood in Czechoslovakia during the Cold War. Great Graphic Novels for Teens, 2008.

PICTURE BOOKS FOR YOUNG ADULTS

Closely related to graphic novels are picture books for older readers. The appeal of picture books to teens is likely to increase with the rise of popularity in illustrated stories. A picture book collection in middle school and high school can have several purposes to justify its existence besides a close association with graphic novels.

1. Art teachers can use picture books when discussing careers in art and the use of various media and techniques.

2. Classes in parenting can incorporate lessons in reading aloud to young children.

3. English teachers can introduce literary elements using simple stories before students read complex ones. Susan Hall's *Using Picture Story Books to Teach Literary Devices* provides a plethora of examples from alliteration to understatement.

4. For students who are learning English as a second language, picture books can make the text more accessible.

5. Last, there's the sheer pleasure of reading and viewing picture books.

Recommended Picture Books for Teens

Hoops by Robert Burleigh, illustrated by Stephen T. Johnson. Muted close-up illustrations of young men playing basketball combine with brief comments to evoke the feel of playing the game.

I Never Knew Your Name by Sherry Garland, illustrated by Sheldon Greenberg. Rich oil paintings and simple language depict a young boy lamenting the suicide of a lonely neighborhood teenaged boy.

The Invention of Hugo Cabret by Brian Selznick. Part wordless picture book and part novel, Selznick's approach to this 533-page book defies neat categories.

In 1931 12-year-old Hugo, an orphan and a repairer of clocks, lives in a Paris train station keeping a big secret.

Just One Flick of a Finger by Marybeth Lorbiecki, illustrated by David Diaz. A gun, a boy, and a bully narrowly miss tragedy. Quick Picks for Reluctant Young Adult Readers, 1997.

Math Curse by Jon Scieszka and Lane Smith. In this lighthearted approach to math, one boy suffers from math anxiety as he learns that math permeates every phase of his life.

The Mysteries of Harris Burdick by Chris Van Allsburg. Fourteen full-page monochrome illustrations, each with a title and a provocative sentence or two, will pique teens' imaginations as they try to figure out what's happening.

Our Gracie Aunt by Jacqueline Woodson, illustrated by Jon J. Muth. Softly colored illustrations help tell the story of two children abandoned and neglected by their mother but saved by their mother's sister.

Patrol: An American Soldier in Vietnam by Walter Dean Myers, illustrated by Ann Grifalconi. Use this brief, sobering story to booktalk Myers's *Fallen Angels*.

Pink and Say by Patricia Polacco. Through her skillful art and storytelling Polacco relates a dramatic Civil War story of a young white soldier rescued by a young black soldier and destined to be faithful friends.

The Stinky Cheese Man and Other Fairly Stupid Tales by Jon Scieszka and Lane Smith. Brief, wacky versions of familiar fairy tales combine with equally silly illustrations.

Tibet: Through the Red Box by Peter Sis. After finding a diary, Sis learns about his father's trek through Tibet in the 1950s and communicates this knowledge to readers through imaginative and sometimes bizarre illustrations.

Woolvs in the Sitee by Margaret Wild, illustrated by Anne Spudvilas. Lurking terror relentlessly screams from the pages of this rendering of a post-apocalyptic world in which a teen boy ventures from his apartment to rescue an elderly friend.

SERIES BOOKS

Through the years, series books have been both praised and maligned. Perhaps you grew up reading Nancy Drew mysteries or Babysitter Club stories or Sweet Valley High romances. For many readers, series books hook them on reading. The delight of being totally absorbed in the antics of characters, both good and bad, keep readers waiting excitedly for the next book in the series. Yet series books haven't always been favored by educators. In 1913 Franklin K. Mathiews, the chief librarian of the Boy Scouts of America, wrote an article comparing the act of reading books such as the Rover Boys series, to "blowing out the boy's brains." Mathiews closes his article with a letter from a runaway's parent. "He has a good home, and his parents seem quiet but thrifty. The only possible clue I can find is 'cheap reading'" (Watson 1991, 58).

Even today, some librarians question the wisdom of spending book funding on paperback series. They may ask themselves, "Isn't it better to spend my limited funding on award-winning titles and books that support school curriculum?" If one of your library's goals is to encourage and increase reading among young adults, series books offer enticing plots and characters that appeal to both genders. Cliff-hangers at the end of each book compel readers to anticipate sequels. Readers find comfort in the familiar structure of a particular series. Reading levels are usually low, allowing readers to practice their reading skills while they enjoy reading. Eventually, readers will leave series books and move to more sophisticated writing, but they won't change until they're ready. Librarians need to respect a young adults' desire to read series books, and parents need to be assured that their children will outgrow this reading stage or at least expand their reading when they are ready.

There is some variety in the format of series books. Some are published as original paperback series, such as <u>Buffy the Vampire Slayer</u>, <u>X-Files</u>, and <u>Sweet Dreams</u>. Some series are clearly numbered, like the Circle of Three series about a group of teen Wiccans, joined by magic and bound by nature. Published in 2001 and 2002, there are 15 books in the series. Other series, like <u>Sweet Valley High</u>, may have more than 140 titles. Some series are originally published in hardcover and may remain in that format or be published later in paperback editions. That's the case with the <u>Harry Potter</u> series, the <u>Alex Rider</u> series, and <u>The Sisterhood of the Traveling Pants</u> series.

History in Action: Early Series Books

To better understand series books and their impact on young adult reading, a brief look at Edward Stratemeyer's legacy, is useful. Horatio Alger, Jr. and Oliver Optic, two early writers of series books, were predecessors of Edward Stratemeyer, whose fertile mind produced plot lines for boys' and girls' novels at an astonishing rate, and whose publishing empire was unrivaled in the business of producing series books for children and adolescents. His story begins simply. After Stratemeyer sold a story for $75 to a weekly boys' magazine, his future in writing and publishing began in earnest. Stratemeyer's first successful series began with *Under Dewey at Manila; or, The War Fortunes of a Castaway* (1898) about two boys on a battleship. Stratemeyer capitalized on boys' interest in war and continued similar adventures in <u>The Old Glory</u> series and in the <u>Soldiers of Fortune</u> series (Nilsen and Donelson 2000). Stratemeyer became a "literary machine," a term used in a 1991 *Smithsonian* article (Watson 1991) examining Stratemeyer's literary contribution. From 1890 through 1980 Stratemeyer and his syndicate created more than 125 original children's series and published over 1,300 books (Plunkett-Powell 1993). Four of his series are still published today in updated form: <u>The Bobbsey Twins</u> (begun in 1904), <u>Tom Swift</u> (1910), <u>The Hardy Boys</u> (1927), and <u>Nancy Drew</u> (1930) (Plunkett-Powell 1993). On Stratemeyer's death in 1930, his daughter Harriet S. Adams took over managing his publishing empire with continued success until 1980 when the syndicate was purchased by Simon & Schuster. Part of the phenomenal economical success of the syndicate was due to Stratemeyer's system. He and his daughter wrote plot outlines, hired ghostwriters who were sworn to secrecy, and paid a flat rate for each manuscript. He influenced the writing of modern series through his rigid adherence to three rules. First, each series began with three titles to test their potential popularity. Second, each book ended in a cliff hanger. Third, each book advertised the next book in the series.

<u>Nancy Drew</u>, Stratemeyer's most successful character and series, was written under the name Carolyn Keene. In 1926 Stratemeyer outlined a plot that included a girl superteen as the main character and hired Mildred A. Wirt, a journalist and respected author, to write the first book, *The Secret of the Old Clock*, published in 1930 by Grosset & Dunlap. For 50 years Wirt's identify as

the original writer of the Nancy Drew series was kept secret, yet she wrote 22 of the first 25 titles (Plunkett-Powell 1993).

Popularity of Series Books

When I was a librarian in Houston, Texas, I surveyed middle school students about what they would like to do after reading a book they enjoyed. Among the choices were "tell a friend about the book," "visit with the author," "write a book report," "make a diorama," and more. The majority of sixth, seventh, and eighth graders chose "go to the library and get another book just like the one I read." (Their last choice was "write a book report.") The key to reading series books is enjoyment. Young adults like the fast-paced plots, the familiar characters in each book, and the anticipation of reading more about characters they enjoy. Young adults like being able to go to a library or book store and select the next book in a series, knowing it's a book they'll want to read. Successful series are set in a high school, a neighborhood, or a special world. Main characters have access to unlimited travel. They don't grow or change, they always prevail; and they never die. Books in a series must have the same reading level, length, and covers to continue the comfort of familiarity found in the series.

Series books may frighten readers through supernatural stories or tease them with wish-fulfillment through romances and adventure. For most series the average reading level is fifth through seventh grade, making them easy reading for middle school and high school readers (Makowski 1998). Series books offer escape reading; the chance for YAs to immerse themselves in stories and be swept along with characters their same age.

A closer look at two recent series illustrates some elements of appeal. The Alex Rider Adventure series by Anthony Horowitz, begins with *Stormbreaker* (2004) and takes readers on a wild, James Bond-type, thrill-laden ride. Alex Rider, the 14-year-old British hero, is a good guy able to survive one unbelievable trial after another. Young adults who love breathless action and are willing to suspend disbelief for sheer fun will clamor for the next sequel, currently numbering six with the publication of *Ark Angel* (2006). Alex Rider and his adventures are especially appealing to boys. A second series, the Clique novels, that's currently popular, but geared to girls only, begins with *The Clique* by Lisi Harrison. Not only is this quick reading, but it's light reading. The plot is a simple one: Claire, a newcomer to the school, is snubbed by a clique of rich girls. Full of brand names, bullying, and manipulating, girls will recognize the personality types. Despite the negative possibilities, the story reveals some secrets of friendship, too. A third series, a scary, creepy one, will appeal to both genders. *Cirque du Freak: A Living Nightmare* by Darren Shan is the first title in the series. The freaky sideshows feature oddities and low-key horror with appropriate macabre covers, sure to appeal to fans of horror and scary stories. Cirque du Freak will keep them waiting for the next fright.

Selecting Series Books

It may be overwhelming to think about the numbers of titles found in series books. Reviews are available, of course, for most series or at least for the first title in a series. If you are a librarian who wants to read what the young adults are reading, be assured that all you have to do is read the first title in a series, and you will know what the entire series is like. That works to your advantage and to the young adults' advantage. One of the reasons young adults like series books is the comfort of knowing what each book in the series will be like. They won't know the exact plot, and there might be a new character introduced, but style and main characters will be the same.

SHORT STORIES

For busy young adults and for librarians who want to share a quick story with young adults, a short story collection offers a quality reading experience in a brief amount of time. A short story is more than the simple telling of an incident or anecdote. Like a novel, it has a beginning, middle, and ending. Short story collections for young adults focus on teen characters and situations that they can relate to.

Benefits of short story collections include the following:

1. Fewer characters and a straightforward plot make short stories accessible to reluctant readers and to readers who have little time to read for pleasure.

2. In a brief span of pages the short story entertains and (hopefully) leaves the reader satisfied with the conclusion.

3. Short story collections encourage browsing. It's okay for a reader to select only one story out of an entire collection. A reader doesn't have to read the book cover to cover.

4. Reading a short story encourages young adults to search for other books written by a particular author. Fans of Chris Crutcher's *Athletic Shorts* will want to read his novels: *Running Loose, The Crazy Horse Electric Game, Stotan, Whale Talk,* and *Ironman*.

Basically, there are two types of short story collections for young adults: (1) those written by one author and (2) those written by many authors. Some of the most popular short story collections are those written by Kathi Appelt, Martha Brooks, Robert Cormier, Chris Crutcher, Richard Peck, and Gary Soto. Readers of Soto's short story collections (*Baseball in April and Other Stories, Help Wanted, Local News,* and *Petty Crimes*) about growing up Hispanic in California, will look for his novels: *Accidental Love, The Afterlife, Jesse,* and *Pacific Crossing.*

Topics in Short Story Collections

Individual short story collections may be themed or show a full gamut of topics. Themed collections offer a wide range of topics, including love and romance, sexual relationships, horror, diversity, and special topics, such as the examples below.

1. Love, romance, and sex: In Appelt's collection, *Kissing Tennessee and Other Stories from the Stardust Dance*, Tennessee Jones kisses Peggy Lee three times: once in first grade on the playground, once during a Little League game when she was in fourth grade, and then at the Stardust Dance when she floats right off the cafeteria floor. In Sharon Flake's *Who Am I Without Him?* teen girls question their self-worth, and in *Love & Sex: Ten Stories of Truth*, edited by Michael Cart, Joan Bauer's "Extra Virgin" addresses abstinence with her light sense of humor.

2. Horror: For horror fans, there's Judith Gorog's *When Nobody's Home: Fifteen Baby-sitting Tales of Terror* and Bruce Coville's *Oddly Enough* and *Odder Than Ever.*

3. Diversity: Stories of diversity include *Am I Blue? Coming Out from the Silence*, edited by Marion Dane Bauer, and *Join In: Multiethnic Short Stories*, edited by Don Gallo.

4. Special Topics: Judy Blume's collection, *Places I Never Meant to Be* has original stories by frequently challenged writers, such as Chris Lynch, Jacqueline Woodson, and Paul Zindel. In *Time Capsule*, edited by Don Gallo, young adults are treated to stories about their peers in the twentieth century. *Twelve Shots: Outstanding Stories about Guns*, edited by Harry Mazer, includes "Hunting Bear," a surprisingly humorous story by Kevin McColley. In *Young Warriors: Stories of Strength*, edited by Tamora Pierce and Josepha Sherman, 15 young adult authors answer the question, "What would I fight for?"

As with graphic novels, there are shelving options. Short story collections can be shelved with fiction so that young adults who have a favorite author can easily find all fiction in one location. A disadvantage to shelving the collections in fiction is that quite wonderful collections may be overlooked. The ideal situation is to maintain a story collection near fiction and shelve all story collections in it, but add an additional copy to fiction for those authors who are especially popular. Young adults tend to be unaware of story collections and need to be reminded they exist, where they're located, and the advantages of being able to browse the book for an appealing story.

Authors in Action: Teleconferencing with Chris Crutcher

Chris Crutcher is a psychologist as well as an award-winning author. Would your students like to talk to Chris Crutcher, but you can't afford a face-to-face visit? Consider using an old technology: the telephone. Arrange a teleconference between Crutcher and a group of students. Authors don't usually charge for these sessions and all it costs you is the price of a long distance call. Follow these steps for a rewarding experience:

1. Contact the author's publisher with times and dates in mind.

2. Once the author agrees, students need to read at least one book by the author.

3. Enlist the help of an interested teacher.

4. Students should research the author's life and works.

5. Then they can suggest a few questions they would like to ask him or her.

6. Choose the best questions and arrange them in order like a script.

7. Arrange for a speakerphone and a microphone (if there are more than 30 students participating).

8. The day of the teleconference, be prepared with copies of the script for each person.

9. Record it and photograph it, but most of all, enjoy it!

10. The next day, hold a debriefing session to find out what students learned from the teleconference.

11. Send thank-you notes from students to the author.

This is such a rewarding activity! Over the years I have managed teleconferences between authors and students from 6th grade through 12th grade. Always there's the sense of wonder from the students and sometimes from the authors as well!

Librarians in Action: Reading Aloud to Young Adults

Picture 25 seventh graders gathered around you in the library. Some are watching you, listening raptly while you read. Others are quietly doodling on pieces of paper. You finish reading, and say, "Next week we'll see what Grandma Dowdel has in mind for another adventure." There's a moan as you close the book. "Aw, just one more chapter?" You've just finished reading the first chapter of *A Long Way from Chicago* by Richard Peck, one of the wittiest storytellers writing for middle school young adults today. "Shotgun Cheatham's Last Night above Ground" has three of the best ingredients for a read-aloud: humor, suspense, and readability. From the first sentence, "You wouldn't think we'd have to leave Chicago to see a dead body" (Peck 1998, 3) to the last, "It was a story that grew in the telling in one of those little towns where there's always time to ponder all the different kinds of truth" (Peck 1998, 16). Middle school students love this story!

Older young adults enjoy short story collections, such as *Athletic Shorts* by Chris Crutcher. With less time to spend in the library, it makes sense to read short stories to high school students and to encourage their teachers to read aloud as often as they can.

At this point you or parents of young adults or school administrators may question spending school time to read aloud to young adults who already know how to read. The benefits are many. Studies show that reading aloud increases listening skills and vocabulary, establishes classroom rapport in a shared experience, and encourages young adults to find more books to read on their own (Follos 2007; Krashen 2004). For young adults to realize benefits from reading aloud, pleasure should always be the motivation to listen. For lists of read-alouds for youth, no-nonsense do's and don'ts of reading aloud, and information on the importance of reading aloud, consult the latest edition of Jim Trelease's *The Read-Aloud Handbook*.

MAGAZINES AND ZINES

Magazines offer young adults something that other genres and formats discussed in this chapter do not: timeliness. They offer school curriculum connections and a print source of pleasure reading for teens who won't read books willingly. Magazines are "real" reading and are tailored to special interests, such as fashion, sports, games, news, hobbies, music, science, history, and so forth. Special interest topics and curriculum-related topics may overlap. For instance, news magazines like *Newsweek* and *Time* have curricular connections for current events and will appeal to teens who want to read about current news. Obviously, there are magazines published specifically for the teen population, but many magazines teens want to read are published for a general or adult population.

Traditional school curriculum-related magazines include news, history, science, and consumerism. You will want to subscribe to other topical magazines related to specific class assignments as suggested by teachers. Depending on your budget for leisure reading subscriptions, you'll want to include as many high interest magazines as you can to entice young adults into school and public libraries. The best way to decide on leisure reading magazines is to ask the teens you serve. You can distribute a written survey, informally interview teens, and discuss magazines with your youth advisory council. A combination of these three strategies will give you the best results.

Magazines for Leisure Reading

Blackgirl Magazine (African American teens/elementary, middle, high school)
Careers & Colleges (snazzy and witty/high school)
Career World (current job market/middle, high school)
Computer Gaming World (high school/adult)
Cosmo Girl (fashion, interviews, teen life style/middle, high school)
Electronic Gaming Monthly (elementary, middle, high school/adult)
ELLEgirl (teen style with global sensibility/middle, high school)
ESPN Magazine (sports enthusiasts/high school/adult)
Hot Rod (automobiles/high school/adult)
Latina (bilingual fashion and lifestyle/adult)
Mad Magazine (parody and satire/high school/adult)
Ready Made (crafts/high school/adult)
Realms of Fantasy (fiction and more/high school/adult)
Rolling Stone (music/adult)
Rush Hour (short stories/high school)
Seventeen (fashion and girls' lives/high school)
Spin (rock/alternative music/adult)
Teen Vogue (fashion/life style/high school)
Transworld Skateboarding (skateboarding/high school/adult)
Wizard (comics price guide and more/elementary, middle, high school/adult)
Young Money (national money and finance/high school/adult)

Note: Some magazines for teens come and go. For the latest magazine news and trends, consult current issues of VOYA, School *Library Journal,* and other professional journals.

What Are Zines?

If you want to encourage reading and writing, you will want to include at least a few "zines" in your collection. Zines are handmade, sometimes crudely assembled, sometimes professionally created. The variety of approaches is endless, and they can be created by the teens in your school or community. For a thorough look at zines, consult *Whatcha Mean, What's a Zine? The Art of Making Zines and Mini-Comics*, written by Mark Todd and Esther Pearl Watson. This book is a must-have if you want to understand zines and want your students or patrons to make them.

Professional Resources for Selecting Magazines

Bartel, Julie. 2005. Annotated List of Magazines. *School Library Journal* 51: 37–41.

Borne, Christine, and Kevin Ferst. 2004. Zines for Teens. In *Thinking Outside the Book: Alternatives for Today's Teen Library Collection*, ed. C. Allen Nichols. Westport, CT: Libraries Unlimited, pp. 1–20.

Katz, Bill, and Cheryl Laguardia, eds. 2008. *Magazines for Libraries*. 16th ed. New Providence, NJ: Bowker.

Todd, Mark, and Esther Pearl Watson. 2006. *Whatcha Mean, What's a Zine? The Art of Making Zines and Mini-Comics*. Boston: Houghton Mifflin.

POETRY

Poetry for young adults has been increasing in popularity during the last 25 years. The publication of Paul Janeczko's *Poetspeak* and Mel Glenn's *Class Dismissed!* signaled a need for poetry that speaks to adolescents. Both men understand the emotions and crises of being a teenager and translate that understanding into their collections: Janeczko, as a poet and collector of modern poetry; Glenn, as a poet and high school English teacher. Since those beginnings, more and more poetry collections have been published especially for teens. Increased interest in poetry is due to those initial volumes written especially for young adults and, in more recent years, to poetry slams and to publications of poetry written by young adults. More poetry collections are being published than ever before, and librarians have the luxury of selecting the ones right for their teen population.

"Poetry," as discussed in this chapter, is an open term including both poetry and verse. Literarily, poetry is considered to be of higher merit than verse. For example, Shakespeare's sonnet, "Shall I Compare Thee to a Summer's Day?" is a classic romantic poem, while Edward Lear's limericks and Shel Silverstein's "Hammock" are fun to read verse but can't be considered great poetry by any stretch of the definition. Figurative language, emotional intensity, and universal themes are hallmarks of great poetry, while verse amuses with its rhythm, rhyme, and silly humor.

In this chapter focusing on easily accessible reading experiences for teens, poetry offers special features.

1. Many poems for teens are short, less than a page in length.
2. Poetry collections offer the browsing feature of short story collections and magazines.
3. Poetry offers relevancy to teens' lives.
4. Poetry begs to be read aloud by teachers, librarians, and, most of all, by teens.
5. Poetry offers exposure to rhyme, rhythm, figurative language, and imagery.
6. Poetry can be humorous or intense, providing emotional outlets through laughter or tears or at least through feelings of empathy.
7. Through the experiences of adult poets, young adults can experience the feelings and emotions of adolescence, learning they are not alone in their feelings. The best poets remember what it was like to be caught in the emotional maelstrom of puberty and early adulthood, and they have the writing talent to express those feelings.
8. Poetry offers young adults a chance to express themselves by writing their own poetry.

As children transition to adolescence, their poetry preferences change. In childhood they want clear rhyme and rhythm and silly humor like the poetry of Shel Silverstein and Jack Prelutsky, but in adolescence teens are looking for clues to their own behavior and that of their friends and families. They want to express their own confusion and frustration with their world. Poetry is suited perfectly as an outlet to these emotions.

Topical categories of poetry collections published for young adults provide a sampling of the types of collections with teen appeal available today: romantic love; sports; teen tragedy, angst, and joy; neighborhoods; humor; and classic poetry.

Poems of Romantic Love

When I was a middle school librarian in Houston, Texas, the most consistently stolen books were poetry collections about love. I speculated that some students were too shy or too embarrassed to check them out. The volumes were slim and easy to slip into a notebook or a purse, and without a security system, they slipped right through the doors. Paul Janeczko's 2004 collection, *Blushing: Expressions of Love in Poems & Letters*, would be grabbed right off the shelf in that Texas middle school today. A combination of classic and modern poetry with sections devoted to first love, more mature love, alone in love, the end of love, and, finally, "the resilience of the human heart" (Janeczko 2004). Arnold Adoff's *Slow Dance Heart Break Blues* is a slim volume of brief, down-to-earth, free verse about young love and other mysteries of growing up. From the perspective of six teens, Ralph Fletcher explores love in *Buried Alive: The Elements of Love*. Many voices through time and around the world express the passion and agony of love in *Love Is Like the Lion's Tooth: An Anthology of*

Love Poems, edited by Frances McCullough. A final example, *Going Over to Your Place: Poems for Each Other*, selected by Janeczko, includes poems of romantic love as well as poems on other topics and emotions. Even a poem with the title, "Reading Room, the New York Public Library" carries the romance of a young man who sees his love, "a faun with light steps and brilliant eye" (Janeczko 1987, 126). Each of these volumes is worthy of being stolen from a library collection by a boy wanting to express his love to a girl who wants to hear it.

Sports Poetry

Teens with an interest in sports can find slim volumes expressing how it feels to play football, soccer, baseball, tennis, and basketball and what it's like to wrestle, run track, perform gymnastics, canoe, golf, and more. The exhilaration of physical activity and the pain of injury are intense in the following sample collections and offer a voice to athletes and vicarious experiences to teens who want to know what it's like to compete. Compiler and poet Lillian Morrison offers the whole range of sports in *Sprints & Distances: Sports in Poetry and the Poetry in Sport*, including the classic poem "Casey at the Bat." Arnold Adoff's *Sports Pages*, a Reading Rainbow Book, combines his signature blank verse poems with Steve Kuzma's pencil drawings showing teens in action running, biking, tackling, stretching, jumping, throwing, and catching. Basketball and illustrations combine in three volumes that will appeal to a wide range of ages. Adoff's *The Basket Counts*, illustrated by Michael Weaver, begs to be read aloud, teen to teen. Twenty-eight poems reflect the action and sensation of playing the game, including "The Hoop Behind the Bedroom Door" where "any soft round fuzzy ball that fits the hand will feed the game" (Adoff 2000, 7). Lillian Morrison's *Slam Dunk* features basketball poems by well-known writers, such as Richard Peck, Mel Glenn, Jack Prelutsky, Eloise Greenfield, Jerry Spinelli, and Ralph Fletcher. Then there's the bonus of poems about Shaquille O'Neal, Wilt Chamberlain, and other basketball heroes. Sports poems have the potential to catch the attention of reluctant poetry readers. It will be a relief to young adults to discover that not all poetry is about flowers and emotional depression.

Poems about Teen Tragedy, Angst, and Joy

For poems that speak to teens about life, most collections are written by adults, but an increasing number of collections include poetry written by teens. All of it is immediately relevant to their lives at school, at home, in their communities, and in the larger world. This type of poetry speaks directly to teens about sadness, abandonment, depression, loneliness, death, running away, and more. Ruth Gordon's collection *Pierced by a Ray of Sun: Poems about the Times We Feel Alone*, share sobering experiences from classic poets and poets from many countries, a testimony to difference and sameness. Kathi Appelt's *Poems from Homeroom* are at once up-to-date and universal. In the first part of the collection Appelt shares poems that express adolescent longings, evident in individual titles: "In the Nurse's Office," "The Fat Girl," "Cyberlove," and "The Driver's License." In the second part Appelt takes each one of her poems, relates it to teen situations and longings, and gives specific advice to developing writers. For writing starters, she suggests teens describe their test to get a driver's license, begin a poem with a funny line written on a bathroom wall, and write about a secret love (Appelt 2002).

Literature in Action: Poetry Slams and Open Mics

Librarians who want to provide excitement about poetry should try a poetry slam! A poetry slam is a competition giving young adults the opportunity to perform their own poems before a live audience. In schools, poetry slams are held in individual classrooms or in the library, during school hours or even after school or at night. Poetry slams have rules, structure, judges, scoring, time limits, and prizes or certificates. Poetry slams offer teens the joy of self-expression and the exuberance of competition. Poetry slams can be small, local events at a public library or major events held in cities, such as those organized by the Youth Poetry Slam League in San Francisco and Washington, DC and the Urban Word Annual Teen Poetry Slam in New York City. A tip sheet on poetry slams is available from Poets House at www.poetshouse.org. To sample poems being read or recited at slams, read *Slam* (edited by Cecily von Ziegesar), a compilation of classic poems and those written by young adults. For promotional materials borrow "Slammin' @ Your Library," a 2003 Teen Read Week theme.

In contrast to poetry slams, open mic sessions don't have rules or judges. They are informal times for sharing poetry written by teens. For a glimpse at how this works, get to know 18 high school students who share their poetry with each other and who come to know and respect one another better in Nikki Grimes's *Bronx Masquerade*, winner of the 2003 Coretta Scott King Author Award.

Poetry Written by Young Adults

For teens who want to read poetry written by teens, there are excellent collections available. Betsy Franco collected poems and prose written by young women, ages 12 through 18, from across the country in *Things I Have to Tell You: Poems and Writing by Teenage Girls*. They share their feelings about lacking self-confidence, keeping secrets, telling the truth, dressing with style, trying to be perfect, having a bad hair day, and wanting to be loved for their flaws and beliefs. *The Pain Tree and Other Teenage Angst-Ridden Poetry* includes brief poems written by both boys and girls. Inspired by his raw emotions in adolescence, Mark Todd collected 25 poems and illustrated the boys' poems, while Esther Pearl Watson illustrated the girls' poems. Teen poetry in a third collection, *Movin': Teen Poets Take Voice* (edited by Dave Johnson), was selected from workshops developed in a cooperative effort between Poets House and The New York Public Library. Visit their sites at www.poetshouse.org and www.nypl. org/branch/teen to learn how teens can submit poems. In a fourth collection, *Paint Me Like I Am*, poetry was written by teens who participated in a national nonprofit organization called WritersCorps. Titles of some of the poems finely express the essence of what is means to be a teen: "You Were Fine Till I Met

Your Mind," "Friendship," "Diary of an Abusive Stepfather," and "The Spring in Your Voice." If you haven't been privileged to be around teens in the last few years, reading these collections will move you closer to an understanding of their thoughts and the challenges they face.

Poems about Neighborhoods

To understand young adults from many geographical locations, delve into this group of poems about neighborhoods, each one a special culture, a unique way of viewing the world. Through poetry encourage young adults to visit Africa, the Middle East, the Caribbean, and neighborhoods across the United States: Harlem; Fresno, California; Fredericksburg, Texas; Detroit, Michigan; and many more. In Gary Soto's *Neighborhood Odes* experience the deliciousness of a tortilla dripping with butter and the intimacy of a public library. Young and old share their voices in Walter Dean Myers's *Here in Harlem: Poems in Many Voices*. Poetry in several collections describes the Latino/Latina culture: Lori M. Carlson's *Cool Salsa: Bilingual Poems on Growing Up Latino/a in the United States*, Gary Soto's *A Fire in My Hands*, and Pat Mora's *My Own True Name: New and Selected Poems for Young Adults*.

Humorous Poetry

While young adults outgrow the humorous poetry they love as children, some young adults will appreciate poetry that makes them laugh. Older and more sophisticated teens may not admit they like reading the poetry of Shel Silverstein, Jack Prelutsky, and Judith Viorst, but I have seen teens in the library reading collections from their childhood and grinning to themselves. Perhaps they read humor out of nostalgia for their younger, less complicated selves or perhaps they read humor for the sheer fun of it! Humorous poetry collections make good choices for readings and performances in speech classes and contests. A few collections written for young adults include humorous poems, but you have to search for them. *Looking for Your Name: A Collection of Contemporary Poems*, selected by Paul B. Janeczko, includes "Gone Astray: Little Miss Muffet" by David James and "Help Is on the Way" by Herbert Scott, in which Frankenstein's wife writes to Ann Landers and Ann replies. Surprisingly, there's humor in Carol Ann Duffy's collection, *Stopping for Death: Poems of Death and Loss*, even though the poem by Cynthia Rylant is titled "When My Grandaddy Died."

Classic Poets

Contemporary poetry and poetry written by young adults is more likely to appeal to teens than classic or traditional poetry. Poetry typically taught in English classes carries the stigma of assignments and interpreting poetry rather than pleasure in reading it and hearing it read. Collectors, selectors, and compilers of poetry for young adults have carefully chosen poetry from Shakespeare, Emily Dickinson, e. e. cummings, and many others. Poems chosen for relevancy to the lives of young adults and blended into a thematic collection have a better chance of appealing to youth. The following four collections are examples of classic poetry with appeal to teens: *Earth-Shattering Poems*, edited by Liz Rosenberg; *Step Lightly: Poems for the Journey*, collected by Nancy Willard; *Light-Gathering Poems*, edited by Liz Rosenberg; and Langston Hughes's *The Dream Keeper and Other Poems*, illustrated by Brian Pinkney.

Verse Novels

Feeding teens' appetites for experiencing poetry, and all of its emotional ups and downs, is the verse novel. Each one a series of narrative poems, verse novels are most popular with girls. What teenage girl can resist titles like *Bad Boys Can Be Good for a Girl, What My Mother Doesn't Know*, and *Girl Coming in for a Landing*? Verse novels deal with serious topics: death, suicide, murder, life-threatening illnesses, love, and sex, all set within the background of growing up.

Verse novels are a relatively new type of fiction, mostly modern realistic. Three significant verse novels started this popular trend. In 1993 Virginia Euwer Wolff's *Make Lemonade* was a groundbreaking novel of 66 short chapters of prose that looked like poetry. Wolff introduces readers to 17-year-old Jolly, an unwed single mother of two young children. Jolly desperately needs help and she finds it in 14-year-old Verna LaVaughn. The two young women and the two young children become a family of sorts, and Jolly begins to see better possibilities for her life. Mel Glenn's *Who Killed Mr. Chippendale? A Mystery in Poems*, published in 1996, slowly reveals the solution to an English teacher's murder. Written in free verse, individual voices of students, the principal, neighbors, a guidance counselor, and a detective paint a realistic picture of high school life. A third title, Karen Hesse's *Out of the Dust* won the 1998 Newbery Medal. In a series of poems dated by month and year, 14-year-old Billie Jo relates her story of heartbreak in Oklahoma during the Great Depression.

This technique of writing novels by assembling separate poems works remarkably well. Plot moves along, characters are defined, themes flow through the poetry, setting is clear, tone is set, and the style is musical. Verse novels offer the same benefits of reading poetry collections, except for the option of browsing. As you would expect, verse novels are more about emotions than about fast action. For that reason, their appeal is mostly to girls. In Tanya Lee Stone's *A Bad Boy Can Be Good for a Girl*, three high school girls fall for the same sexy senior boy, one girl at a time. It becomes clear that he's using the girls, and their fury at him is unleashed on the blank pages of Judy Blume's *Forever* so all the girls in the high school can be forewarned. Jen Bryant's quiet novel, *Pieces of Georgia*, is a collection of 62 poems telling Georgia's story of recovery from her mother's death and making a connection with her grieving father through art. In Mel Glenn's *Split Image: A Story in Poems*, popular, beautiful, and smart Laura Li commits suicide when she can no longer tolerate her loss of freedom. For a break from the seriousness of other modern realistic fiction, Linda Oatman High delivers plenty of laughs in *Sister Slam and the Poetic Motormouth Road Trip*. Laura (Sister Slam) and her best friend Twig head for adventure and a poetry slam in New York City after graduating from high school. Word play, rhyming, love, humor, and liveliness will make teen girls want to take this trip, too. Creativity in the poetry and in the stories and the wonder of fitting so many elements together make verse novels great additions to teen literature.

Poetry in Action: More Activities

Besides holding slams and open mics, what more can you do with fabulous poems written by and for young adults?

1. Arrange book displays of verse novels and poetry collections. Incorporate poetry collections into displays for holidays and topics. Valentine's Day is an obvious one for poetry about love and romance.
2. April is National Poetry Month. Celebrate by holding a poetry writing contest. Each year *VOYA* holds a Teen Poetry Contest and publishes the results in the April issue along with "Poetry Picks," a list of recommended poetry collections published during one year. To hold a local contest read Jan Bridges's suggestions in "Making Your Teen Poetry Contest a Winner."
3. Read brief poems, especially humorous ones, out loud to a class that has come to the library for instruction in the online catalog, databases, research, or almost anything. If the poem is a serious one, duplicate it on a bookmark and hand it out to students for silently reading.
4. Select favorite poems, print them attractively, frame them inexpensively, and place them on the tops of bookcases like works of art.

CONCLUSION

You can help adults of all ages find reading pleasure in quick reads: comic books, graphic novels, series books, magazines, short stories, and poetry. These genres and formats offer accessibility through brevity, illustration, extra white space, currency, relevancy, emotional punch, and reading entertainment. Encouraging and engaging young adults in reading can be accomplished by reading short stories and poetry aloud, forming manga clubs, collaborating with teachers to teleconference with an author, and planning and offering poetry slams and writing contests.

ASSIGNMENTS IN ACTION: QUICK READS FOR DISCUSSION

1. Literary Graphic Novel. *Maus: My Father Bleeds History* by Art Spiegelman. Explain your personal response to this nonfiction graphic novel in both format and content. Give a specific example of a part of the story that moved you in some way. Was this graphic novel easy reading for you? Did you find the book disturbing or inspiring? Interpret the symbolism of the animal characters. Compare the format to a manga, a comic book, and a picture book. What are the differences

and similarities? Speculate on the reasons format, style, genre, and topic of *Maus* might interest young adults.

2. Manga. *Fruits Basket* by Natsuki Takaya. Choose any book in the series. Was this manga difficult for you to read? Why or why not? Why do you think manga is so popular with middle school students?

3. Series Book. Choose a series and read the first book. What makes you want to keep reading? What specifically will young adults like about the series you chose?

4. Short Story. *Athletic Shorts* by Chris Crutcher. After reading his collection, do you want to share it with teens? Why or why not? Do you want to read his novels? Why or why not? What are some of the opinions and beliefs expressed by Crutcher through his short stories?

5. Magazines. Look at two or three magazines for girls. How are girls portrayed in advertising and in articles? Look at a few magazines typically read by boys. What's the appeal?

6. Poetry. *Stop Pretending* by Sonya Sones. To understand more about this verse novel and Sonya Sones, visit her web site at www.sonyasones.com. Then answer these questions: Where did Sonya get the idea for writing *Stop Pretending*? Find out about the cover photo. Why is the photo blurry? What is the appeal to teens of this verse novel, considering both content and format?

3

Realistic Fiction

Demi.

My conspirator. My first true friend. A spirit made of equal parts ambition and razzle-dazzle. A big baritone that slides easily into falsetto. And a future as bright as the lights on 42nd Street.

Demi believed that the Wildwood Summer Institute would be heaven. Believed he would be king there, and I would be queen, and we would live all summer in utter fabulousness.

And he was right—about himself, at least.

From *Dramarama* by E. Lockhart (2007, 7)

Realistic fiction consists of stories that could happen. These stories reflect a wide variety of experiences by young adults. Stories show what happens in small towns and cities, to boys and girls, and to families, friends, and enemies. Characters have different values, different ethnic backgrounds, different religions, and different sexual orientations. Plots and characters are humorous, romantic, mysterious, adventurous, and sometimes violent. In this chapter realistic fiction includes two general types of modern realistic fiction, light and dark, and one specific type, historical fiction.

LIGHT MODERN REALISTIC FICTION

Light realism is humorous, mysterious, adventurous, romantic, or focuses on sports, sometimes combining all of these elements. It's tricky to try to place young adult novels into specific categories or topics, but for the purpose of presenting excellent examples, categories are a necessity of organization. Be aware that many titles could fit into several categories at once. For example, in Catherine Gilbert Murdock's *Dairy Queen*, D. J. has to do the heavy work at her family's Wisconsin dairy farm after her father breaks his hip. Then Brian, a cute quarterback from a rival team, begins helping out at the farm, and D. J. starts to fall in love with him even though he compares her to a cow. This romantic comedy based on farming and football primarily appeals to girls despite the descriptions of football training. If a teen asks for an entertaining (good) novel about love or about girls who play sports, this book fills both needs.

Humor

Not all vegetables are this draining. Lettuce doesn't bring heartache. Turnips don't ask for your soul. Potatoes don't care where you are or even where they are. Tomatoes cuddle up to anyone who'll give them mulch and sunshine. But giants like Max need you every second. You can forget about a whiz-bang social life.

From *Squashed* by Joan Bauer (1992, 6)

What do teens think is funny? How do we know what they think is funny? One way to determine what amuses teens in the books they read is to look at the titles in Young Adults' Choices. On the 1999 list, 30 percent of the 23 novels use humorous devices to carry the stories. Chris Lynch's *Slot Machine* and Christopher Paul Curtis's *The Watsons Go to Birmingham—1963*, a 1996 Newbery Honor, are two such novels. Ten years later, 19 percent of the 26 novels on Young Adults' Choices for 2006 uses humor as a major device. Teens actively choose books with humor, although their choices will depend on what is accessible to them. Sarcasm, teasing, grossness, lewd jokes, exaggeration, word play, plus humor at the expense of adults are staples of humor for grades 6 through 10. In the last years of high school teens begin to appreciate satire and parody, while some continue to prefer more infantile devices. Some authors engage every literary element to make laugh-out-loud humor. Situational humor, characters whose thoughts and speech are funny, writing style full of figurative language and imagery, a lighthearted tone, even setting and theme may be humorous. Other authors include enough humorous elements to alleviate the weight of tragic or serious circumstances. In Carolyn Mackler's *Love and Other Four-Letter Words*, 16-year-old Sammie struggles with her parent's separation and the necessity for her to relocate to New York City with her mother. Mackler softens Sammie's distress through understatement, hyperbole, and other figurative devices. Before the move Sammie and her mother have a disagreement over the volume of the music that Sammie's playing. "I folded my arms across my chest and faced Mom. We stared at each other for a few seconds, like gunslingers in an Old West showdown" (Mackler 2000, 17).

Chick Lit

In recent years, humor for girls has become a trend termed "chick lit." Chick lit burst upon the adult literary scene with Helen Fielding's *Bridget Jones's Diary* (Alderdice 2004). Teen chick lit morphed into something different with a few similarities. Early novels include Louise Rennison's *Angus, Thongs and*

Full-Frontal Snogging, Meg Cabot's *Princess Diaries*, and Ann Brashares's *Sisterhood of the Traveling Pants* (Adams 2004). Unlike adult chick lit, young adult novels are not about careers but about the hilarity and tragedy of being a teenaged girl. The girly trappings of preoccupation with clothes and boys, cell phones and computers, parties and ladies' rooms, lots of crying, and the color pink frequently and persistently show up in the pages of chick lit. Patty Campbell, author of "The Sand in the Oyster" column for *The Horn Book Magazine*, reminds us that "chick-lit novels are dramas of social class, not love stories" (Campbell 2006, 489).

For a thorough dose of chick lit, read several of Rennison's books for confessions of 14-year-old Georgia Nicolson, written in diary format: *Angus, Thongs and Full-Frontal Snogging; Knocked Out by My Nunga-Nungas; On the Bright Side, I'm Now the Girlfriend of a Sex God; Away Laughing on a Fast Camel*, and more. Rennison won a 2001 Printz Honor for her first title in the series, also on the 2002 Young Adults' Choices list. Georgia, the character she created, is funny, irreverent, scornful of her parents and teachers, devoted to her best friends, and interested in boys. There's a glossary of British words at the end of each book that's as humorous as Georgia's crazy adventures in teen land. Rennison's fans will want to visit her Web site at www.georgianicolson.com to find out about her most recent titles and engage in the author's brand of hilarity.

Besides diaries, manifestations of chick lit include, but are not limited to, letters, blogs, and e-mail messaging. In Julia DeVillers *How My Private, Personal Journal Became a Bestseller*, 14-year-old ordinary Jamie Bartlett suffers when her diary is read aloud in her English class. Then she's amazed when it's published, thanks again to her English teacher. Overnight Jamie is a sensation. Jaclyn Moriarty's *The Year of Secret Assignments* is almost an Australian version of Rennison's books. In this case, there are letters and e-mails between three girls and three boys in rival Australian high schools. At once funny and sad, their correspondence affords them the joy and strife of friendship with a mystery about the identity of Matthew. Combining many devices of chick lit, *Cathy's Book* by Sean Stewart and Jordan Weisman will amuse girls with the added bonus of supplemental material and will give librarians headaches trying to decide how to make the material available without losing it. For more chick lit, consult YALSA's Popular Paperbacks for Young Adults, specifically a 2003 list titled, "Lock It, Lick It, Click It: Diaries, Letters, and Email."

Guy Humor

Although there isn't a corresponding genre to chick lit for boys, there are a few novels with humor for young adult boys. We'll call these books "guy humor." Some classic titles will keep them laughing and asking for more. Gary Paulsen's *Harris and Me* is one of the funniest books for young adults today. Action, mischief, a little cursing, and a developing friendship between cousins add up to a great read-aloud or a book to be read again and again for the laughs. Two humorous novels about boys and puberty are unequaled in targeting the mysteries of puberty: Jerry Spinelli's *Space Station Seventh Grade* and Sue Townsend's British novel, *The Secret Diary of Adrian Mole, Aged 13¾*.

Mysteries

"I wanted to go out with her," Zeke continued, "but she didn't want to. So I killed her. What should I do?"

From *Wolf-Rider* by Avi (1986, 3)

Perhaps it seems odd to include murder mysteries and psychological thrillers in light modern realistic fiction, but young adults who love mysteries read them for the fun of trying to puzzle out the answer. Unlike chick lit, mysteries appeal to readers of both genders, according to a reading interest survey given to sophomore boys and girls (Thomason 1983).

History in Action: Early Mysteries

Nancy Drew, Judy Bolton, and the Hardy Boys paved the way to modern mysteries with fast-paced action and scary moments. As amateur crime solvers, they showed youth how to be brave, clever, and self-confident. They were heroes ridding the world of criminals, giving readers a rush of wish-fulfillment. While Judy Bolton, a red-haired amateur detective similar to Nancy Drew, has disappeared from publishing, the other two series have continued to struggle over the years. Publisher Simon & Schuster continues to update Nancy Drew stories, trying to appeal to modern girls. Nancy Drew uses a computer and drives a gas/electric hybrid car in recent books. The new versions expect to appeal to 8- to 12-year-olds, making them too young for most young adults. Despite efforts to update Nancy's adventures, *The Secret of the Old Clock*, the first title of the original 56 hardcover novels, continues to be popular (Strauss 2004).

Types of Mysteries

Mysteries that are well-plotted and well-written will grab students at the beginning and not let them go until the mystery is solved and every detail worked out. Mysteries for young adults integrate meaningful themes and realistic concerns of teens into the stories. Joan Lowery Nixon, one of the premier authors of mysteries for young people, explained that the plot of a mystery should have two levels: "the main character's personal problem, which she must solve; and the mystery, which she must also solve. Both of these elements use suspense to keep readers in doubt, but it's the mystery itself in which writers can pull out all stops and create scenes so nerve-wracking and compelling that teenagers must keep reading to find out what happens next" (Nixon 1991, 2). Two of Nixon's mysteries represent one type of mystery commonly read by young adults today: puzzling mysteries. In puzzling mysteries there are no murders. Instead, the mystery revolves around a problem that seemingly cannot be solved. In *The Kidnapping of Christina Lattimore*, Christina is kidnapped from a parking lot and held in a basement for ransom. Once she's released, her family accuses her of staging her own kidnapping. Now she must try to prove her innocence. A second mystery, *Who Are You?*, revolves around the possible theft of a painting and a man who thinks that Kristi Evans, the main character, is his granddaughter. Kristi learns that the man, Mr. Merson, is a professional artist. She wants to study art and has gotten little support from her parents. His offer to send her to art school is tempting, but she discovers his role in art forgeries and ends their relationship. *Who Are You?* was chosen for Quick Picks for Reluctant Readers in 2000.

Two other titles of puzzling mysteries for older readers are *The Body of Christopher Creed* by Carol Plum-Ucci, winner of a 2001 Printz Honor, and *Double Helix*, a 2005 Best Book for Young Adults by Nancy Werlin. In the first title, a class geek, Christopher Creed, suddenly disappears. Sixteen-year-old Torey Adams wonders about Christopher and feels guilty for having mistreated him. The entire community wonders if he ran away, committed suicide, or was murdered. A mysterious open ending will intrigue some readers and frustrate others. In the second book, *Double Helix* by Nancy Werlin, it's possible that 18-year-old Eli Samuels has inherited a gene for Huntington's Disease. Instead of attending college, he defies his father and decides to work for Wyatt Transgenetics. Once there, he learns about genetic engineering and how it affects his family. This book is one with overlapping genre characteristics; it can also be considered science fiction.

Murder Mysteries

The most familiar type of mystery is the murder mystery. In young adult murder mysteries, the detectives are usually amateur sleuths, à la Nancy Drew. Readers want a catchy title, an initial hook, fast action, plenty of suspense, lots of details to help solve the crime, and a clear-cut conclusion. Predictable plots and revelation of the killer half-way through the novel will lose readers faster than you can say, "Welcome to the library!" Four novels closely fit the description of an ideal murder mystery for young adults: *The Christmas Killer* by Patricia Windsor, *Facing the Dark* by Michael Harrison, *Ruby in the Smoke* by Philip Pullman, and *Who Killed Mr. Chippendale?* by Mel Glenn. Two of the four novels have great hooks in the first sentence of the book. *The Christmas Killer* begins simply with "Nancy Emerson disappeared the Wednesday before Thanksgiving" (Windsor 1991, 3). *Facing the Dark* begins with this simple sentence: "Dad was arrested for murder on Tuesday" (Harrison 2000, 1). In *Ruby in the Smoke*, the last sentence of the second paragraph is the hook. "Her name was Sally Lockhart; and within fifteen minutes, she was going to kill a man" (Pullman 1985, 3). It's the third poem of the verse novel, *Who Killed Mr. Chippendale?*, before the hook is set. "He does not see, hear, or feel the bullet/That explodes his brain like a star-burst rocket" (Glenn 1996, 5). Murder is quickly established, and the hunt for the killers can begin.

The intriguing plots of these four murder mysteries will keep young adults guessing. In *The Ruby in the Smoke*, a 1986 Best Book for Young Adults, Sally Lockhart is searching desperately for the murderer of her father. The novel is set in Victorian London, where Sally encounters scalawags, opium dens, a legendary ruby, and the term "seven blessings." Two sequels follow for those who want to find out what happens to Sally next: *The Shadow in the North* and *The Tiger in the Well*. In *The Christmas Killer*, a serial killer leaves plastic poinsettias with each victim, and Rose, the main character, is horrified. Using her psychic ability to help solve the crimes, she tries to contact the dead women. This eerie story made the Young Adults' Choices for 1993 list. Narration bounces back and forth between two teens in *Facing the Dark.* Simon's dad is accused of murder; Charlotte's dad was the victim. The teens sort through evidence for a solution while their lives are in danger. This mystery was chosen as a Young Adults' Choices for 2002. The fourth mystery, *Who Killed Mr. Chippendale?*, departs from the first three in style. Written in free verse, Glenn's novel presents multiple voices, revealing high school life and, ultimately, the murderer of an English teacher. Recognized in 1997 as a Best Books for Young Adults and a Quick Pick for Reluctant Readers, this verse novel appeals to middle school and high school age teens who are looking for a quick read.

Psychological Thrillers

The most numerous and popular type of mystery today is the psychological thriller. Terror, suspense, sociopaths, and psychopaths are the hallmarks of these mysteries. An excellent example of this type of novel is Avi's *Wolf-Rider: A Tale of Terror*, an unusually intriguing thriller. It begins with a phone call. Fifteen-year-old Andy picks up the phone one evening to hear a voice confessing to the murder of a young woman. Andy believes the caller is going to murder her and finally locates the college student but can't convince her of the danger she's in. He's accused of stalking her. Once he discovers the man making the calls, Andy's life is in eminent danger. Written at an easy level but with plenty of tension and an inconclusive ending, this novel is meant for older readers.

Three authors are particularly adept at writing psychological thrillers: Robert Cormier, Lois Duncan, and Nancy Werlin. Cormier's *Tenderness* tantalizes readers through the viewpoint of two characters: Eric Poole, 18, who has killed his mother and stepfather and is preying on young women; Lori, 15, a runaway who is fascinated with Eric, even after she knows he's a killer. Cormier's telling is masterful, understated and terrifying. In Duncan's *Killing Mr. Griffin*, readers know who killed Mr. Griffin, an English teacher. A group of high school seniors want revenge for his meanness to them, and they decide to teach him a lesson. After kidnapping him and leaving him alone all night, they return to find that he has died. The most intriguing parts of this psychological thriller are the discovery of the leader's past and the possibilities for lively discussions about the consequences of the teens involved. Werlin's *The Killer's Cousin* features two scary characters: David, who accidentally killed his girlfriend, and Lily, his 11-year-old cousin who hates him. They live together in a dysfunctional family while Lily harasses him until he believes that she is truly dangerous. With the increase of tension to a sensational climax, Werlin's novel satisfies, surprises, and stuns its readers. Fans of these three psychological mysteries will be scrambling to find and read the authors' other novels.

Wilderness Adventure/Survival Stories

Too late? The plane was already into the first choppy waves of the rapids. I caught a glimpse of Raymond's face, the whites of his eyes: he knew we were dead.

From *Far North* by Will Hobbs (1996, 46)

Think of Robinson Crusoe, a man stranded on an island for many years. Will he survive? How does he survive? What adventures does he have? Written in 1719 by Daniel Defoe, *The Life and Surprising Adventures of Robinson Crusoe of York, Mariner* is based on the true story of Alexander Selkirk, a sailor who lived on an uninhabited island from 1704–1709. Defoe's elaborate story is considered a forerunner of adventure/survival stories. Crusoe's tale is preachy and racist but intrigued young readers for his ability to create his own world. Spin-offs of Defoe's story are termed "robinsonades." Gary Paulsen's *Hatchet* is an excellent example of a novel closely following Defoe's basic concept. Brian, the protagonist of *Hatchet*, is stranded in the Canadian wilderness and must learn to find his own food and build his own shelter. *Hatchet* became so popular that Paulsen wrote several sequels to satisfy his readers' requests to learn more about Brian. He reappeared in The *River* (1991), *Brian's Winter* (1996), and *Brian's Return* (1999). Other classic robinsonades carrying survival themes and actions are William Golding's *Lord of the Flies* (1954), Jean George's *My Side of the Mountain* (1959), Scott O'Dell's *Island of the Blue Dolphins* (1961), and Theodore Taylor's *The Cay* (1969).

Stories of surviving hardships in the wilderness share characteristics that appeal to young adults. These stories are peopled with heroes who survive on their own against great odds, or they save someone else's life at great risk to their own life. Heroes exhibit admirable qualities of loyalty, courage, honor, faith, and sacrifice. They are self-reliant, independent problem-solvers who may have to spend long periods of time alone. They face physical hardships from weather, starvation, and injuries. Sometimes animals play significant roles in their adventures; sometimes animals are the focus of the stories. Wilderness adventure stories have the potential to appeal to male readers (Gill 1999). *The River*, the first sequel to *Hatchet*, was voted onto the Young Adults' Choices for 1993.

One Book in Action: **The Big Wander** *by Will Hobbs*

One of the most notable adventure writers for young adults is Will Hobbs, a former teacher and a nature enthusiast who lives in Colorado. He's known for his coming-of-age novels, usually featuring a 14-year-old boy. His stories are classic survival adventures, sometimes predictable, occasionally sentimental, but always suspenseful page-turners. Typically, in a classic coming-of-age novel, an inexperienced boy has a goal in mind, takes risks to achieve it, is isolated by circumstances, manages some success, suffers from at least one risk, shows his courage throughout his ordeal, and emerges a wiser and more mature person. For example, in *The Big Wander*, 14-year-old Clay and his older brother Mike take a long-planned road trip from Seattle, Washington to the southwest. Missing his girlfriend, Mike returns home, and Clay stays in Utah to earn a little money and to search Monument Valley for his favorite uncle, an ex-rodeo star. His search leads him and his burro into the canyons of Navajo country where the humorous and romantic touches with vibrant details of the land flesh out the story. Clay meets a beautiful girl and her family, learns his uncle is in jail for stealing wild horses, and breaks his uncle out of jail. Clay and his uncle race for the state line avoiding pursuers. It's implied that if his uncle leaves Utah and never returns, he won't be prosecuted. Clay emerges a hero, having accomplished his goal, not only finding his uncle but rescuing him. Two other novels written by Hobbs follow similar patterns. *The Maze* takes place in Canyonlands National Park of Utah; *Far North* is a winter survival story in Canada's Northwest Territories. Readers will want to explore Hobbs's official Web site at www.willhobbsauthor.com for information about him and insights into the creation of his books.

Four other titles are notable examples of traditional adventure survival. Joe Cottonwood's *Quake!*, a Young Adults' Choices for 1997, shows 14-year-old Franny's courage when an earthquake destroys their home on Loma Prieta Mountain in California. Eric Campbell's *The Place of Lions* takes readers to Africa, where 14-year-old Chris is stranded on the Serengeti Plain, followed by an aging lion. In Roland Smith's *Peak*, 14-year-old Peak Marcello attempts to gain the summit of Mount Everest and attempts to be the youngest person to ever reach it. *Peak* makes a worthwhile companion book to Jon Krakauer's *Into Thin Air*, a true story of people who have climbed or attempted to climb Mount Everest.

Sports Stories

> I hope all you here in Kennisaw, in this small town in the Oklahoma hills, will remember the greatness that lies within. Stick together. Do good and then push yourself to do even better. The Knights of the hill country stand for honor and integrity, inner fortitude and grit, and the triumph that comes from hard work, and all of you here are a part of that magnificent tradition!
>
> From *Knights of the Hill Country* by Jim Tharp (2006, 32)

The popularity of sports in the United States continues to expand and to encompass an impressive variety, from traditionally popular ones like football and baseball to newer extreme sports, such as snowboarding and off-roading. As with wilderness adventure stories, sports stories can be coming-of-age stories, suspenseful, and with physical challenges and risks. The best sports stories incorporate significant themes and well-developed characters who grow, learn, and have the potential of improving their lives. No one manages this dynamic combination better than author Chris Crutcher. His knowledge of psychology and his experience counseling disturbed young adults has prepared him to bring characters to life, characters with serious problems. Readers of Crutcher's books come away understanding their own lives better than they did before delving into his books. Crutcher's books are much more than sports fiction, of course. His novels fit better under the category of "serious realistic fiction," but I couldn't resist including them in sports fiction with apologies for my own need to categorize. It's a librarian thing. With the understanding that within Crutcher's books human emotions are brewing—anger, racism, abuse, grief, revenge, and prejudice for starters—adults and young adult readers will be caught in the maelstrom and spit out a bit dazed but knowing more about life than before they read the opening lines. Here is a list of his books and the featured sport: *Running Loose* (football, track), *Stotan!* (swimming), *The Crazy Horse Electric Game* (baseball), *Chinese Handcuffs* (basketball), *Staying Fat for Sarah Byrnes* (swimming), *Ironman* (triathlon), and *Whale Talk* (swimming). Read more about Chris Crutcher in a later section on challenged materials.

Sports stories have a history of popularity with boy readers. Journalist and sports announcer John R. Tunis was one of the early writers who captured boys' imaginations with an extensive list of novels. His earliest one was *All-American*, published in 1942, and featured professional football players. Writers in the last few decades produce more sophisticated stories with fully developed characters, integrated themes, and enough details for the flavor of the sport without long, tedious descriptions. Current, popular sports writers include Bruce Brooks, Carl Deuker, Thomas J. Dygard, David Klass, Robert Lipsyte, Chris Lynch, Will Weaver, and more. Not surprisingly, few girls were the heroines of sports fiction in the early days of the genre. That situation is improving with the publication of books like *Dairy Queen* (see humor section); *In Lane Three, Alex Archer* by Tessa Duder; *Going for the Record* by Julie A Swanson; and *River Thunder* by Will Hobbs. Respect for the athletic abilities of girls is evident in these positive stories.

To better understand the quality writing and the versatility of sports fiction, three novels have particular appeal to young adults. Each novel was selected by teens for a Young Adults' Choices list: Edward Bloor's *Tangerine*, John Ritter's *Choosing Up Sides*, and Carl Deuker's *Night Hoops*. There's a lot going on in Bloor's novel about seventh grader Paul, who's legally blind but plays soccer, and his brother Erik, who's an extraordinary football player. Paul has great instincts and "sees" that Erik is far from being the hero everyone thinks he is. In Ritter's novel Luke Bledsoe, a left-hander, is vilified by his own father, a fire-and-brimstone preacher who forbids Luke to use his left hand. Imagine Luke's anger and frustration as a boy with an amazing fast ball whose left arm is broken during a vicious beating by his father. Because the story is told by Luke in a homey first-person voice, readers have a chance to be inspired by this insightful, dramatic story. In *Night Hoops*, sophomore Nick Abbott loves to play basketball but has to deal with his parents' divorce, his brother Scott, his father's disapproval, and a disturbed teammate's anger and aggressiveness. Shooting hoops in the quiet of the night helps. Blow-by-blow basketball plays mixed with complex characters and their dilemmas has the potential to guide readers to see that there are no easy answers in life.

Romantic Love Stories

Because they both feel intense love but there is no way either one can express it. She is not with the man she loves, and he loves her but realizes she loves someone else. Suffering—that's what love is all about.
From *If I Love You, Am I Trapped Forever?* by M. E. Kerr (1973, 61)

Hearts and roses, longing gazes and lingering kisses are signs of first love, of young emerging love, and of awakening sexuality. To state the obvious, romantic love is a universal experience. The search for a partner begins early in one's life, usually with the onset of puberty. Young adult literature mirrors a joyful, painful, complex time in young people's lives. In the 1940s and 1950s the most popular romantic novels for girls were those written by Sally Benson, Betty Cavanna, Maureen Daly, Rosamond Du Jardin, Anne Emery, Mary Stoltz, and James Summers (Dunning 1959). Maureen Daly's *Seventeenth Summer* (1942) is beautifully written with lush descriptions of scenery. For modern girls, Angie's dating restrictions will seem bizarre because they are so outdated: Don't call a boy. Waiting to hear the phone in the house ring. References to "necking." Angie is considered too young to be dating seriously, yet she has recently graduated from high school. Young adults will be amazed at her passivity and shyness. Still, it's a romantic story of a summer romance that can touch the most cynical heart.

Many romantic novels for young adults contain bits and pieces of romance. In Jim Tharp's *Knights of the Hill Country* star football player Hampton Green gradually falls for Sara, a girl with bushy brown hair but with "sad soulful brown eyes. I noticed them from day one but never figured they had much to do with me till a few weeks back when she come up after class and talked to me" (Tharp 2006, 37). Despite the slowly developing romance between Hampton and Sara, the story is primarily about Oklahoma football and Hampton's coming of age. Surprisingly, as universal as love is to young people, few young adult books are all about romance. There are romantic elements in novels across the genres, however. For instance, in Annette Curtis Klause's *Blood and Chocolate*, two werewolves fall in love. This section on romantic love concentrates on a few titles using a basic formula:

Teen meets teen.

They fall in love.

There are misunderstandings.

They make up.

They live happily, continuing to date and to be in love.

In Louise Plummer's *The Unlikely Romance of Kate Bjorkman*, we see this formula unfold. Kate falls in love with her older brother's friend Richard during Christmas vacation, and to her delight, he loves her. During an elaborate party, Kate goes looking for Richard and finds him kissing her ex-best friend Ashley. She won't speak to him or look at him, but they make up after he digs a snow cave in her Minnesota backyard and holds up a sign "Will work for food." After six weeks, she considers their relationship a "real romance," and it is. "I want to gloat and bask in this lovely feeling of being in love. And if I do not have long, silky legs and long, blonde locks, I do have sensuous, full lips, and if I have not written three-paragraph kisses, I have kissed them" (Plummer 1995, 2).

Boys and Girls in Love

Most teen romances are written from a girl's point of view and read by girls, but there are also titles available with male characters. Romances may be considered exclusive reading material for girls, but novels with a boy narrator have a better chance of being read by boys, although there's no guarantee boys will read them. A sample of romances feature some with girl narrators, some with boy narrators, and a few with both.

Annie on My Mind by Nancy Garden. Two high school girls fall in love and live happily.

Much Ado about Prom Night by William D. McCants. Laughter, love, and social issues combine for Becca and Jeff, as they antagonize each other and long for each other.

My Heartbeat by Garret Freymann-Weyr. A bisexual love story of Ellen and her brother's best friend Link who is gay.

Nick and Norah's Playlist by Rachel Cohn and David Levithan. At a Manhattan bar Nick grabs Norah and asks her to be his girlfriend for five minutes to provoke a recent ex-girlfriend.

Tom Loves Anna Loves Tom by Bruce Clements. For Tom and Anna it is almost love at first sight, and that love continues comfortingly throughout the novel.

Weetzie Bat by Francesca Lia Block. Weetzie Bat, a child of Hollywood, finds her Secret Agent Lover Man, and her gay friend Dirk finds a blond surfer. They all live happily together in an off-beat world of their own design.

Fairy Tale Characters in Love

A sure way to attract young adults to novels based on fairy tales is to read a picture book fairy tale to them. Not all children grew up hearing familiar tales and appreciating beautiful illustrations. Under the guise of reviewing a familiar story, read *Beauty and the Beast* by Jeanne-Marie Le Prince de Beaumont, an eighteenth-century French version, lavishly illustrated by Hilary Knight. Share Marianna Mayer's version of *Beauty and the Beast*, movingly illustrated by Mercer Mayer. The addition of beautifully illustrated versions will add an enriching layer to your booktalk. Then briefly booktalk romantic novels based on fairy tales such as these:

Beast by Donna Jo Napoli. Prince Orasmyn of Persia is turned into a lion, treks to France, and finds a haunted castle to occupy. Then the lovely Bella appears.

Beastly by Alex Flinn. Cursed by a witch and betrayed by his father, an arrogant 16-year-old is isolated and despairing in New York City. Lindy, a 16-year-old girl is his redemption.

Beauty: A Retelling of Beauty & the Beast by Robin McKinley. Still the loveliest version of them all.

Rose Daughter by Robin McKinley. Also a retelling of "Beauty and the Beast" but fuller than McKinley's 1978 version.

Spindle's End by Robin McKinley. Based on the story of Briar Rose, better known as Sleeping Beauty. Share Trina Schart Hyman's *The Sleeping Beauty* for its detailed depiction of the familiar story.

The Tower Room by Adele Geras. In an all-girls boarding school, Simon climbs the scaffolding of the tower room to rendezvous with Megan. Share Paul O. Zelinsky's Italian-themed picture book, *Rapunzel.*

Zel by Donna Jo Napoli. Zel, her mother, and a young nobleman each tell their stories as they are drawn closer together by conflicting emotions in this retelling of "Rapunzel."

Be sure to include in your book collection picture book versions of the tales you plan to booktalk. A combination of novels and picture books makes a good-looking display for the tops of book cases and will intrigue potential readers.

Classic Characters in Love

In recent years there has been a small surge of novels based on Shakespearean dramas and Shakespeare's life. For high school students who are reading *Romeo and Juliet* and *Othello*, these novels may have special appeal. They are well-written and more accessible than the plays. High school English teachers may appreciate knowing about the books. Consider offering to booktalk these titles in their classrooms and handing out bookmarks with a list of the following books:

Cyrano by Geraldine McCaughrean. The classic story of a witty man with an enormous nose who falls in love with beautiful Roxanne.

Loving Will Shakespeare by Carolyn Meyer. The imagined complex life of Anne Hathaway and her frustration with her husband.

Othello by Julius Lester. A tragic romance.

Romeo's Ex: Rosaline's Story by Lisa Fiedler. Romeo loved Rosaline before he fell for Juliet. This is Rosaline's story.

Romiette and Julio by Sharon Draper. For this modern-day tragedy romance, the setting is Corpus Christi, Texas.

Someone Like Summer by M. E. Kerr. An interracial Romeo and Juliet story.

Literature in Action: Love Letters to Authors

For Valentine's Day or during Teen Read Week in October, invite teens to write love letters to their favorite authors. Collaborate with an English or reading teacher interested in teaching the art of letter writing. Booktalk epistolary novels (those written in letter form) to use as models for letters and for reading pleasure. Stephen Chbosky's *The Perks of Being a Wallflower* is an example of a coming-of-age epistolary novel. Fifteen-year-old Charlie writes to an unnamed "friend" about the best friend who committed suicide the previous year, his new gay best friend, his pregnant sister, his new social set at school, and the sexual abuse he suffered as a child. Chbosky's novel isn't a love story, but students will find the rhythm of letter writing. To get students started on their own letters ask: "How much do you love your favorite author? What would you like to tell him or her?" Display love letters in the library next to novels by the authors students wrote to.

Stories of Sexual Orientation

Since the publication of Nancy Garden's *Annie on My Mind*, young adult fiction has encompassed former taboos about featuring gays, lesbians, bisexuals, transsexuals, and those questioning their own sexual identity. Possibly "twenty percent of all teenagers have some degree of same-sex orientation" (Whelan 2006, 46). With a population that large, school and public libraries need to include gay-themed fiction and nonfiction books in their collections if they are intent on serving all young adults. According to Debra Lau Whelan's article, "Out and Ignored," young adults find identity, safety, and comfort in reading about characters with similar sexual orientation. Whelan recommends steps for building a gay-themed collection, including advice for avoiding book challenges. The following recommended fiction titles explore issues of same-sex relationships:

Am I Blue? Coming Out of the Silence edited by Marion Dane Bauer. This anthology of original stories by well-known children's and young adult authors has become a classic.

Boy Meets Boy by David Levithan. Charming, surreal, and upbeat aptly describe this novel about a gay high school sophomore in a contemporary world of tolerance.

Deliver Us from Evie by M. E. Kerr. Told from the viewpoint of Evie's 15-year-old brother, readers witness Evie's infatuation with Patty, a banker's daughter, and the resulting conflicts in a rural community.

Empress of the World by Sara Ryan. Nicola attends a summer program for gifted students and finds friends of both genders, both platonic and romantic.

Geography Club by Brent Hartinger. Russel is delighted to be included in a support group of seven friends who accept each other for who they really are.

Hard Love by Ellen Wittlinger. John Galardi and Marisol become friends and bond over issues of zines while Marisol explores her identity as a lesbian, inevitably disappointing John as he becomes more and more enamored with her.

Luna by Julie Anne Peters. Regan supports her transgender brother as he pursues his desire to be a girl.

Parrotfish by Ellen Wittlinger. Angela "comes out" at home and at school as Grady, a girl who has always known she was a boy inside.

Peter by Kate Walker. Peter struggles with his identity when he doesn't want to have sex with a girl and feels drawn to his older brother's gay friend.

Rainbow Boys by Alex Sanchez. Three senior gay teens are realistically portrayed as they deal with love and sexual orientation issues at school.

So Hard to Say by Alex Sanchez. Frederick, a transfer student from Wisconsin, is absorbed into Latina Xio's group of girlfriends, yet he's attracted to Victor, his soccer buddy, not to Xio.

Concerns about Sexuality in Young Adult Fiction

It seems appropriate to end a section on light realistic fiction and begin one on dark realistic fiction with a topic that may straddle the two types. Romantic love that ends happily fits the lighter side; sexual abuse is the darker side. In between there are concerns about unwanted pregnancies, single parents, and sexual experiences. All of these concerns may be resolved favorably or not. One certainty is that sexual relations at one level or another are in the minds, hearts, and bodies of teens. Tanya Lee Stone, the author of *Bad Boys Can Be Good for a Girl*, expresses her feelings about an author's role: "I would like to see books for teens reflect male and female main characters who are allowed to be healthy sexual beings, able to experience sex and intimacy without feeling ashamed or being punished" (2006, 465). Judy Blume's *Forever* was (and still is) enthusiastically embraced by teen girls for its honest view of one girl's healthy sexual experience.

At least there is more being offered to young adults than pregnancy as a terrible consequence of sexual relations. Having said that, the reality of teen pregnancy continues to be a topic in young adult fiction as it is in life. Ruth Pennebaker's *Don't Think Twice* tells the story of a group of girls in a home for pregnant teens in Texas in the 1960s. Each girl's story is uniquely heartbreaking, and narrated by 18-year-old Anne. Her acerbic view provides dark humor and covers up the sympathy she feels for many of the girls, most of whom will give up their babies for adoption. Harriet is one girl who manages to alienate everyone with her confidence. "It must be nice to go through life thinking you have all the answers and dying to tell everybody about them. Harriet spends most of her days looking so smug, I want to hit her. I keep hoping that she'll read a book about saints and decide to become a martyr and throw herself on a pitchfork instead of torturing us to death by preaching all the time" (Pennebaker 1996, 152). Angela Johnson presents a unique point of view in *The First Part Last*. Instead of the story of a single mother, Bobby, a 16-year-old boy is determined to be a father to their newborn baby. The baby's mother is in a coma after the delivery. Johnson articulates the realism of taking care of a baby and

Bobby's devotion to their baby, Feather. Beautifully written, *The First Part Last* won the 2004 Printz Award and the 2004 Coretta Scott King Author Award.

Two books demonstrating sexual experiences that go far beyond Katherine's and Michael's "first time" in *Forever* are Melvin Burgess's *Doing It* and Ellen Wittlinger's *Sandpiper*. In *Doing It* three teenaged boys are obsessed with sex and take the opportunities presented to them to engage in every aspect they can. The strength of the novel is the honest portrayal of sexual situations and how the characters react. Adults will be shocked by the content, but teens will be mesmerized. In *Sandpiper*, a 15-year-old girl known for her blow jobs is threatened by one of her former partners, Derek. He attempts to rape her, but she's rescued by Walker (later known as Aiden), a recent friend of hers. As with many young adult novels, there's more substance to this novel than Sandpiper's sexual escapades. As she and Aiden develop a true friendship, gradually revealing themselves, they form a strong bond that comforts them both.

DARK MODERN REALISTIC FICTION

> She's dead, isn't she? If she was alive, I wouldn't be handcuffed to a table in an interview room. You'd take her statement before you'd come at me for a confession, right?
>
> From *What Happened to Cass McBride?* by Gail Giles (2006, 1)

Like light modern realistic fiction, dark modern realistic novels tell stories that could happen. Dark modern realistic fiction integrates controversial topics and previous taboos into well-written, well-developed stories. These novels are disturbing, sometimes shocking, but they reflect the lives of today's teens—not the lives of every teen but of enough teens for the stories to be authentic. Today's well-written dark fiction is not the typical "problem novel" of the 1960s. Typically, novels "focused on one social issue and how it complicated the protagonist's life" (Hart 2004, 40). S. E. Hinton's *The Outsiders* is an example of this type of novel. The Socs, a gang of rich kids, continually push and challenge a group of "greasers." Ponyboy, one of the greasers, is a likeable protagonist who becomes fully engaged in the battles between the two groups with tragic results. Young adult fiction is maturing. It's better written, more sophisticated, and more intense than those early novels. Authors of the 1970s, such as Robert Cormier, Paul Zindel, and Madeleine L'Engle, wrote novels "with complex characters and rich, layered plots—key ingredients in any serious piece of literature—and they included social issues pertinent to the era" (Hart 2004, 39).

Today's dark fiction centers on violence. Murder, rape, sexual abuse, suicide, shootings, bullying—the list could be taken from continually running news programs. Other topics, seemingly less violent, include drug abuse, homelessness, and incarceration and inevitably include some level of violence.

Rape

She put the survival knife down on the table. It pointed across at him.

She couldn't breathe.

"From now on—" she said. "I'll have this knife." Her knees were watery, and her mouth trembled. "All the time."

From *When She Hollers* by Cynthia Voigt (1994, 1)

Recent novels about sexual abuse and rape reflect changing knowledge as well as an avoidance of stereotypes discussed in Carolyn Lehman's article, "Hero, Victim, or Monster?" Lehman uses four questions when evaluating stories:

1. Does the story perpetuate stereotypes?
2. Does the survivor have agency?
3. Are the complexities of abuse dynamics portrayed in age-appropriate ways?
4. Is the potential for healing acknowledged? (Lehman 2006, 36–37)

Positive approaches to these traumas can be found in novels by Chris Lynch, Cynthia Voigt, Leslea Newman, and Laurie Halse Anderson. In Voigt's *When She Hollers*, 17-year-old Tish rebels against continuous raping by her stepfather. Readers breathlessly follow Tish through one day as she confronts her stepfather and asks for help from a friend's lawyer father. Depiction of this rape victim is raw and unrelenting. Melinda, the victim in Anderson's *Speak*, responds differently from Tish. Melinda gets drunk and is raped at a party. She calls the police, who break up the party, making her a school pariah, and then she goes mute. She gets justice by writing messages in the blank pages of Judy Blume's *Forever* about Andy, the student who raped her, and through a final confrontation. In Lynch's *Inexcusable*, Keir, a senior, date rapes his girlfriend but denies it. The viewpoint of a rapist is an unusual but effective one as readers get to know Keir but understand that he's being dishonest with himself. Gigi, his girlfriend, is no victim as she tells him clearly, "You raped me" (Lynch 2005, 140). Newman's *Jailbait* brings yet another aspect to this crime against young women. Andi's loneliness makes her vulnerable to the advances of a 30-year-old drifter, Frank. They meet when she's 15, and once she's 16, they have sexual intercourse, and he becomes physically and emotionally abusive. Andi becomes wiser and gains enough self-worth to get away from Frank. Hopefully, these novels will be eye-openers to teen girls and will make them more cautious in their relationships with the opposite sex.

As in life, girls are not the only sexually vulnerable ones in young adult fiction. In Catherine Atkins's *When Jeff Comes Home*, a 16-year-old boy was abducted and abused mentally, physically, and emotionally. He's brought home by his kidnapper two and a half years later but refuses to talk about his trauma initially. Then there's Barry Lyga's *Boy Toy*. Josh, a seventh grader, is seduced and sexually abused by his beautiful history teacher. The novel, shocking in details yet skillfully written, is chillingly uncomfortable to read.

School Violence

He giggles. "Just wanted to see the look on yer face." And again. Same spot. Pounding me. Punching. My fingers itch and curl. I want to gouge his eyes out. I want to bite into his throat. I want to rake furrows into his stupid, doughy face.

From *The Astonishing Adventures of Fanboy and Goth Girl* by Barry Lyga (2006, 33)

Bullying, frustration, and anger only begin a list of reasons that some young adults lash out at teachers, administrators, and students. School violence has been prominently in the news since the Littleton, Colorado tragedy, and this timely topic has become increasingly available in young adult literature. Through sharing young adult literature, school personnel and public librarians have opportunities to discuss issues involved in bullying and related violence and to explore avenues of aid and alternate ways for students to be heard. Discussing novels like Todd Strasser's *Give a Boy a Gun*, Nancy Garden's *Endgame*, and Barry Lyga's *The Astonishing Adventures of Fanboy and Goth Girl* can open these dialogues, giving teens a chance to talk about hypothetical situations and how they would respond.

As with the best young adult literature, there is more within the pages of a book than a topic. The novels of Strasser, Garden, and Lyga are more than forums for teaching about school violence. That's what makes them particularly suitable for recommending to teens. In *The Astonishing Adventures of Fanboy and Goth Girl*, 15-year-old Fanboy is a geek who is being bullied at school and mistreated at home. He can't drive yet, and he can't get away from either setting. Fortunately for Fanboy, he has three advantages that keep him from tragedy. First, he meets Kyra (aka Goth Girl), who sees him being hit in gym class and IMs him; they become friends. Second, he's creating a graphic novel. Third, he carries a bullet with him at all times and uses it like a worry stone when he gets anxious or when his rage flares. Dark humor relieves the tension of the story. For Fanboy, ignoring the bullies doesn't work for him, but letting his frustrations feed his art saves him. In *Endgame*, Gray Wilton is not as fortunate as Fanboy. The three bullet holes in a student's metal locker get your attention first. The dust jacket lets the reader know what's coming. By moving to another town and another school, Gray was hoping to leave the bullying behind. He finds nonstop harassment and eventually takes his dad's semi-automatic to school and starts shooting. As Gray awaits his trial, his defense lawyer interviews him, trying to understand why he did it. The road Gray is traveling is tragically predictable, but the reader's view of Gray's confused and violent thoughts is horrifying. *Give a Boy a Gun*, a documentary novel combining information and fiction, chronicles the journey of two outcast boys who have been bullied and want revenge. In the gymnasium of Middletown High School, the boys hold their classmates hostage at a school dance. Gary shoots, and then commits suicide. Brandon is beaten into a coma by his classmates. Strasser's unique approach to the topic of school violence opens up pathways for questions, reflection, and discussion among students, faculty, administrators, and parents.

Street Violence, Drug Abuse, and Homelessness

It's not uncommon for dark realistic fiction to combine street violence, drug abuse, and homelessness all in one novel. These novels are further characterized by raw language, crowded cities, poverty, despair, and glimmers of hope. In Coe

Booth's *Tyrell*, all of these characteristics are at work. Tyrell is carrying more pressure than is reasonable to expect of a 17-year-old. His dad's in jail, his mother's useless, his little brother's needy, and his girlfriend expects more than he can give. Evicted from the projects, Tyrell has dropped out of school to take care of his mother and brother. With no money they live in the worst motel possible while waiting for a decent shelter to open. Tyrell has an idea to make enough money to move them into an apartment, but it takes plenty of luck to manage it. In Paul Volponi's *Rooftop*, Clay and his cousin Addison enter a drug treatment program. Addison is fatally and mistakenly shot by police. Clay sees what happens but doesn't tell the whole truth. In Todd Strasser's *Can't Get There from Here*, Maybe has run away from home and is living on the streets of New York City with other homeless teens who have banded together to make a sort of family. Maybe's first-person view of life on the streets is chilling. There is hope though in the kindness of a librarian and the possibility that Maybe can get help and leave the streets. These stories and more like them paint a heart-breaking picture of desperate lives. While they are imbued with current societal issues, the stories remain gripping and unforgettable.

Dealing with Grief

Death by cancer and suicide are relatively common topics in young adult novels. In these novels, teens grieve for their lost loved ones—grandparents, parents, friends, and siblings. Death takes a huge toll on the health of the survivors. Today's stories are heartbreaking, but they're stories of hope, too. A few years ago, my sister-in-law's Yorkshire Terrier died, and she cried for days. A few weeks later her five-year-old granddaughter came to visit her and told her, "You've got to do three things. One, stop crying. Two, get over it. Three, buy a hamster!" Somewhere in that spunky advice is a message of love and the need to recover from loss. Young adult novels have the potential to bring comfort and understanding.

Naturally, books about grief are going to cover a full range of emotions. We know that books expressing characters' thoughts and feelings are going to appeal more to girls than to boys (Carlsen 1980). While a middle school librarian, I kept an ongoing bibliography for girls titled "Books to Make You Cry." This list was at the request of a group of sixth-grade girls. They cheerily said they got together at sleepovers, read passages from books about death, and cried together. I often wondered what their parents thought. A 2005 Popular Paperbacks list is just right for this type of reader: "Read 'em & Weep." Two novels dealing with death from cancer are particularly moving. In Margo Rabb's *Cures for Heartbreak*, unlucky Mia, a ninth-grader, suffers from the death of her mother and then her father's heart attack. Against the backdrop of these tragedies, Mia experiences typical young adult events and emotions with some humor to relieve the sadness. One of the most touching experiences is her friendship with Sasha, a boy with leukemia who's confined to a wheelchair. In the second novel, Davida Wills Hurwin's *A Time for Dancing*, best friends Jules and Sam learn that Jules has lymphoma and must undergo chemotherapy. The closeness of the two friends and Sam's devotion to Jules as she is dying is heart-wrenching but inspiring.

Violent death leaves wounded survivors, but suicide adds a dose of guilt. Survivors wonder why they didn't recognize the signs of an impending suicide. They wonder what they could have done to stop it. And they wonder why. Why did this young person want to die? Richard Peck's *Remembering the Good Times* offers the positive comfort of friends in the midst of a mysterious tragedy. Buck, Trav, and Kate have been inseparable friends throughout junior and senior high school. Then good-looking, smart, popular Trav, aged 16, hangs himself. It's hard for his parents and friends to understand why. In a second title, John Green's *Looking for Alaska*, friends at an Alabama boarding school are fascinated with Alaska Young, a confident, provocative feminist. Sixteen-year-old Miles is mesmerized by her, even as she indulges in self-destructive behavior. Tragically, she ends her life after drinking and crashing her car into a police cruiser, killing her instantly. In this powerful coming-of-age novel, the grieving process is acted out with questions about suicide hovering in the background.

HISTORICAL FICTION

I speak seldom, if ever, of those terrible months of 1692. Nor does my husband. Indeed, I thought I had put them behind me until I came into this church today. When I did, once I entered these portals, it all came rushing back.

From *A Break with Charity: A Story about the Salem Witch Trials*
by Ann Rinaldi (1992, 1).

Historical fiction takes readers to the past through setting, events, and characters that clearly evoke a time from at least 20 years ago. Although young people may learn from fiction about history, the emphasis is on the pleasure of the story. To journey with Eleanor and Thomas on a religious pilgrimage from England across France to Spain in 1299 in Frances Temple's *The Ramsay Scallop* is to encounter pilgrims and learn their incredible stories. To follow Adam in Napoleon's army across Europe to Russia is to know the horror and discomfort of war in Josef Holub's *An Innocent Soldier*. Yet there can be humor and joy in stories of historical fiction, too. Richard Peck's *A Long Way from Chicago*, *A Year Down Yonder*, *The Teacher's Funeral*, and *Here Lies the Librarian* are embedded with history and laughter.

Characteristics of the Best Historical Fiction

It's expected that the best historical fiction will have those qualities of any "good" story: well-developed characters and plot, a believable setting, a readable and exciting style, and a worthwhile underlying theme. In historical fiction settings, characters, and events are especially vital to develop the feeling that readers are experiencing the past.

1. Setting should be steeped in accurate details of place and time. In Katherine Paterson's *Lyddie*, a young girl journeys to a mill town in Lowell, Massachusetts to earn money to help her family. Conditions

for factory girls in the 1840s are severe, and Lyddie wonders if she can survive the hard work and illness. "Lyddie went to work in the icy darkness and returned again at night. She never saw the sun. The brief noon break did not help. The sky was always oppressive and gray, and the smoke of thousands of chimneys hung low and menacing" (Paterson 1991, 101).

2. Significant events establish a story in a particular time and place. In Graham Salisbury's *Under the Blood-Red Sun* the Japanese attack on Pearl Harbor in 1941 changes Tomikazu's world forever. "An ear-shattering roar suddenly thundered down on us, a plane flying way too low. A dark fighter. It blasted over the trees. I ducked, and covered my head with my glove" (Salisbury 1994, 105).

3. Characters personalize history by showing how societal conditions affect their lives. In Carolyn Meyer's *White Lilacs*, the white folks of Dillon, Texas decide to move the black community to an ugly area outside of town to make room for a park. Rose Lee Jefferson, 12 years old, lived in Freedomtown, observing and experiencing how the relocation affected those closest to her. "In my memory Juneteenth 1921 was the last good day for Freedomtown, all of us together in one place. It seemed fitting that the day had ended with a flaming cross in the church grove. It was a sight I'd never forget" (Meyer 1993, 111).

Those same elements of setting, characters, and events can become traps for poor writing. Setting can fail to thoroughly integrate the historical scene into other story elements. Characters may be stereotypes of a particular period. Emphasis may be on teaching history rather than on story. Mistakes or anachronisms may occur, incorrectly assigning certain values or technology to a time period (Donelson and Nilsen 2004).

Authors in Action: Richard Peck

In 1971 Richard Peck quit his job teaching English in New York City and began writing his first young adult novel, *Don't Look and It Won't Hurt.* In the beginning phase of his writing career, Peck was informed by the current trend of "problem novels" for teens. These were realistic stories that had a societal problem at the core. *Are You in the House Alone?* is the story of a teen girl who is raped; *Father Figure* focuses on a missing father and a teen who takes care of his younger brother; and *Remembering the Good Times* is the heartbreaking story of a teen suicide and the effect the tragedy has on his friends and family. Peck empathizes with young adults who rely on their peers for support and advice rather than on their families and teachers. In the latest phase of his writing, he reflects on the past with great wit, mixing together hyperbole, slapstick, understatement, and nostalgia. For *A Long Way from Chicago* he won a 1999 Newbery Honor followed by the 2001 Newbery Medal for *A Year Down Yonder*, its sequel. The first novel delights readers with the antics of Grandma Dowdel each summer when her two grandchildren visit her. The sequel takes place in 1937 and tells Mary Alice's story when—much to her horror—she has to spend a year with her unpredictable Grandma Dowdel. Other historical novels that followed are *The River Between Us*, set along the banks of the Mississippi; *Fair Weather*, a visit to the World's Fair; *The Teacher's Funeral: A Comedy in Three Parts*, set in 1904 Indiana in a one-room schoolhouse; *Here Lies the Librarian*, a 1914 tribute to living librarians; and *On the Wings of Heroes*, a home front view of World War II.

In his writing career, Richard Peck has published more than 30 books for young people and garnered many book awards and special awards for his contribution as an outstanding author. He was honored with a 2001 National Humanities Medal, presented by the President and First Lady Laura Bush; a National Council of Teachers of English/ALAN Award; the 1990 Margaret A. Edwards Award; and a 1991 Silver Medallion from The University of Southern Mississippi.

War

Inevitably, many historical novels focus on war. War offers the opportunity for great drama, excitement, heroes, and tragedy. Esther Forbes's *Johnny Tremain* (1943), a classic story taught for many years in classrooms across the United States, won the Newbery Medal in 1944. The story is set at the outbreak of the American Revolution with a well-drawn main character, an apprentice silversmith, who immediately captures the reader's attention. Johnny meets famous people, such as Paul Revere, John Hancock, and Samuel Adams, as they are caught up in dangerous and exciting events in Boston. Forty-five years later, Walter Dean Myers's *Fallen Angels* (1988) offers readers another quality experience in historical fiction with a realistic depiction of the Vietnam War told through the view of Perry, a Harlem teenager. Perry and his comrades face the terrible violence of war through combat on the front lines. Readers can't avoid being caught up in the riveting action and the fate of this group of young black men. In an interview, Meyers says he reminds himself when writing "to keep my focus on the characters," and to ask himself, "How do my characters react to what's going on around them?" (Miller and Parker 2007, 688).

Stories of the Holocaust

Young adults are fascinated with the Holocaust. They are drawn to it with curiosity and a sense of horror. A high school girl in Kansas told me that she couldn't read *Maus I* because it was too real, too frightening. That may be the case for some students. The list below includes nonfiction as well as fiction telling of unspeakable acts and tragedy in Germany and Poland from very different approaches.

Anne Frank: The Diary of a Young Girl by Anne Frank. Nonfiction. At 13 years old, Anne enters her hiding place with her family on July 5, 1942; Anne and her sister Margot die of typhus at Auschwitz concentration camp sometime between late February to early March, 1945.

Anne Frank: A Hidden Life by Mirjam Pressler. Nonfiction. In this companion to *Anne Frank: Diary of a Young Girl*, Pressler fleshes out the details of daily life for the two years that Anne hid in the Secret Annex.

The Book Thief by Markus Zusak. Fiction. In Nazi Germany Liesl steals books and learns of cruelty and kindness as death tells the story and releases souls from their misery. A 2007 Printz Honor.

Briar Rose by Jane Yolen. Fiction. This remarkable fantasy, a version of "Sleeping Beauty," makes a surprising connection with Rebecca's grandmother and a woman who survived the Holocaust.

Hitler Youth: Growing Up in Hitler's Shadow by Susan Campbell Bartoletti. Nonfiction. The account of children who were forced to participate in the Third Reich's youth program and of those who resisted is fascinating but heartbreaking.

Maus I, A Survivor's Tale: My Father Bleeds History by Art Spiegelman and *Maus II: Here My Troubles Began* by Art Spiegelman. Nonfiction. These two black-and-white graphic novels won the Pulitzer Prize in 1992 for their stunning view of triumph and tragedy of a Holocaust survivor.

Milkweed by Jerry Spinelli. Fiction. Told from the perspective of a young orphaned boy, this story of Warsaw is matter-of-factly brutal.

Night by Elie Wiesel. Nonfiction. Wiesel's memoir of surviving the evil of the Holocaust but questioning his belief in God is riveting.

No Pretty Pictures: A Child of War by Anita Lobel. Nonfiction. This memoir of a young girl who survived the Nazis trap in Poland is heart-wrenching.

Other Historical Eras

Of course, historical fiction is about more subjects than war. The following novels are presented, not with summaries but with a few lines quoted from their openings. They represent notable historical time periods that are not focused on war and include a notable selection of novels. Use the quotes for 10-second booktalks!

The Astonishing Life of Octavian Nothing, V. I: The Pox Party by M. T. Anderson. "The men who raised me were lords of matter, and in the dim chambers I watched as they traced the spinning of bodies celestial in vast, iron courses, and bid sparks to dance upon their hands; they read the bodies of fish as if each dying trout or shad was a fresh Biblical Testament, the wet and twitching volume of a new-born Pentateuch" (Anderson 2006, 4). Revolution Era.

Catherine Called Birdy by Karen Cushman. "I am commanded to write an account of my days: I am bit by fleas and plagued by family. That is all there is to say" (Cushman 1994, 1). Middle Ages.

The Land by Mildred D. Taylor. "I loved my daddy. I loved my brothers too. But in the end it was Mitchell Thomas and I who were most like brothers, with a bond that couldn't be broken. The two of us came into Mississippi together by way of east Texas, and that was when we were still boys, long after we had come to our understanding of each other" (Taylor 2001, 3). Post-Civil War.

Lizzie Bright and the Buckminster Boy by Gary Schmidt. "Turner Buckminster had lived in Phippsburg, Maine, for fifteen minutes shy of six hours. He had dipped his hand in its waves and licked the salt from his fingers. He had smelled the sharp resin of the pines. He had heard the low rhythm of the bells on the buoys that balanced on the ridges of the sea. He had seen the fine clapboard parsonage beside the church where he was to live, and the small house set a ways beyond it that puzzled him some.

Turner Buckminster had lived in Phippsburg, Maine, for almost six whole hours. He didn't know how much longer he could stand it" (Schmidt 2004, 1). 1960s.

The Ramsay Scallop by Frances Temple. "Four times now, Carla had let Elenor make the long walk into Peterborough market with Father Gregory. This time was best of all: Michaelmas, last festival of the year before Advent, in the last year of the century, 1299. Excitement and fear were in the wind" (Temple 1994, 2). Crusades.

Sarny: A Life Remembered by Gary Paulsen. "The reading didn't spread so fast at first. Took on to be slow, like watching spilled molasses smearing across a table. Nightjohn he was gone but I got to where the letters meant more all the time and pretty soon I was working words with two and even three parts in them, writing whole sentences helping others and before too long some were doing the same" (Paulsen 1997, 9). Sequel to *Nightjohn*. Post–Civil War.

Wolf by the Ears by Ann Rinaldi. "Only twice in all my years on this place have I ever been inside the master's private quarters. No one is allowed in there. Only my mama. And that's because she is the mistress of his wardrobe" (Rinaldi 1991, 3). Pre–Civil War.

LIBRARIANS IN ACTION: BOOKTALKING

What is a booktalk? Simply stated, it's a teaser, a bit of advertising to intrigue readers, like a movie trailer. A booktalk is an effective and inexpensive way to encourage young adults to check out books and read! It can be daunting to teens to enter a library of 10,000 plus books and try to choose something "good" to read. In schools they may have limited time to do so. By booktalking frequently and briefly, librarians give teens places to start looking. Hearing booktalks helps teens determine what they might like to read. Booktalks offer the opportunity to build a relationship between a teen and a librarian.

The content of a basic booktalk can be expressed by answering the following questions:

1. What's the title?
2. Who's the author?
3. What's the basic plot?
4. Who's the main character?
5. What's the problem faced by the character?
6. What's an intriguing way to end the booktalk?

Once those questions are answered, you have an outline of your booktalk. Next, write a draft of your booktalk, keeping the following steps in mind:

1. Show enthusiasm for the book.
2. Make eye contact with individuals in the audience.
3. Describe a fascinating character, setting, event, or conversation.
4. Read a few sentences or a paragraph from the book.
5. Reflect the tone of the book in everything that you say.
6. Make a concluding comment or transition to another book.

A Checklist to Successful Booktalking

What should you, the librarian, do to make sure your booktalks are successful and have potential readers clamoring for books?

_____Read the book, the whole book!

_____Read reviews of the book.

_____Love the books you booktalk! Skip those you personally don't like.

_____Introduce and end each booktalk with the title and the author's name.

_____Don't tell about events past a third to a half of the book. Leave some surprises for the readers.

_____If you read a section from the book, choose a short one.

_____Keep it brief—3–5 minutes for each book.

_____Don't deliver a review of the book! Literary criticism isn't the point of a booktalk.

_____Practice your booktalk so that you are confident.

_____Choose a variety of genres, including poetry and informational books.

_____Be sure you have books that will appeal to both boys and girls.

_____If you booktalk several books, use a general theme, such as Survival, New Books, Creepy Books, or Tough Decisions to loosely tie the books together.

_____Develop smooth transitions between books. A general theme can help with this.

_____Include both lighthearted and serious books.

_____Stay true to the viewpoint of the book. If it's a serious story, let your audience know by the selections you choose and the way you talk about the book.

_____Keep a record of your booktalks so you can use them with the same grades another year if appropriate.

_____Keep a written version of your booktalk to refresh your memory in case you booktalk the same book next year.

_____Check Young Adults' Choices Awards lists for titles popular with teens at www.reading.org

_____Peruse Popular Paperbacks for Young Adults annual lists for quirky topical lists online at www.ala.org/yalsa

Survival! A Booktalking Topic in Action

One way to approach booktalking 6–12 books is to choose a broad theme, such as growing up or survival. Broad themes allow you to choose many different genres, including poetry and nonfiction. There's no need to announce the theme to your audience or to try to teach the theme. On the other hand, you can have a preliminary discussion and surprise students with what fits that theme. Booktalking is all about variety and using your own style. Take survival, for instance. Get a hiking backpack or better yet an old Army surplus backpack. Place some books in it, and you're ready to booktalk! Ask young adults to pretend they're going camping overnight in a wilderness area. All they can take with them is one backpack. What do they need to take to survive? You can bet that cell phones and hair dryers will be suggested, but guide them to think about basics (with no electricity) like matches, food, water, flashlight, and so forth. Then pull out the books one at a time and very briefly booktalk a few typical wilderness titles, like Paulsen's *Hatchet* and Hobbs's *The Big Wander.* Then ask your young adult audience if there are other kinds of survival besides in a wilderness situation? You may need to prompt them with a few questions: What do you have to do to survive in school? How about in your own family or on a date? What will you need to do to survive on your own after high school or after college? Pull books out of the backpack that address the answers to these questions and how characters responded. Titles could include *Beauty Shop for Rent* by Laura Bowers, *Speak* by Laurie Halse Anderson, *Can't Get There from Here* by Todd Strasser, *The Schwa Was Here* by Neal Shusterman, *Nothing to Lose* by Alex Flinn, and *Contents under Pressure* by Lara M. Zeises. There's no need to try to teach lessons based on each book. As always, you want to stress the pleasure of reading. The backpack with a survival theme is a hook to hold your audience's attention. Even the small bit of suspense as you take books out of the backpack works with teens. The beauty of using the survival theme or any other general theme is the flexibility for age levels and types of books. Figure 20 to 30 minutes for the entire session.

Professional Booktalking Resources

Bodart, Joni R. 2002. *Radical Reads: 101 Young Adult Novels on the Edge.* Lanham, MD: Scarecrow.

Bromann, Jennifer. 1999. The Toughest Audience on Earth. *School Library Journal* 45, no. 10 (October): 60–63.

Charles, J. V. 2005. Get Real! Booktalking Nonfiction for Teen Read Week 2005. *Young Adult Library Services* 4, 12–16.

Clark, Ruth Cox. 2002. *Tantalizing Tidbits for Teens: Quick Booktalks for the Busy High School Library Media Specialist.* Columbus, OH: Linworth.

Gillespie, J. (2006). *Classic Teenplots.* Westport, CT: Libraries Unlimited.

Jones, Patrick, Michele Gorman, and Tricia Suellentrop. 2004. *Connecting Young Adults and Libraries: A How-to-Do-It Manual.* 3rd ed. New York: Neal-Schuman.

Keane, Nancy J. 2006. *The Big Book of Teen Reading Lists: 100 Great, Ready-to-Use Book Lists for Educators, Librarians, Parents, and Teens.* Westport, CT: Libraries Unlimited.

Lesesne, Teri. 2003. *Making the Match: The Right Book for the Right Reader at the Right Time, Grades 4–12.* Portland, ME: Stenhouse.

Mahood, Kristine. 2006. *A Passion for Print: Promoting Reading and Books to Teens.* Westport, CT: Libraries Unlimited.

Rochman, Hazel. 1987. *Tales of Love and Terror: Booktalking the Classics, Old and New.* Chicago: American Library Association.
Schall, Lucy. 2007. *Booktalks and Beyond: Promoting Great Genre Reads to Teens.* Westport, CT: Libraries Unlimited.

CONCLUSION

The best contemporary realistic fiction and historical fiction have the ability to draw readers into situations that are so real that readers will think the events have actually taken place. Those written in first-person point of view make the characters easy for young adults to identify with, as if the characters are real friends and enemies. Realistic fiction encompasses such a wide variety of genres and topics that most readers can find a type of book or a title that appeals to them.

ASSIGNMENTS IN ACTION: REALISTIC FICTION FOR DISCUSSION

1. How realistic is realistic fiction? Does it matter if it's realistic? Can it be too real for youthful readers?

2. Do young athletes read sports fiction? Interview or survey a basketball team or a football team. If ball players and other athletes don't read sports fiction, who does?

3. Can a dialogue about school violence be useful after the reading and discussion of books like *The Astonishing Adventures of Fanboy and Goth Girl*, *Give a Boy a Gun*, and *Endgame*?

4. How does humor for adults differ from humor for young adults? Why does knowing that difference matter to librarians?

5. How can young adults benefit from comparing a historical novel to a nonfiction history book on the same topic or time period?

6. What do young adults who have lost a loved one want to read? Are they comforted by reading fiction about grieving teens or do they want to read something totally different to escape their own situation? How can a librarian find out?

7. Are the dark realistic books published today a reflection of our society or do they influence society?

8. Why are young adults attracted to mysteries and psychological thrillers?

9. Are there benefits to young adults reading about war? What are they?

10. What were your favorite realistic novels when you were a young adult? Why?

4

Fantastic Fiction

"We have never taken on a librarian whom we haven't already Seen as being a librarian," she said, tilting her head, like someone puzzling over how to hang a painting. "But no one has ever Seen you at all, have they?"

Lirael felt her mouth dry up. Unable to speak, she nodded. She felt the sudden opportunity that had been granted her slipping away. The reprieve, the chance of work, of being someone—

"So you are a mystery," continued the Librarian. "But there is no better place for mystery than the Great Library of the Clayr—and it is better to be a librarian than part of the collection."

From *Lirael* by Garth Nix (2001, 58)

In fantastic fiction, imagination rules. In any fiction authors use their imagination to create characters and events and to describe settings. Imagination is at the core of writing. In fantastic fiction, the author has the freedom to take bold leaps into the bizarre, the strange, and the otherworldly. Imagination is unleashed to entertain and to mesmerize readers. Classic novels have taught readers to embrace the unusual, to savor oddity, and to want to read more. Such milestones as Jules Verne's *Twenty Thousand Leagues Under the Sea* (1870), Mary Shelley's *Frankenstein* (1818), and J. R. R. Tolkien's *The Hobbit, or There and Back Again* (1938, rev. 1951) have created fans of science fiction and fantasy. Fantastic fiction encompasses three major genres: fantasy, horror, and science fiction. Included in those major genres are a variety of subtypes: high fantasy, animal fantasy, fairy tales, magic realism, supernatural, paranormal, and time travel. Writers of fantasy have given readers Diagon Alley in J. K. Rowling's *Harry Potter and the Sorcerer's Stone*, the Dragonriders of Pern in Anne McCaffrey's *Dragonflight*, and a sensuous vampire in Stephenie Meyer's *Twilight*. Recent writers of science fiction have shown readers the devastation

75

caused by a meteor hitting the moon in Susan Beth Pfeffer's *Life As We Knew It*, a human clone in Nancy Farmer's *The House of the Scorpion*, and a lanky color-shifting alien in Kate Gilmore's *The Exchange Student*. Intriguing and mind-boggling only begin to describe fantastic fiction for today's young adults. In this chapter, genres, definitions, and recommended titles will be explored.

FANTASY

In the land Ingary, where such things as seven-league boots and cloaks of invisibility really exist, it is quite a misfortune to be born the eldest of three. Everyone knows you are the one who will fail first, and worst, if the three of you set out to seek your fortunes.

From *Howl's Moving Castle* by Diana Wynne Jones (1986, 1)

Characteristics of High Fantasy

When we think of fantasy, we usually are thinking about high fantasy, and there are certain distinct characteristics that define this popular genre.

1. A complete world is created with specific and consistent rules. The world may be bizarre, but in that bizarre world what happens must make sense.

2. Closely related to the first characteristic, readers should be so thoroughly convinced of the logistics of the created world that they can suspend their disbelief enough to be drawn into the story. There must be a basis in reality. Grounding the story in reality by beginning and ending the story in a real world or by using dates and events from the real world or even fake newspaper articles that give the sense of reality helps readers in their journey through a world spun from the imagination of a writer's fertile mind. On her Web site readers can see Ursula Le Guin's "Plausibility in Fantasy to Alexei Mutovkin: An Open Letter": "The more realistic, exact, 'factual' detail in a fantasy story, the more sensually things and acts are imagined and described, the more plausible the world will be. After all, it is a world made entirely of words. Exact and vivid words make an exact and vivid world." For more information about her writing, visit www.ursulakleguin.com.

3. There is always a quest and a hero who must complete the quest no matter the dangers or the impossibility of the tasks set before him or her.

4. Good, in the guise of the hero, and evil, in the guise of an antihero or villain, must engage in battle, usually back and forth throughout the story until the hero wins.

5. There must be plenty of suspense to propel the story forward and compel the reader to keep turning pages.

6. Fantasy often features a character or a creature to add humor and relieve tension or despair. In Garth Nix's fantasy, Lirael turns a small dog statuette into a real dog, an irreverent, smart dog that

becomes her companion and protector. "I am the Disreputable Dog. Or Disreputable Bitch, if you want to get technical. When are we going for a walk?" (Nix 2001, 101).

One Book in Action: *The Golden Compass* by Philip Pullman

In the best-written fantasy, literary elements should attain the highest narrative standards. In fantasy, characters should be well-developed, setting should be detailed, plots should be believable, themes should be universal, and style should sustain an entertaining story and convey the appropriate tone and mood. Combining special characteristics of fantasy and the best writing, consider Philip Pullman's *The Golden Compass*. The first in a trilogy, the story carries readers into a world with similarities to our own as it was in the nineteenth century. Lyra Belacque lives in Jordan College, Oxford, free to scamper about with her friend Roger. She appears to be an orphan who is educated in a slapdash fashion by scholars. The first sentence of the novel informs readers that Lyra has her own daemon, and this fact plunges the story into fantasy and into the heart of the tale. In Lyra's world, all humans have their own daemons, which are not pets but are alter egos with unique personalities. Early in the story it's revealed that Lyra will save the world, but she must be unaware of what she is doing. Of course, she fights for good and against evil, in the guise of Mrs. Coulter, Gobblers, her Uncle Asriel, and a cast of unusual creatures. Pullman's skillful writing smoothly navigates between characters and events while cranking the level of suspense tighter and tighter as Lyra tries to rescue kidnapped children without being taken herself. Lyra's daemon, Pantalaimon, usually appearing as a white ermine, brings some levity and comfort, as they journey through peril together, trying to understand the mysteries of the aurora borealis and a substance referred to simply as Dust. Pullman's language is clever and visual as seen in a paragraph on an idea Lyra has for saving her friend, an armored bear. "The idea hovered and shimmered delicately, like a soap bubble, and she dared not even look at it directly in case it burst. But she was familiar with the way of ideas, and she let it shimmer, looking away, thinking about something else" (Pullman 1995, 334). This well-crafted fantasy hinges on the curiosity, intelligence, and brave heart of a girl and the alethiometer, or golden compass, that guides her.

Favorite Authors of Fantasy

Many British authors, as well as Americans, writing for children and young adults, like Philip Pullman, share their expansive imaginations through high fantasy. Their works and awards are too extensive to list here, but visits to their Web sites and to author reference sources provide easily accessible information.

Lloyd Alexander (1924–2007)

Best known for <u>Chronicles of Prydain</u>: *The Book of Three*, *The Black Cauldron*, *The Castle of Llyr*, *Taran Wanderer*, and *The High King*.
Awarded 1969 Newbery Medal for *The High King*.

T. A. Barron (1952–)

Best known for <u>Lost Years of Merlin</u> series: *The Lost Years of Merlin, The Seven Songs of Merlin, The Fires of Merlin, The Mirror of Merlin,* and *The Wings of Merlin.*

Home: Colorado
Official Web site: www.tabarron.com

Susan Cooper (1935–2008)

Best known for <u>The Dark Is Rising</u> series set in and around England and Wales: *Over Sea, Under Stone; The Dark Is Rising; Greenwitch; The Grey King;* and *Silver on the Tree*
Awarded the 1976 Newbery Medal for *The Grey King.*

Home: Connecticut

Diane Wynne Jones (1934–)

Best known for *Howl's Moving Castle, Castle in the Air, Dark Lord of Derkholm,* and *Year of the Griffin.*
Awarded the 2004 Phoenix Award *for Howl's Moving Castle,* which was made into a Japanese animated movie in 2004.

Home: England
Official Web site: www.leemac.freeserve.co.uk

Ursula K. Le Guin (1929–)

Best known for her four books of <u>Earthsea</u>: *Wizard of Earthsea, The Tombs of Atuan, The Farthest Shore,* and *Tehanu.*
A recent trilogy: *Gifts, Voices,* and *Powers.*
Honored with the 2004 Margaret A. Edwards Award for her lifetime contribution to young adult readers.

Home: Portland, Oregon
Official Web site: www.urslakleguin.com

C. S. Lewis (1898–1963)

An Irish author and scholar, best known for <u>The Chronicles of Narnia</u>: *The Lion, the Witch and the Wardrobe, Prince Caspian, The Voyage of the Dawn Treader, The Silver Chair, The Horse and His Boy, The Magician's Nephew,* and *The Last Battle.*

Garth Nix (1963–)

Best known for his books <u>The Abhorsen</u> trilogy: *Sabriel, Lirael,* and *Abhorsen* and the <u>Seventh Tower</u> series: *The Fall, Castle Aenir, Above the Veil, Into Battle,* and *The Violet Keystone.*

Recently published: The <u>Keys to the Kingdom</u> series, featuring Arthur Penhaligon, who fights to save his world as he struggles and battles through seven adventures, one for each day of the week: *Mister Monday, Grim Tuesday, Drowned Wednesday, Sir Thursday, Lady Friday, Superior Saturday* (2008), and *Lord Sunday* (2009).

Home: Australia

Official Web site: www.garthnix.co.uk

Christopher Paolini (1983–)

Known for <u>The Inheritance</u> trilogy: *Eragon, Eldest,* and a third book yet to be published.

Wrote *Eragon* after graduating from high school at 15 years old.

Home: Montana

Terry Pratchett (1948–)

Known in England as a prolific fantasy writer, he's best known in the United States for a few children's/young adult novels: *The Wee Free Men, A Hat Full of Sky,* and *Wintersmith.*

Awarded the 2001 Carnegie Medal for best children's novel: *The Amazing Maurice and His Educated Rodents.*

Home: England

Official Web site: www.terrypratchettbooks.com

Philip Pullman (1946–)

Best known for <u>His Dark Materials</u>: *The Golden Compass, The Subtle Knife,* and *The Amber Spyglass.*

Awarded the 1995 Carnegie Medal for *Northern Lights* (titled *The Golden Compass* in the United States); the 2001 Whitbread Prize and the 2002 Whitbread Book of the Year for *The Amber Spyglass.*

Home: England

Web site: www.philip-pullman.com

J. K. Rowling (1965–)

Known for the <u>Harry Potter</u> series, a 10-year publishing phenomenon, making Rowling a billionaire: *Harry Potter and the Sorcerer's Stone, Harry Potter and the Chamber of Secrets, Harry Potter and the Prisoner of Azkaban, Harry Potter and the Goblet of Fire, Harry Potter and the Half-Blood Prince*, and *Harry Potter and the Deathly Hallows*.

Home: Scotland and England

Official Web site: www.jkrowling.com

J.R.R. Tolkien (1892–1973)

An English philologist, writer, and university professor, he is known worldwide for *The Hobbit, or There and Back Again* (1937) and <u>The Lord of the Rings</u> trilogy: *The Fellowship of the Ring* (1954), *The Two Towers* (1954), and *The Return of the King* (1955). Tolkien's full name is John Ronald Reuel Tolkien. Fans of his novels may want to learn about Tolkien's life and how he became such a famous writer. Anne E. Neimark's brief biography, *Myth Maker: J.R.R Tolkien*, may satisfy readers' interest.

Web site: www.tolkiensociety.org

British Literature Awards for Young Adult Literature

British awards for young adult literature include books of a variety of genres, especially fantasy. Three awards that include titles for young adults are the Carnegie Medal, the Phoenix Award, and The Costa Book Awards. The Carnegie Medal has been awarded annually by the Library Association since 1936 in memory of Andrew Carnegie, Scottish-born philanthropist. A self-made industrialist, Carnegie made a fortune in steel in the United States. According to the Web site, The CILIP Carnegie & Kate Greenaway Children's Book Awards, "His experience of using a library as a child led him to resolve that 'if ever wealth came to me that it should be used to establish free libraries.'" As of 2002, the award is now sponsored by the Chartered Institute of Library and Information Professionals. The Carnegie Medal is awarded to an outstanding book for children, including books for young adults. The 2007 winner of the medal was Meg Rosoff's *Just in Case*, which also was a Best Books for Young Adults in the United States.

The Phoenix Award was established in 1985 and is "awarded annually to a book originally published in English twenty years previously which did not receive a major award at the time of its publication," according to the Web site The Children's Literature Web Guide. Recent winners are Margaret Mahy's *Memory* (2007), Diane Wynne Jones's *Howl's Moving Castle* (2006), and Margaret Mahy's *The Catalogue of the Universe* (2005).

The Costa Book Awards, formerly known as the Whitbread Literary Awards, the most prestigious book prize in the United Kingdom, have been awarded annually since 1971 in five categories: first novel, novel, biography, poetry, children's book. Since 1985, there has also been a Book of the Year chosen. In 2001 Philip Pullman's *Amber Spyglass* was the first children's book to win a Book of the Year Award. Interestingly, in 2006, Costa Coffee, makers of the leading brand of coffee in the UK, took over the sponsorship of the award. The company offers large cash prizes to the winning author in each category. For complete lists of the winning titles, visit www.costabookawards.com.

HORROR

> The night is full of mystery. Even when the moon is brightest, secrets hide everywhere. Then the sun rises and its rays cast so many shadows that the day creates more illusion than all the veiled truth of the night.
> From *Demon in My View* by Amelia Atwater-Rhodes (2000, 1)

The world of horror fiction shares some components of high fantasy. Magic and supernatural elements are the most common ones. Ghosts, witches, and mythical creatures, such as elves, trolls, giants, dragons, vampires, and werewolves, are popular characters. It's impossible to draw clear lines between types of fantasy, but for the purpose of examining books written for young adults and popular with young adults, dominant traits can be isolated. Be aware that horror stories have different levels of scariness and creepiness. Take the advice given in a recent *School Library Journal*: "If students request scary stories, find out what they mean by scary. Remember, horror is a subjective term—what sends shivers down one person's spine may not make another even blink. Kids enjoy different degrees and types of 'scary,' and you'll want to make sure you recommend books that match their interests and expectations" (Luedtke, Wentling, & Wurt 2006, 36).

Author Paul Zindel explained why horror stories appeal to young adults. At a book conference in Huntsville, Texas on November 7, 1998, Zindel shared his philosophy about the benefit of reading horror. Essentially, to young adults, horror is so exaggerated in movies and books that it's humorous. It makes readers and viewers shiver at the creepiness and laugh at the silliness, whether it's rats crawling around inside someone's body at the town dump or a creature exploding from the depths of a Vermont lake. According to Zindel, horror stories provide laughter and escapism, as shown by the popularity of his horrific thrillers beginning with *Loch* and continuing with other scary novels, such as *The Doom Stone*, *Rats*, *Raptor*, and *The Gadget*. In *The Doom Stone*, an ancient spirit comes to life. Fifteen-year-old Jackson travels to Stonehenge to visit his aunt on an archeological dig. There he witnesses a bloodthirsty hominid on the loose, attacking, mutilating, and killing people. After his aunt has been attacked, Jackson and a young girl solve the mystery of the creature, surviving dangerous encounters in one quick action after another.

Other stories of ghosts and evil spirits that will intrigue readers are William Sleator's *The Boy Who Couldn't Die*, Vivian Vande Velde's short story collection, *Being Dead*, Joan Lowry Nixon's *The Haunting* and *Whispers from the Dead*, Dorothy and Thomas Hoobler's *The Ghost in the Tokaido Inn*, Gary Soto's *The Afterlife*, and Rosemary Clement-Moore's *Prom Dates from Hell*. *Prom Dates from Hell* combines the best elements of horror and begins like this: "As an interactive horror experience, with beasts from Hell, mayhem, gore, and dismemberment, it was an impressive event. As a high school prom, however, the evening was marginally less successful" (Clement-Moore 2007, 1). Maggie, the main character and narrator, isn't kidding. She does not want to go to the prom, but circumstances get out of control. A demon is loosed from Hell by her fellow classmates and begins embarrassing and seriously injuring a group of jocks and their girlfriends. Maggie's sarcastic sense of humor and the weird happenings will compel readers through this entertaining novel, the best of evil spirits, laughter, and escapism.

Witches and Wizards

"Are you sure that's a real spell?" said the girl. "Well, it's not very good, is it? I've tried a few simple spells just for practice and it's all worked for me. Nobody in my family is magic at all, it was ever such a surprise when I got my letter, but I was ever so pleased, of course, I mean, it's the very best school of witchcraft there is, I've heard—I've learned all our course books by heart, of course, I just hope it will be enough—I'm Hermione Granger, by the way, who are you?"

From *Harry Potter and the Sorcerer's Stone*
by J. K. Rowling (1997, 105–106)

Witches and wizards figure prominently in horror fiction. Of course, everyone in the world knows about the Hogwart's School of Witchcraft and Wizardry in the Harry Potter books, but there are other types of books featuring witches.

1. There are stories of young women and men who have paranormal abilities that cause accusations of witchcraft. In Vivian Vande Velde's *Witch Dreams*, 16-year-old Nyssa can enter people's dreams. She watches and listens but doesn't harm anyone. She wants information about the deaths of her parents and brother. If townspeople knew her paranormal abilities, she would be condemned as a witch. In Lois Duncan's *Gallows Hill*, Sarah is clairvoyant, but after playing the role of a fortune-teller who looks into a crystal ball and reads the future, students accuse her of being a witch.

2. On the other hand, there are stories about women who acknowledge they are witches. Some are kind and well-intentioned; others are evil or at least mean-spirited. In Ann Turner's *Rosemary's Witch*, a 150-year-old witch tries to get her house back through magic. Rosemary gets rid of the ancient witch by showing her love and understanding. Certainly, C. S. Lewis's White Witch in *The Lion, the Witch and the Wardrobe* wields evil magic against the good and powerful Aslan. Monica Furlong's trilogy begins with *Juniper*, the story of a young girl who leaves her home to study herbs, healing, and the magic of nature with a wise woman. *Wise Child* and *Colman* complete this trilogy of a gentle craft that seeks harmony with nature and defense against sorceresses in medieval Scotland.

3. Then there are stories of Wiccans. Wicca is a modern religion based on pagan beliefs that is practiced throughout the world. It entails the practice of magic, a pentagram within a circle (a pentacle) as a symbol of faith, secrecy for its rituals, and organization into covens. Isobel Bird launched a series in 2001 titled Circle of Three, based

on Wicca, in which teenaged girls learn and practice "the craft." In the first novel, *So Mote It Be*, Kate finds a book of spells and tries a love spell. Gradually, she finds two other girls who are interested in the craft, and they begin to learn.

Harry Potter, a Wizard Hero

He began as a sad, orphaned boy and emerged seven books later as a hero. In between the first and the last book he battled the evil Voldemort again and again, barely escaping death, knowing his grip on triumph was tenuous, at least until J. K. Rowling resolved everything in *Harry Potter and the Deathly Hallows*. Ten years ago, Rowling started a publishing phenomenon. In Scotland, out of work, a single mother, almost destitute, she slipped her writing onto the top of an editor's stack of manuscripts in a café and anxiously waited. Immediately, he loved the book, making her a household word and a rich woman. Children and teens craved the lengthy books and read like Americans had never seen them read before. *Harry Potter and the Half-Blood Prince* with 652 pages? Not a problem. *Harry Potter and the Goblet of Fire* with 734 pages? And, *Harry Potter and the Order of the Phoenix*, the thickest one of all at 870 pages, confirmed that Americans are readers, and thick books won't keep them from reading if the story is exciting enough. After reading six books, American youth were willing to read 759 more pages to know the final ending of Harry's adventures in *Harry Potter and the Deathly Hallows*.

With the popularity of a wizard hero, not only are young adults reading lengthier books, they're reading more fantasy. They ask for books similar to Rowling's to quench their thirst for adventure in between Harry Potter books. Besides the few fantasy books mentioned in this chapter, there are more titles to draw readers into magical, fascinating worlds. In Terry Pratchett's *Wintersmith*, Tiffany faces the challenge of being wooed by Winter in the guise of a boy. For help and humor the Wee Free Men try their best to save her. In Matthew Skelton's *Endymion Spring*, Blake picks up a book that has fallen to the floor in an Oxford, England library where he and his sister are waiting for their mother. The book is old-looking with blank pages but it literally pricks him and pulls him into a dangerous quest. In Michael Scott's *The Alchemyst*, twins Sophie and Josh are caught between rival alchemists as they struggle for possession of an ancient and powerful book.

Dragons

In his dragon form, Draconas was armored in scales that were harder than any steel man had yet created. His eyes could spot a rodent in the pitch darkness fifty feet away. He had a massive tail that could fell a tree with one swipe, razor-sharp claws and sword-sharp teeth, and the fire of magic blazed in his blood. He was invincible to every creature in the world with the exception of his own kind.

Or at least, he had been.

From *Master of Dragons* by Margaret Weis (2005, 116)

Dragons are consistently popular in literature for youth. Perhaps it's partly due to wishful thinking. What teen wouldn't love to be a dragon rider and have command of such a magnificent creature as the one described in Margaret Weis's Dragonvarld trilogy? Dragons possess terrifying beauty, intelligence, deadliness, and sometimes great humor. And imagine the rush of flying through the air and going anywhere you wanted to anytime. Dragons symbolize absolute power and freedom. What teen wouldn't want to identify with the dragon or its rider?

Examining books on the Young Adults' Choices lists of the last 10 years, no fictional dragon books appear until the 2005 list, with *Eragon*, by the young writer Christopher Paolini. Then the 2006 list has two titles: *Dragon Rider* by Cornelia Funke, a German author, and *Mistress of Dragons* by Margaret Weis, the first book in the Dragonvarld trilogy. Paolini's phenomenally successful book encouraged a renewed interest in dragon fantasies. Of course, there have been previous dragon fantasies written for young adults. In 1999 Anne McCaffrey was honored with the Margaret A. Edwards Award for her outstanding contributions to young adult literature. She was honored for the following titles about dragons: *Dragonflight, Dragonquest, White Dragon*, and the Harper Hall trilogy—*Dragonsong, Dragonsinger*, and *Dragondrums*. McCaffrey steadfastly maintains that her books are science fiction, not fantasy. They are set on the planet of Pern, which provides the science fiction part, but her books are included in fantasy here because of the overwhelming focus on dragons, considered mythical creatures. Devoted fans of McCaffrey's Pern stories hungry for details of the dragons and people who inhabit Pern will want to read *The Dragonlover's Guide to Pern* written by Jody Lynn Nye with Anne McCaffrey, illustrated by Todd Cameron Hamilton, and with maps and illustrations by James Clouse. Two other writers have contributed previously to popular dragon stories: Jane Yolen and Patricia C. Wrede. Yolen's Pit Dragon Chronicles—*Dragon's Blood, Heart's Blood*, and *A Sending of Dragons*—feature Jakkin Stewart, a young man who bonds with a dragon. Wrede's Enchanted Forest series begins with *Dealing with Dragons* and continues with *Searching for Dragons, Calling on Dragons*, and *Talking to Dragons*. Her books have a whimsical touch, as the main character, Cimorene, relinquishes being a princess and becomes a dragon's librarian and chief cook. Original cover illustrations by Trina Schart Hyman convey whimsy along with humor and the expectation of exciting adventures. Current paperback covers show action and imply more serious adventures.

Two recent titles, Janet Lee Carey's *Dragon's Keep* and Silvana De Mari's *The Last Dragon*, will intrigue readers with very different dragon stories. In *Dragon's Keep*, Wilde Island is plagued by dragons, and Princess Rosalind Pendragon is born with a dragon claw in place of one finger. When she's taken by a dragon to its cave to care for four young dragons, a prophecy is set in motion. For younger readers, *The Last Dragon*, winner of a 2007 Batchelder Award, also holds the promise of a prophecy. The last dragon and the last elf come together for a new beginning. An elf and two humans set out on a quest complete with humor and danger. These two titles should suffice to draw readers back to classic titles and to more recent well-written, popular titles.

Librarians in Action: Connect Dragons with Art!

Propose to an art teacher a collaboration with you on art and fantasy books about dragons. The art teacher chooses the medium and technique to teach students; as the librarian, you offer to collect resources of information about dragons, to booktalk the best dragon fantasies in the teacher's class, and to display the art in the library. When you booktalk, be sure to read a few pages describing the dragons so that students add to their mental visuals of dragons. Turn the displays into a contest by numbering each piece of art and asking students school-wide to vote for their favorite ones. Winners each receive a paperback copy of a dragon book. Have as many winners as you can afford dragon books!

Several resources can help you with this project. Print out a copy of Deborah Lenny's article titled "Dynamic Dragons" in the December 2005 issue of *Arts & Activities*, full text accessible online through Academic Premier, an Ebscohost database. The article provides gorgeous examples of dragon artwork, a list of materials and learning objectives, and a narrative describing the overall project. Additionally, make available how-to-draw books that focus on dragons. I recommend Damon J. Reinagle's *Draw Medieval Fantasies: A Step by Step Guide* with a chapter devoted to drawing dragons.

Vampires and Werewolves

About three things I was absolutely positive. First, Edward was a vampire. Second, there was part of him—and I didn't know how potent that part might be—that thirsted for my blood. And third, I was unconditionally and irrevocably in love with him.

From *Twilight* by Stephenie Meyer (2005, 195)

Bram Stoker's *Dracula*, published in 1897, set the stage for future vampire stories. Dracula, as an evil force, epitomizes the shivery horror of being turned into a vampire by a terrifying creature. Anne Rice continued the vampiric horror and mystic in her adult series beginning in *Interview with the Vampire*, the first in her Vampire Chronicles. Some conventions of vampire stories, such as the power of garlic and crucifixes to ward off vampires, are being altered in novels written for the young adult audience. The biggest recent success has been Stephenie Meyer's *Twilight* and its two sequels, *New Moon* and *Eclipse*. If there's any question of the popularity of vampire stories, especially for girls, six titles have appeared on Young Adults' Choices lists beginning with the 2002 list: Amelia Atwater-Rhodes's *Demon in My View*, Pete Hautman's *Sweetblood*, Ellen Schreiber's *Vampire Kisses*, Douglas Rees's *Vampire High*, Kate Cary's *Bloodline*, and *Twilight*. Six titles may not seem like many, but considering that few fantasy titles, compared to the overwhelming number of realistic titles, are chosen by young adults, vampire stories represent a significant reading interest of teens. Besides being scary, creepy, and fun to read, there's much to be gained by young adults who read vampire stories, at least according to Joseph De Marco in his article titled, "Vampire Literature: Something Young Adults Can Really Sink Their Teeth Into."

Young adults can identify with vampires since they share similar problems: bodily changes teens can't control and new desires and cravings that are potentially frightening (De Marco 1997). An even better attraction is a sort of wish fulfillment: "The vampire is suave, sophisticated, certain of himself, rooted in history, poised to take the future with neither fear nor reluctance, self-possessed, sexual, powerful, sometimes cruel and sometimes kind, not possessed by doubts, not burdened with conscience, cool and resourceful, supremely intelligent and, best of all, immortal. This is everything the young adult is not and everything they aspire to be" (De Marco 1997, 26). Thanks to the publication of *The Silver Kiss* and *Twilight*, we can add romantic, sensual, and sexually desirable (in an almost innocent manner) to the list of desirable traits. In Annette Curtis Klause's *The Silver Kiss*, Zoe feels isolated as her mother dies of cancer and her father distances himself from her. She meets Simon, an ancient vampire, in a neighborhood park late one night.

> He was young, more boy than man, slight and pale, made elfin by the moon. He noticed her and froze like a deer before the gun. They were trapped in each other's gaze. His eyes were dark, full of wilderness and stars. But his face was ashen. Almost as pale as his silver hair.

> With a sudden ache she realized he was beautiful. The tears that prickled her eyes broke his bonds, and he fled, while she sat and cried for all things lost. (Klause 1990, 12)

Alternating viewpoints of Zoe and Simon add depth to the tale as the two form a tentative alliance. In Vivian Vande Velde's *Companions of the Night*, 16-year-old Kerry makes the choice to defend Ethan, a vampire, putting herself and her family in danger. In Amelia Atwater-Rhodes's *Demon in My View*, senior high school student Jessica begins writing a novel about vampires, only to discover that they really exist. Aubrey, a vampire character from Atwater-Rhodes's *In the Forest of the Night*, tries to avoid Jessica's efforts to discover the secrets of his existence. On the other hand, Scott Westerfeld's *Peeps* departs from the romantic vampire icon to join a parasite-positive character in New York City trying to track down others who are infected. Horrible, gory, scary, and sexy—this novel mixes fantasy and science fiction.

Werewolves are not as popular in fantasy as vampires are, but in Meyer's *New Moon*, werewolves enter the vampire scene and become firmly entrenched in the story. Annette Curtis Klause's *Blood and Chocolate* will intrigue readers with a combination of sensuality and identity crisis, as beautiful Vivian Gandillon learns to accept herself as a werewolf and as part of the pack.

Authors in Action: Stephenie Meyer

Stephenie Meyer, a devout Mormon, lives in Phoenix, Arizona with her husband and three young sons. She shook the young adult publishing world with the publication of her first novel, *Twilight*, a sensual tale of a high school girl and the vampire she falls in love with. According to the *Phoenix New Times* article on her Web site, Meyer earned an advance of $750,000 from Little, Brown and Company for a three-book deal, beginning with *Twilight*. As a result of her first book and its sequels, such popularity and wildly enthusiastic fans have not been seen since the publication of Rowling's <u>Harry Potter</u> books. In an interview with her on Amazon.com, Meyer reveals a few facts her fans will love: *Twilight* was inspired by a vivid dream; her favorite vampire story is Anne Rice's *The Vampire Lestat*; and her favorite author of books for young people is L. M. Montgomery, author of *Anne of Green Gables* (Meyer 2008).

To promote Meyer and her books, public libraries have been hosting "proms." The first book ends with Edward taking Bella to her high school prom. In a children's and young adult literature symposium at Brigham Young University (Meyer's alma mater) a fancy party was held to honor Meyer. Use your imagination and resources to create your own event by inviting girls to wear prom dresses and boys to wear tuxedos (You can always try!). Decorate with black and red crepe streamers. Have readings from Meyer's books, skits, book-talks of other vampire stories, refreshments, games, and, of course, music and dancing.

Brief teasers to Meyer's Twilight Saga:

Twilight. Bella Swan, a beautiful high school senior with a strong sense of her own personality, meets and falls in love with Edward Cullen, as irresistible as he is mysterious. Awards: Teens' Top Ten 2006, Best Books for Young Adults 2006, and Young Adults' Choices for 2007.

New Moon. Bella celebrates her birthday at Edward's home with disastrous results. Convinced that Bella is endangered by him, Edward leaves. Jacob becomes Bella's friend and confidant in Edward's absence.

Eclipse. Does Bella choose a human life or a vampire's life? Does she choose Edward or Jacob? These are the big questions answered in the third highly anticipated story.

Breaking Dawn. The fourth and last book in the <u>Twilight Saga</u> will be published in 2008.

Other Fantastic Creatures

Other creatures besides dragons and vampires show up in fantasy to entertain young adults: unicorns, leprechauns, trolls, giants, goblins, and elves, primarily. In Christopher Pike's *Alosha*, a collection of creatures gather as Ali Warner sets out to try and understand the fantastic mysteries around her and within herself. Bruce Coville's *Into the Land of the Unicorns* and *Song of the Wanderer* will satisfy middle school students who are intrigued with the beauty and mystery of unicorns. For fans of fantasies featuring ordinary animals that talk and act like humans, Brian Jacques's <u>Redwall</u> series begun in 1986 and Richard Adams's classic adult story *Watership Down* show the authors' skill in creating believable characters.

Librarians in Action: Celebrate Halloween!

October is the perfect month for displays of horror fiction and nonfiction! Liberally lace your book display with fake spiders, plastic vampire teeth, and rubber rats and bats. Combine creepy displays with telling or reading ghost stories with a flashlight shining on your face, and add a creepy quiz about traditional and current characters in horror. Reward listening to the stories and completing the quiz with treats from a plastic cauldron. Emphasize fun!

Short Stories for Quick, Fantastic Reading

Do you work with young adults who don't want to read an 870-page book? These story collections can be read aloud, browsed through, or checked out to teens anytime of the year.

Book of Enchantments by Patricia C. Wrede.
Curses, Inc. and Other Stories by Vivian Vande Velde.
Here There Be Unicorns by Jane Yolen, illustrated by David Wilgus.
Here There Be Witches by Jane Yolen, illustrated by David Wilgus.
Short Circuits: Thirteen Shocking Stories by Outstanding Writers for Young Adults, edited by Donald R. Gallo.
Thirteen: 13 Tales of Horror by 13 Masters of Horror, edited by T. Pines.
Truly Grim Tales by Priscilla Galloway.
Twelve Impossible Things Before Breakfast by Jane Yolen.
Vampires: A Collection of Original Stories, edited by Jane Yolen and Martin H. Greenberg.

SCIENCE FICTION

> The creatures are tall, taller than Tim and me, with two long, pale arms that seem boneless, like tentacles. I can tell they are very thin, even though they are wearing loose sleeveless robes that hang from their long necks to the floor. The truly horrible thing about them is their heads, simply because they are so tiny in relation to their height, about the size of tennis balls. The heads are smooth and gray and almost featureless, with one lidless eye in the front and another in the back, and underneath the eyes a mouth like a line without lips that seems to go all the way around the head.
> From William Sleator's *The Night the Heads Came* (1996, 8)

Science fiction is much more than weird aliens with heads the size of tennis balls. It fits under the umbrella of fantastic fiction, sharing the umbrella with fantasy. Very simply, science fiction has a basis in science; fantasy does not. Then there are stories that include both. Anne McCaffrey's dragons and fire lizards live on the planet of Pern, combining mythical creatures with life on another planet. In science fiction there are tales of aliens and tales of universes and planets other than ours. There are stories of technological discoveries and time travel, of utopias and dystopias, and stories of potential futures, including disasters and wonders. Just as fantasy releases the imagination to dwell on dragons and vampires, science fiction envisions the future of intelligent robots and the disaster of planets colliding.

History in Action: Classic Science Fiction Titles

Adult writers of science fiction carved a path filled with classic tales of the genre still popular with young adults today.

Frankenstein (1818) by Mary Shelley.
Journey to the Center of the Earth (1874) by Jules Verne.
Twenty Thousand Leagues Under the Sea (1870) by Jules Verne.
The Time Machine (1895) by H. G. Wells.
War of the Worlds (1898) by H. G. Wells.
Out of the Silent Planet (1938) by C. S. Lewis.
Foundation trilogy (1942–1950) by Isaac Asimov.
The Martian Chronicles (1950) by Ray Bradbury.
Stranger in a Strange Land (1960) by Robert Heinlein.
The Ship Who Sang (1961) by Anne McCaffrey.
2001: A Space Odyssey (1968) by Arthur C. Clarke.
Dragonflight (The Dragonriders of Pern, vol. 1) (1968) by Anne McCaffrey.
The Hitchhiker's Guide to the Galaxy (1979) by Douglas Adams.

In addition to the fine titles listed above, two science fiction movies established the science fiction genre as a popular one: *Star Wars* in the 1970s and *Star Trek: The Next Generation* in the 1990s. Huge numbers of fans flocked to subsequent releases, much as enthusiastic fans flock to Harry Potter movies as each one is released.

Science Fiction Written for Young Adult Readers

Young adult fans who are devoted to the genre are likely to be reading adult science fiction. Still, science fiction written especially for young adults is gradually increasing. Entice middle school and high school readers with samples from the variety of science fiction types and topics in the following list arranged by copyright dates:

A Wrinkle in Time (1962) by Madeleine L'Engle. On a quest to find their father, three children search through space and time. Winner of the 1963 Newbery Medal, L'Engle also won the 1998 Margaret A. Edwards Award for the Austin Family Series and the Time Fantasy Series.
The White Mountains (1967) (Tripods Trilogy, vol. 1) by John Christopher. Huge three-legged machines rule the earth.
The Left Hand of Darkness (1969) by Ursula K. Le Guin. An emissary to an alien world tries to bridge the cultural gaps between galaxies. Winner of the 2004 Margaret A. Edwards Award.
Dragonsong (1976) (The Harper-Hall trilogy, vol. 1) by Anne McCaffrey. Fire lizards on Pern share the look of dragons but on a much smaller scale.
The Keeper of the Isis Light (1980) by Monica Hughes. Born on the planet of Isis, she has lived there alone for many years.
Ender's Game (1985) by Orson Scott Card. He's taught to kill real aliens while playing a video game.
Eva (1988) by Peter Dickinson. A terrible car crash results in a teenaged girl occupying the body of a chimpanzee.
The Giver (1993) by Lois Lowry. Utopia becomes dystopia. 1994 Newbery Medal.
Lost in Cyberspace (1995) by Richard Peck. Sixth-graders travel through time at their New York City prep school.
Shade's Children (1997) by Garth Nix. In a postnuclear world no child is allowed to live past a 14th birthday.
The Exchange Student (1999) by Kate Gilmore. Fen is a color-shifting exchange student from another planet.
Feed (2002) by M. T. Anderson. An implanted transmitter is vital to Titus's life.

dystopia —

The House of the Scorpion (2002) by Nancy Farmer. Matteo is cloned for his body parts by a drug lord. A 2003 Newbery Honor.

Midnighters: The Secret Hour (2004) by Scott Westerfeld. In Oklahoma a group of teens have special abilities to fight ancient creatures.

Double Identity (2005) by Margaret Peterson Haddix. Bethany is the clone of an older sister who died.

Life As We Knew It (2006) by Susan Beth Pfeffer. A meteor hits the moon, causing world-wide disasters

Streams of Babel (2008) by Carol Plum-Ucci. Terrorists contaminate a small community's water source.

Literature in Action: Guys Read Science Fiction!

Science fiction is the perfect genre for boys' leisure reading. Science fiction has fast-paced action and suspense. Read Anderson's *Feed*. It's exciting! Suggest Sleator's *Singularity*. There are weird characters! Recommend Sleator's *The Night the Heads Came*. Sometimes it's gross. Booktalk Nix's *Shade's Children*. Sometimes there's humor. Check out Douglas Adams's *The Hitchhiker's Guide to the Galaxy* for science fiction humor.

Follow Jon Scieszka's lead in promoting books boys will read! Visit his Web site at www.guysread.com and "Join the Guys Read Cause":

1. Make plenty of noise on a national level to call attention to the questions of boys' literacy.

2. Motivate adults (parents, teachers, librarians, booksellers, and publishers) to examine the role gender plays in the book choices we give to boys.

3. Reach boys directly with books recommended by other guys.

4. Challenge men to step up and be role models for literacy.

5. Try to help boys explore the possibilities of a wider emotional range and connection to feelings through reading.

The Guys Read initiative addresses reading habits of boys, especially their penchant to read nonfiction, newspapers, magazines, graphic novels, and humorous and adventurous short stories and novels. For brief writings by boys' favorite authors, be sure to have at least one copy of *Guys Write for Guys Read*, edited by Scieszka.

Authors in Action: William Sleator

Thirty high school students sat quietly in a classroom section of the school library and listened to William Sleator speak about his life and his writing. Occasionally, there were snorts of laughter. Teachers and librarians cringed when a student asked him how much money he made. Then Sleator told them. He explained about royalties and not knowing exactly how much money he would get each six months. They were fascinated. As the students filed out of the library I overhead a young man say, "He was weird...I liked him."

That comes close to summing up William Sleator. At least, he writes weird stuff, and young adults who like reading weird stuff will like his science fiction books.

For more than 30 years Sleator has been writing science fiction with particular appeal to boys. In *House of Stairs*, five 16-year-old orphans live in a house of endless stairs as a psychological experiment. In the *Green Futures of Tycho*, an 11-year-old boy travels back and forth in time, observing various futures for his family and himself. In *Interstellar Pig*, Barney's three adult neighbors play a role-playing game with him that turns out to be a dangerous struggle with three aliens. Its sequel, *Parasite Pig*, once again places Barney in danger as he's captured by a disgusting alien parasite that inhabits the body of a dinosaur. Barney and his friend Kate end up captives of intelligent crabs who enjoy eating human flesh. Suspense, humor, and grossness fit together well to entice readers. In *Singularity*, twins Harry and Barry stumble onto a gateway into another universe. In *The Duplicate*, David uses a machine to clone himself twice, resulting in three conflicting personalities. With *The Beasties*, a brother and sister discover a world of naked mole rats underground and get drawn into their strange lives, including amputating body parts. In *The Boxes*, Annie is given a box by her uncle, and out of the box come telepathic crab-like beasts she can't control. In *Marco's Millions*, the sequel, a brother and his younger sister journey to other universes. For boys, or any readers, who want stories that are fast-paced, suspenseful, imaginative, and usually bizarre and creepy, recommend William Sleator's novels. If science fiction is not your personal favorite and a problem for you to booktalk, enlist a small cadre of teens willing to booktalk popular or quality books from genres other than your favorites.

MOVIES BASED ON YOUNG ADULT BOOKS

Young adults have strong opinions about viewing movies based on books. Some are outraged that their favorite scenes are eliminated from the movies; others don't want their own vision of the characters to be disrupted by a producer's view. Still others like to see how a producer envisions the setting, plot, and characters. For some young adults, viewing a movie based on a book encourages them to read the book. Librarians can capitalize on interests in movies based on books by arranging displays of books that have been made into movies. They can collaborate with a classroom teacher to discuss contrasting elements in the book and the movie, an activity that can be expanded into formal debates and essays. Of course, Harry Potter movies and books are obvious targets for comparison, but there are other interesting titles.

Angus (based on a short story, "A Brief Moment in the Life of Angus Bethune," from *Athletic Shorts* by Chris Crutcher)

Blood and Chocolate by Annette Curtis Klause

Confessions of a Teenage Drama Queen by Dyan Sheldon

A Cry in the Wild (based on *Hatchet* by Gary Paulsen)

Drive Me Crazy (based on *Girl Gives Birth to Own Prom Date* by Todd Strasser)

Eragon by Christopher Paolini

The Golden Compass by Philip Pullman

Holes by Louis Sachar

How to Deal (based on *Someone to Love* and *That Summer* by Sarah Dessen)

Howl's Moving Castle by Diane Wynne Jones

I Know What You Did Last Summer by Lois Duncan

The Lion, the Witch, and the Wardrobe by C. S. Lewis

Little Women by Louisa May Alcott

The Man without a Face by Isabel Holland

The Mighty (based on *Freak the Mighty* by Rodman Philbrick)

The Outsiders by S. E. Hinton

The Princess Diaries by Meg Cabot

The Sisterhood of the Traveling Pants by Ann Brashares

Speak by Laurie Halse Anderson

Tex by S. E. Hinton

CONCLUSION

For fans of fantastic fiction, the biggest problem for young adults will be finding time to read all of the books they want to read. The librarian's pleasurable job is to guide them to their favorite genres. What will it be? Fantasy like Tolkien's or Rowling's? Dragons, witches, or vampires? Classic science fiction, such as Heinlein's *Stranger in a Strange Land*? Or young adult science fiction, such as Anderson's *Feed* or Pfeffer's *Life As We Knew It*? No matter which type of fantastic fiction young adults choose, they'll find imaginative writing at its best, books to take them to places they've never been.

PROFESSIONAL RESOURCES FOR FANTASY AND SCIENCE FICTION

Fichtelberg, Susan. 2007. *Encountering Enchantment: A Guide to Speculative Fiction for Teens*. Libraries Unlimited.

Herald, Diana Tixier. 2003. *Teen Genreflecting: A Guide to Reading Interests*, Second Edition. Libraries Unlimited.

Lynn, Ruth Nadelman. 2007. *Fantasy Literature for Children and Young Adults: A Comprehensive Guide*. 5th ed. Libraries Unlimited.

Spratford, Becky Siegel, and Tammy Hennigh Clausen. 2004. *The Horror Readers' Advisory: The Librarian's Guide to Vampires, Killer Tomatoes, and Haunted Houses*. American Library Association.

Voice of Youth Advocates (VOYA), published bi-monthly, April through February, by Scarecrow Press. The journal publishes excellent reviews of fantasy, horror, and science fiction; an annual list of the best fantasy, horror, and science fiction; and online access at www.voya.com.

ASSIGNMENTS IN ACTION: FANTASTIC FICTION
FOR DISCUSSION

1. Why are young adults attracted to the supernatural and paranormal?

2. What are the benefits of reading fantasy and science fiction?

3. Describe novels from other genres featuring heroes on quests.

4. Which author of fantastic fiction would you like to learn more about? What resources would you use?

5. After reading about the wide range of fantasy and science fiction titles, which novels do you think you would like to read? Why?

6. Which fantastic fiction titles do you think would appeal to teens you work with?

7. Which titles would you consider booktalking? Why?

8. How could a public librarian and a school librarian collaborate on promoting fantastic fiction?

5

Informational Books

[Americans] spend more on fast food than on movies, books, magazines, newspapers, and recorded music—combined.

From *Chew on This: Everything You Don't Want to Know about Fast Food* by Eric Schlosser and Charles Wilson (2006, 10–11)

Biography, autobiography, memoir, nonfiction, science, history, facts, self-help, true crime, true survival, true stories, atlases, dictionaries, encyclopedias— informational books read by young adults are a wonderful hodgepodge of popular and classic categories, subgenres, formats, and topics. Melvil Dewey organized it all into his famous Dewey Decimal Classification (DDC) System. He selected 10 major classes and introduced them to the world in 1876. According to the *Abridged Dewey Decimal Classification and Relative Index, Edition 14* (Dewey 2004), the 10 classes are as follows:

000—Computer science, information and general works

100—Philosophy, parapsychology and occultism, psychology

200—Religion

300—Social sciences

400—Language

500—Natural sciences and mathematics

600—Technology (Applied Science)

700—The arts   Fine and decorative arts

800—Literature (Belles lettres) and rhetoric

900—History, geography, and auxiliary disciplines (Dewey 2004).

Skip most of the 810–899 (poetry and fiction), 398s (folklore), and 741.5 (cartoon fiction and graphic novels), and what's left is an astonishing range of informational books. Topics are published and arranged for every individual taste, whether a student is seeking informational reading or pleasure reading. The informational collection in the library relates directly to the school curriculum. Roughly half of the library book budget and half of the book shelves are devoted to informational books. This chapter groups together types of informational books young adults typically want to read. It examines quality informational books, providing a few titles and topics as examples within the framework of the DDC.

Titles used as examples of popular interest, quality writing, and book design, and worthwhile curricular-related materials were chosen from book awards and award-winning lists. These are primarily the Orbis Pictus Award, sponsored by the National Council of Teachers of English (NCTE), and the Robert F. Sibert Award, sponsored by the Association of Library Services to Children (ALSC).

HISTORY IN ACTION: FIRST NEWBERY MEDAL

In 1922 the first John Newbery Medal was awarded. The creation and implementation of this award had a huge impact on literature for youth. It was the first award for children's literature in the world, and it recognized and encouraged quality writing in children's books. Also remarkable about this award was the first chosen winner, an informational book titled, *The Story of Mankind* by Hendrik Willem van Loon, a professor at Antioch College (1882–1944). This history of the world has been updated three times—in 1972, 1984, and 1998. It was last updated by professor John Merriman of Yale University, when pen-and-ink illustrations were added by Adam Simon. At 674 pages in length, it includes an "Animated Timeline" and a detailed index. Also, to emphasize the uniqueness of this winner, in the intervening years only fiction has won the Newbery Medal except for six biographies and one poetry collection:

Invincible Louisa: The Story of the Author of "Little Women" by Cornelia Meigs (1934).
Daniel Boone by James H. Daugherty (1940).
Amos Fortune, Free Man by Elizabeth Yates (1951).
Carry On, Mr. Bowditch by Jean Lee Latham (1956).
I, Juan de Pareja by Elizabeth Borten de Trevino (1966).
A Visit to William Blake's Inn: Poems for Innocent and Experienced Travelers by Nancy Willard (1982).
Lincoln: A Photobiography by Russell Freedman (1988).

THE ORBIS PICTUS AWARD

The Orbis Pictus Award and the Robert F. Sibert Award are uniquely dedicated to excellence in informational books, excluding textbooks, historical fiction, folk literature, and poetry. Of the two awards the Orbis Pictus is the older one, first awarded in 1990 to Jean Fritz's *The Great Little Madison*. The name of the award honors Johannes Amos Comenius for his illustrated informational book, *Orbis Pictus: The World in Pictures* (1657), considered the first picture book for children. According to the NCTE Web site, the award recognizes "excellence in the writing of nonfiction for children." Five honor books may be awarded in addition to the winner, and beginning the second year of the award (1991), recommended book titles are available as a useful extension. As with many awards, one year of publications are scrutinized by a committee, and then the award carries the next year's date. Since the award is intended for children in kindergarten through eighth grade, not all books are suitable for young adults, although most are appropriate for middle school students. According to an overview on the NCTE Web site at www.ncte.org, each nomination should meet the following literary criteria:

Accuracy—facts current and complete, balance of fact and theory, varying point of view, stereotypes avoided, author's qualifications adequate, appropriate scope, authenticity of detail

Organization—logical development, clear sequence, interrelationships indicated, patterns provided (general-to-specific, simple-to-complex, etc.)

Design—attractive, readable, illustrations complement text, placement of illustrative material appropriate and complementary, appropriate media, format, type

Style—writing is interesting, stimulating, reveals author's enthusiasm for subject, curiosity and wonder encouraged, appropriate terminology, rich language.

ROBERT F. SIBERT INFORMATIONAL BOOK MEDAL

The Robert F. Sibert Informational Book Medal honors the long-time president of Bound to Stay Bound Books of Jacksonville, Illinois. The award was established by ALSC, sponsored by Bound to Stay Bound, and administered by ALSC. Like the Orbis Pictus Award, the Sibert Medal recognizes informational books only, excluding poetry and traditional literature, such as folktales. To be eligible for a Sibert Medal, a book should be distinguished for its significant contribution to children's literature appropriate for young people, birth through age 14. Again, similar to the Orbis Pictus Award, many titles are appropriate for middle school students; some for high school students. Books eligible for a Sibert Medal must be published in English in the previous year of the announced award. According to the ALSC Web site, criteria for the award are the following "important elements and qualities":

1. excellent, engaging, and distinctive use of language
2. excellent, engaging, and distinctive visual presentation
3. appropriate organization and documentation
4. clear, accurate, and stimulating presentation of facts, concepts, and ideas
5. visual material and book design
6. appropriate style of presentation for subject and intended audience
7. supportive features (index, table of contents, maps, timelines, etc.)
8. respectful and of interest to children

BIOGRAPHIES AND AUTOBIOGRAPHIES

His feeling for the rhythms of life, his sympathy for his fellow man, his yearning for love, and his understanding that what mattered was not worldly success but spirituality and a passion for work all poured into his painting.

From *Vincent Van Gogh: Portrait of an Artist* by Jan Greenberg and Sandra Jordan (2001, 106)

Biographies and autobiographies written for young adults have the potential to benefit readers by:

1. Providing role models.
2. Getting to know people different from themselves.
3. Demonstrating how decisions, opportunities, and changes influence one's life.
4. Entering into the thought processes of people who have made an impact on society.
5. Supplying information on specialized topics for personal interest or for school research.
6. Offering a research model.
7. Offering a pleasurable reading experience.

A modern, well-written biography for youth is a life history, presenting a person's life from birth to death with an effort at interpreting the meaning of the person's life (Holman & Harmon 1992, 54). Greenberg's and Jordan's *Vincent Van Gogh: Portrait of an Artist* is an example of a well-written, well-designed biography. It was awarded a 2002 Sibert Honor, a 2002 Best Books for Young Adults, and a 2002 Recommended Orbis Pictus Title. Using the criteria of the Sibert Award to evaluate the volume, it's easy to understand the accolades. Clearly written without sensationalizing his eccentricities, his possible epilepsy, or the violence van Gogh turned on himself, Greenberg and Jordan have created a biography appropriate for middle school and high school students. A reproduction of van Gogh's self-portrait showing his bandaged ear draws readers quickly into the book. In addition to the compelling narrative, readers will appreciate the 15 pages of color reproductions of his work. These reproductions are carefully chosen to illustrate art that had significance in van Gogh's life, and they are referenced in the narrative. Most fortunate and remarkable from a researcher's viewpoint is the access to hundreds of letters van Gogh wrote to his brother Theo, detailing his life struggles with career choices, with artists and other people he met, and with his own artistic ups and downs. Completing the book are a biographical time line, museum locations, a glossary of artists and terms, notes for each chapter citing Vincent's letters to Theo, a bibliography, photography credits, and an index. *Vincent van Gogh: Portrait of an Artist* is a complete biographical package well suited to the needs of young people.

Other notable biographies for middle school and high school students include *Langston Hughes* by Melvin Meltzer, *Andy Warhol: Prince of Pop* by Jan

Greenberg and Sandra Jordan, and *Eleanor Roosevelt: A Life of Discovery* by Russell Freedman, *Savion: My Life in Tap* by Savion Glover and Bruce Weber, *Surviving Hitler: A Boy in the Nazi Death Camps* by Andrea Warren (Sibert Honor Book), and *Lincoln: A Photobiography* by Russell Freedman (1988 Newbery Medal).

Biography Series

Biography series books can also serve students' needs very well. They tend to be short in length and on easy reading levels. Some examples are the following:

The 14th Dalai Lama: Spiritual Leader of Tibet by Whitney Stewart, A&E Biography series, a Lerner Publication.

Johann Gutenberg: Master of Modern Printing by Michael Pollard, Giants of Science series by Blackbirch Press.

Mary Cassatt: An Artist's Life by Nancy Plain, People in Focus series by Dillon Press.

Maya Angelou: Journey of the Heart by Jayne Pettit, Rainbow Biography series by Lodestar Books.

Maya Angelou: America's Poetic Voice by Nancy Shuker, Giants of Art and Culture series by Blackbirch Press.

Tiger Woods: Golf's Shining Young Star by Bill Gutman, Millbrook Sports World series by Millbrook Press.

Other Biographical Choices

Still other biographical choices include collected biography, picture books, and graphic novels. In the same way that story collections encourage readers to browse through a book and choose stories that interest them, collected biographies offer the same desirable feature. In Andrea Davis Pinkney's *Let It Shine: Stories of Black Women Freedom Fighters*, readers can choose between Sojourner Truth, Harriet Tubman, or Rosa Parks or can read about all of the women in any order they choose. For many years, Diane Stanley has been writing and illustrating picture books about some of the most fascinating people in the history of the world. Her beautifully illustrated, well-researched, well-designed, and well-written biographies are most appropriate for middle school students but may have appeal to high school students because of the excellent presentation of material. Stanley's subjects include Michelangelo, Joan of Arc, Cleopatra, Elizabeth I, Shakespeare, Charles Dickens, Leonardo da Vinci, and more. The increasing popularity of graphic novels (described in chapter 2) extends to autobiography with Art Spiegelman's *Maus I* and *Maus II* (also described in chapter 2), Judd Winick's *Pedro and Me: Friendship, Loss, and What I Learned*, and *To Dance: A Ballerina's Graphic Novel* by Siena Cherson Siegel with artwork by Mark Siegel.

Autobiography

Similar to a biography, an autobiography is a "narrative of the author's life, with some stress on introspection" (Holman & Harmon 1992, 41). In literature for youth, there are few autobiographies of a person's entire life. The closest genre is a memoir. In a memoir, sometimes a writer's entire life is reviewed, but more often there are only slices presented. For instance, in his shocking *Hole in My Life*, Jack Gantos describes how he became a drug user and a smuggler, was arrested, and went to prison as a young adult. Later he attended college and finally became a writer of children's books. Gantos won a 2003 Printz Honor for *Hole in My Life*. In contrast to Gantos's sobering view of his teen years, Chris Crutcher reminisces about his years growing up in Cascade, Idaho. *King of the Mild Frontier: An Ill-Advised Autobiography* is filled with Crutcher's irreverent sense of humor.

Not all memoirs, of course, are humorous or light-hearted. And the best memoirs are judged favorably by eight criteria used in honoring a Sibert award. An excellent memoir that presents both a human and a global tragedy is Anita Lobel's *No Pretty Pictures*, nominated for a National Book Award for Young People's Literature. Young adults are interested in and curious about the Holocaust. Lobel's memoir vividly describes her difficult survival as a Polish Jew during World War II and the aftermath as she and her brother recuperated from tuberculosis in Sweden. Her memoir is especially effective yet heart-wrenching, told in Lobel's naïve voice during a period of about seven years, beginning when Lobel was five years old. "I was afraid to ask what it really meant that all these people had been 'deported.' I was only surprised that my mother could cry that way. The way I had cried one morning when my father was not there" (Lobel 1998, 10). Lobel's ability to write with great detail from the first-person viewpoint of a young child makes her ordeal readable and more chilling. Twelve inset pages of black and white photographs of Lobel and her family at various stages in their lives add yet another dose of reality to her story.

Organizing Biographies and Autobiographies

Biographies and autobiographies allow young adult readers to vicariously experience other people's lives and historical periods. Those experiences can add another dimension to their understanding of human nature and human history. What is the best way to organize these human experiences and make them easily accessible in the school or public library? In most cases biographies and autobiographies are shelved in a special section simply labeled "biography" and shelved by the last name of the person the book is about. This arrangement can create a huge section of books all labeled with a "B." Imagine a fan of baseball or a young artist faced with this section yet wanting to read about a real-life athlete or artist. There are, of course, online catalogs, but a student interested in baseball or art and browsing shelves of books to see what's interesting is more likely to find biographies in a related Dewey number. Instead of a biography section, shelving biographies and autobiographies in Dewey classes automatically groups related materials. This arrangement allows for optimal browsing for both pleasure and curricular purposes. A student wanting to report on music and musicians could find both topics in the 780s. A biography of Dian Fossey, a researcher who worked for many years with the mountain gorillas in the rain forests of Rwanda, would be found in the 590s with books about the behavior of gorillas.

Authors in Action: The Lives of Favorite Young Adult Authors

Anonymously Yours: A Memoir by the Author of Ghosts I Have Been by Richard Peck. Honored with a 1999 Newbery Honor for *A Long Way from Chicago*, the 2001 Newbery Medal for *A Year Down Yonder*, and for consistent recognition of his novels on Best Books for Young Adults, Peck is an icon of a young adult author. His brief memoir describes his transition from teacher to writer and how his early life experiences translated into his popular books.

Authortalk: Conversations with Judy Blume [et al.] compiled and edited by Leonard S. Marcus. Brief interviews with 15 children's/young adult writers, including childhood photographs and a selected list of their books.

Bad Boy: A Memoir by Walter Dean Myers. His personal story growing up in Harlem in the 1950s reflects his turbulent adolescence and eventual path to respected writer. A versatile author, Myers has written both fiction (*Monster*, the first Printz Award winner—2000; *Fallen Angels*) and nonfiction (*Greatest: Muhammad Ali, Amistad: A Long Road to Freedom*, and *Malcolm X: By Any Means Necessary*).

Hole in My Life by Jack Gantos. Gantos is known for his books for children. Nevertheless, Gantos's memoir of his young adult life as a drug user, smuggler, and prisoner will catch the attention of teens.

King of the Mild Frontier: An Ill-Advised Autobiography by Chris Crutcher. At once humorous and poignant, Crutcher's memories of his childhood, his hot temper, and his work as a child and family therapist will enthrall readers. A popular writer whose novels are often challenged, Crutcher can boast an impressive list of books starting with *Running Loose* and continuing with *Stotan!, The Crazy Horse Electric Game, Chinese Handcuffs, Athletic Shorts, Staying Fat for Sarah Byrnes, Ironman, Whale Talk*, and *Deadline*.

Knots in My Yo-Yo String: The Autobiography of a Kid by Jerry Spinelli. The author of *Space Station Seventh Grade; Who Put That Hair in My Toothbrush?; Jason and Marceline; Maniac Magee* (1991 Newbery Medal); *Stargirl; Milkweed*; and *Love, Stargirl*; writes for children and young adults (middle school age) with humor and heart. In 10 years of reminiscences about his childhood in Norristown, Pennsylvania, Spinelli tells about everyday experiences with his family, siblings, school friends, and neighbors, including his triumph as president of his ninth-grade class and king of his ninth-grade prom.

Looking Back: A Book of Memories by Lois Lowry. Best known for her popular, Newbery Medal-winning dystopian novel, *The Giver*, Lowry won the 2007 Margaret Edwards Award for her outstanding contribution to young adult literature. In her introduction to *Looking Back*, Lowry states, "I would like to introduce you to this book. It has no plot. It is about moments, memories, fragments, falsehoods, and fantasies. It is about things that happened, which caused other things to happen, so that eventually stories emerged" (Lowry 1998, introduction unpaged [i-ii]). This memoir with the feel of a scrapbook features black-and-white photos, brief quotes, and brief notes about intimate pieces of her life, with quotes from *The Giver* and some of her other books. In one section she mentions a made-up game she likes to play. When she sees a certain scene, she asks her family and friends, "What book does this remind you of?" According to Lowry, "There are no wrong answers" (Lowry 1998, 137).

Me Me Me Me Me: Not a Novel by M. E. Kerr. Her memoir of her teen years is riveting for its reflection of typical teen angst from the lively viewpoint of a feisty but rebellious girl living in upstate New York. Kerr, growing up as Marijane Meaker, struggles with authority figures yet maintains her sense of humor as she views her life as a teenager in the 1940s. She begins her narrative when she's 15 years old, working her way through stories of dating, literature and reading, music, her two brothers, her parents, friends, World War II, boarding school, college, and of course, her writing efforts. She deftly connects these experiences to realistic novels she has written: *I'll Love You When You're More Like Me; Son of Someone Famous; Is That You, Miss Blue?; Little Little; What I Really Think of You; Gentlehands;* and *Dinky Hocker Shoots Smack!* Kerr won the 1993 Margaret A. Edwards Award.

My Life in Dog Years by Gary Paulsen. This brief view of Paulsen's interactions with his dogs, includes Cookie, his favorite. Paulsen is known for his adventure/survival stories, especially *Hatchet*, and for his sense of humor (read *Harris and Me*). Another of his informational books with particular appeal to boys is *Father Water, Mother Woods: Essays on Fishing and Hunting in the North Woods.* Most of his books are suitable for middle school students; a few are more appropriate for high school (*The Beet Fields*).

Oddballs by William Sleator. A slightly fictional autobiographical account of Sleator's years growing up features hilarious pranks his brother, sister, and he played on each other and sometimes on unsuspecting strangers. See chapter 4 for a list of his science fiction novels.

The Pigman and Me by Paul Zindel. Zindel's wacky sense of humor is reflected in the life he led as a teenager in the small town of Travis, New York. The greatest influence on his year there was Nonno Frankie Vivona, who became his own pigman or mentor. Nonno Frankie told corny jokes and gave funny advice, all with a sparkle in his eyes and plenty of heart. At a time when Zindel's mother threatened suicide a few times a year, he needed his own pigman. Zindel was honored with the 2003 Margaret Edwards Award for *The Effects of Gamma Rays on Man-in-the-Moon Marigolds*, a Pulitzer Prize–winning play; *The Pigman; My Darling, My Hamburger; The Pigman's Legacy;* and *The Pigman and Me.*

Twayne's Young Adult Authors Series offers history and literary criticism of the works of young adult authors, such as Avi, Robert Cormier, Chris Crutcher, Paula Danziger, Rosa Guy, S. E. Hinton, M. E. Kerr, Ursula K. Le Guin, Phyllis R. Naylor, Ouida Sebestyen, Mildred Taylor, and Cynthia Voigt.

Literature in Action: Biographies and Caricatures

Combine research and fun in a collaborative activity between an art teacher and a reading or language arts or English teacher. Follow these basic steps:

1. Students choose an author to research.

2. A language arts teacher explains note-taking and writing processes.

3. A library media specialist helps students locate biographical resources in print and online and reviews research processes and proper citation formats and parenthetical references.

4. An art teacher shows both historical and contemporary caricatures and teaches the basics of drawing a caricature with an emphasis on the importance of knowing details about the author before beginning to draw.

5. For assessment, students self-evaluate; the language arts teacher evaluates students' writing; the art teacher evaluates their caricatures; and the school library media specialist displays writing and art in a secure display cabinet.

See Jean M. Crane's article detailing the activity for middle school students in "Art/Reading/Language Arts: Biographies and Caricatures with Young Adults" in *School Library Media Activities Monthly*, 2005.

OTHER INFORMATIONAL BOOKS

Not so long ago in Montgomery, Alabama, the color of your skin determined where you could sit on a public bus. If you happened to be an African American, you had to sit at the back of the bus, even if there were empty seats up front.

From *Freedom Walkers: The Story of the Montgomery Bus Boycott*
by Russell Freedman (2006, 1)

Certainly biographies and autobiographies are informational books. They inform readers with details of the lives of people of interest. Other informational books may include human stories but the emphasis is not on a single person but on a topic, such as a period in history, a social issue, or a scientific finding or phenomenon. In comparing and contrasting fiction and informational books, we expect fiction to entertain readers and informational books to inform readers. This is an oversimplification of the differences in the two types of books. Readers can learn from fiction about their options in life, such as ways to handle emotional situations. Readers of informational book can gain facts about the world, but for some, maybe many readers, learning information about the world is entertainment as well. The intent of informational books is to provide true and accurate information, but to many young adults it also brings reading pleasure (Carter and Abrahamson, 1990).

One Book in Action: *An American Plague* by Jim Murphy

Referring again to criteria for selecting the Robert F. Sibert Informational Book Award, books can be evaluated through eight basic elements: use of language; visual presentation; organization and documentation; presentation of facts, concepts, and ideas; visual material and book design; style of presentation; supportive features; and suitability for an audience of children. *An American Plague: The True and Terrifying Story of the Yellow Fever Epidemic of 1793* by Jim Murphy is a worthy selection to demonstrate the best in an informational book for young adults, grades 6–12. It won the 2004 Sibert Award, the 2004 Orbis Pictus Award, and a 2004 Newbery Honor. Analyzing *An American*

Plague leads to a better understanding of its success as an award-winning informational book.

1. Excellent, engaging, and distinctive use of language—From the first page readers will be intrigued: "In Philadelphia itself an increasing number of cats were dropping dead every day, attracting, one Philadelphian complained, 'an amazing number of flies and other insects.' Mosquitoes were everywhere, though their high-pitched whirring was particularly loud near rain barrels, gutters, and open sewers" (Murphy 2003, 1). Murphy's narrative is almost conversational as he interweaves historical events with personal tragedies of the disease.

2. Excellent, engaging, and distinctive visual presentation—Visually, the dust jacket will draw readers to this book, especially with the word "plague" in large, heavy, black capital letters on a background that appears to be parchment paper. A colored lithograph of a patient lying in bed after a blood-letting adds to the realism of the epidemic. Once inside the book, readers will appreciate the black-and-white documented facsimiles of drawings and paintings of people, buildings, and events from the time period. Bright, colorful visuals would not have been appropriate to the integrity of the book.

3. Appropriate organization and documentation—The book is organized into 11 chapters with titles capturing the essence of each chapter, sometimes through observers' quotes. The titles are as follows: No One Noticed; "All Was Not Right"; Church Bells Tolling; Confusion, Distress, and Utter Desolation; "It Was Our Duty"; The Prince of Bleeders; "By Twelve Only"; "This Unmerciful Enemy"; "A Delicate Situation"; Improvements and the Public Gratitude; and "A Modern-Day Time Bomb" (Murphy 2003). The title of chapter 2 is a quote from Dr. Benjamin Rush, a 47-year-old physician who observed the rapid deterioration of Catherine LeMaigre, one of the first recognized plague victims. After observing her symptoms and an increase in bilious fevers among other patients, he said, "all was not right in our city" (Murphy 2003, 12). Further, each chapter begins with a brief quotation from a person of the time period or from someone commenting on the time period. A facsimile copy of a section from *The Federal Gazette* (1793) or a list of the dead or a relevant article can be read on a full page adjacent to the beginning page of each chapter. At the beginning of chapter 6 there's a quote from Dr. Benjamin Rush as follows: "In this awful situation, the stoutest hearts began to fail. Hope flickered, and despair succeeded distress in almost every countenance" (Murphy 2003, 57).

Rather than using parenthetical references or footnotes that interrupt the text and can be distracting to young readers, at the end of the book Murphy records the sources he consulted. Most sources are followed with additional interesting facts related to people and the yellow fever. Sources are arranged by the following topics: Firsthand

Accounts: Nonmedical; Firsthand Accounts: Medical; All About Yellow Fever; Yellow Fever: Fiction; Doctoring in the Old Days; Philadelphia, Then and After; George Washington and His Problems; Blacks in Philadelphia; That Buzzing in Your Ear; and Other Plagues.

4. Clear, accurate, and stimulating presentation of facts, concepts, and ideas—Before writing *The American Plague*, Jim Murphy already had a reputation for writing excellent informational books. He won a 1996 Newbery Honor and the 1996 Orbis Pictus Award for *The Great Fire*, and the 1994 Orbis Pictus Award for *Across America on an Emigrant Train*. A list of extensive sources and acknowledgements help assure the accuracy of his information. By integrating historical facts with documented personal accounts of the plague, Murphy clarifies his topic on several levels. Beginning with a date adds to the feeling that the reader is witnessing the terrible progression of the disease. Chapter 1 begins with Saturday, August 3, 1793, and the last chapter begins with September 1, 1858. One of the most chilling stories is the participation of African Americans encouraged "to help nurse the sick and attend to the dead" (Murphy 2003, 17). "One reason they should come forward, Rush contended, was that God had seen fit to grant blacks a special resistance to the dreaded disease" (17). This turned out to be a falsehood and was disastrous for the African American population.

5. Visual material and book design—Appropriately to the late 1700s, all visual material is rendered in black and white. Also appropriately, sources of each of 42 illustrations are indicated following a brief caption. (These are in addition to the initial map of Philadelphia and facsimiles preceding each chapter.) Visual contributions come from The Library Company of Philadelphia, The Historical Society of Pennsylvania, The College of Physicians of Philadelphia, The Philadelphia Museum of Art, The Delaware Art Museum, The Houghton Library/Harvard University, The Abby Aldrich Rockefeller Folk Art Museum, *Harper's Weekly*, plus a few other sources. These visual facsimiles consist of portraits, political cartoons, paintings, and pen-and-ink illustrations of Philadelphia buildings and people. Placement and topic of illustrations closely follow the text and serve to interrupt what might otherwise be a formidable expanse of black print. Visuals range from full pages to a 2 x 2½-inch drawing of a mosquito. This variety in size adds to interest and to a pleasing design.

6. Appropriate style of presentation for subject and intended audience—While Murphy engages the senses in describing how the yellow fever kills people, he avoids sensationalizing their deaths. His simple, clear writing style combined with frequent black-and-white illustrations result in a readable, interesting presentation for grades 6–12.

7. Supportive features (index, table of contents, maps, timelines, etc.)—These include a two-page spread of a drawing of Philadelphia with numbered indications of 12 relevant locations, including St. George's Church, City Hall, and Free African Society. A seven-page, detailed

subject index adds page numbers of illustrations in bold type. Acknowledgments, a note about illustrations, a table of contents (already mentioned), and 13 pages of sources (also mentioned previously) complete supportive features.

8. Respectful and of interest to children—Young people are drawn to true and terrifying stories. *An American Plague* has the added benefit of appropriate visuals and is written in readable language for middle school and high school students.

Format of Informational Books

For the purpose of understanding the format of informational books better, they can be divided into two basic groups: those that are dominated by text and those that are dominated by illustration. As with other categories and genres, this distinction is not always clear. For instance, in Diane McWhorter's *A Dream of Freedom: The Civil Rights Movement from 1954 to 1968*, contents are determined by both a significant year and a title. At first glance, the format is that of a picture book, 10¾″ in length by 9¾″ in height. Visuals are photographs varying from full pages to small shots. At first glance it might appear to be a picture book for children, but subject matter and length (160 pages) quickly show it's written for young adults. On the other hand, *The Tarantula Scientist* by Sy Montgomery with photographs by Nic Bishop, is almost the exact size as *A Dream of Freedom* but is appropriate for a full range of young people from elementary through high school. Instead of being overly concerned with a precise term for formats of informational books, a more useful approach is to understand the many elements that can make a wonderful book, as demonstrated previously by Murphy's book about yellow fever.

Informational books dominated by text, either expository or narrative writing, lack illustrations or have few illustrations. Authors choose the most appropriate style and format for their work. Sometimes a work demands illustrations, sometimes illustrations are either not available or would not be appropriate. In *Dear America: Letters Home from Vietnam* (edited by Bernard Edelman), the emphasis is on the content of the letters. The addition of photographs or illustrations of people and places in Vietnam would detract from the emotions expressed in the letters. Sometimes, although not always, lack of illustration is an indication of reading level or age appropriateness. Other examples of informational books with few or no illustrations are Jon Krakauer's *Into Thin Air: A Personal Account of the Mt. Everest Disaster*, Jon Katz's *Geeks: How Two Lost Boys Rode the Internet out of Idaho*, Eric Schlosser and Charles Wilson's *Chew on This: Everything You Don't Want to Know About Fast Food*, and Milton Meltzer's *Never to Forget: The Jews of the Holocaust*.

REFERENCE SOURCES AND RESEARCH

In school and public libraries, basic print reference sources for information are encyclopedias, dictionaries, atlases, and almanacs. In the past, these were large works in print shelved in a separate section of the library. With the infusion of technology in today's libraries, the way young adults search has changed dramatically. Students still need and want the type of information offered by standard works, but they are finding their information online through databases on the Internet. If a library has enough funding to subscribe to online versions of standard reference works and enough computers available, then the need for reference works in print is drastically reduced. Print sources are declining and e-reference is rapidly replacing print sources. E-reference appeals to the generation of young adults who take laptops, iPods, and cell phones for granted (Polanka 2008). It's all about the technology available in libraries, meaning it's all about funding. Databases can be double the cost of print sources.

Whether or not a library's reference sources are print or electronic, there are two major reasons for supplying reference sources in schools. First, references should support curricular-related lessons and activities. For example, high school students who are writing a research paper on Africa could use the *New Encyclopedia of Africa* (Middleton and Miller 2007), a five-volume set, along with *Africa* (Haugen 2008), a new title in the popular Opposing Viewpoints series. For databases they could search Britannica Online (www.britannica.com), Facts on File (www.factsonfile.com), and ProQuest (www.proquest.com).

Second, reference works should support hobbies and other interests of young adults. Current popular nonfiction interests are reflected in popular magazine topics, such as anime and comics, crafts, entertainment, ethnicity, occultism, teen issues, and trivia. New print reference sources that support at least two of these topics are *Encyclopedia of American Indian History* (Johansen and Pritzker 2007), *The Encyclopedia of Ghosts and Spirits* (Guiley 2007), and *African Americans in the Media Today: An Encyclopedia* (Riley 2007).

For reviews of reference sources, librarians can rely on the same recommended selection tools they use for fiction and informational books: *Booklist*, *School Library Journal*, and *VOYA*.

A Research Process

Reference sources, either print or online, are used for two primary purposes: (1) answering simple questions that students have and (2) assisting students with a research process, usually curriculum related. Librarians and classroom teachers need to direct students in a research process that enables students to go beyond the simple gathering of information. The ultimate goal for a research project is to "learn how to learn" (Carey 2003, 28). One popular and widespread model for teaching and directing student research is the Big6™ model developed by educators Michael Eisenberg and Bob Berkowitz. This is an information and technology literacy model of six process stages based on Bloom's taxonomy, a theory of levels of cognitive learning (Carey 2003). The model's six stages are "task definition, information seeking strategies, location and access, use of information, synthesis, and evaluation" (Eisenberg and Berkowitz 1997, 22). Ideally, Big6 focuses students on the task of solving a problem through a research process. Because Big6 has been used so widely, there are multiple examples of how to understand it and how to implement it.

A trip to the Big6 web page at www.big6.com will yield plenty of information to get you started using the model.

10 Classes of Dewey: Sample Titles

To sample useful and entertaining informational books for young adults, it seems helpful to librarians to consider topics organized into 10 main classes by Melvil Dewey. Librarians want to find the best combination of excellent features with the subjects that address curricular needs and interests of the young adults they serve. Informational books written and published for young adults reflect current societal concerns of adults and especially those of young adults. The following 10 major classification descriptions contain brief samples of book titles published for young adults, including a few published for adults but read by young adults. Lists of topics are not intended to be comprehensive nor are topics taken from a standard subject list, such as *Sears List of Subject Headings*. Lists offer a sample of popular and curricular topics, both specific and general, understanding that new topics capture the imagination of society (and writers) daily. In other words, these are popular topics of popular, well-written books for young adults that provide insight to available reading selections. Each major class describes a few recommended titles.

000—Computer Science, Information and General Works

In *Geeks: How Two Lost Boys Rode the Internet out of Idaho* (2000) by Jon Katz, Jesse and Eric are 19-year-old computer geeks, stuck in a small town without positive prospects for the future, when Katz meets them and decides to write a book about them. Some readers will think the boys' real-life experiences in high school and as young adults bring shame on our public educational system. Others will see that Katz's book offers hope for young adults who are different from the mainstream. A favorite title found in this class is *The Guinness Book of World Records*, published annually, and popular with teens. Although general encyclopedias are classified in the 000s, they are usually shelved in a reference section. Topics include books about aliens, computer technology, the Internet, and miscellaneous facts.

100—Philosophy, Parapsychology and Occultism, Psychology

In *The 7 Habits of Highly Effective Teens*, author Sean Covey speaks to teens in a positive, light-hearted manner while dispensing practical advice for taking control of their own lives. Ed Young's visually beautiful *Voices of the Heart* presents 26 emotions with their Chinese characters. Each emotion, such as rudeness, grace, and aspiration, occupies a full-page illustration with a quick explanation. Topics in the 100s include animal rights, astrology, brain power, dreams, ethics, euthanasia, paranormal, supernatural, and teen survival, success, and inspiration.

200—Religion

This is a small, narrowly focused class. Various editions of the Bible along with descriptions of religions of the world are considered staples. *Bulfinch's Mythology*, a basic work, is an essential choice for this class.

300—Social Sciences

In Ann Bausum's *Freedom Riders: John Lewis and Jim Zwerg on the Front Lines of the Civil Rights Movement*, readers learn about the brave young men and women who rode "freedom buses" to the South as a nonviolent protest against segregation (Sibert Honor Book 2007). Russell Freedman's *Freedom Walkers: The Story of the Montgomery Bus Boycott* has a similar theme. Once Rosa Parks refused to give up her bus seat for a white person, events escalated into a bus boycott in Montgomery, Alabama, which ended bus segregation and was a major victory for the civil rights movement (Orbis Pictus Honor 2007). Ann Bausum's *With Courage and Cloth: Winning the Fight for a Woman's Right to Vote* describes the suffragettes and the events leading to a woman's constitutional voting right (BBYA 2005). On a completely different topic, Janet Bode discussed real-life rape scenarios with teens, recorded the results, and gave teens advice in *The Voices of Rape: Healing the Hurt*. Fans of Lois Duncan's suspense novels will want to read her real-life search for justice and for answers in *Who Killed My Daughter?* In *Chew on This: Everything You Don't Want to Know about Fast Food*, authors Eric Schlosser and Charles Wilson are on a mission to expose gruesome details of feedlots and poultry farms that supply fast food restaurants. Carefully documented information combined with a history of the industry will be eye-opening to most readers.

The social sciences include folk literature, but since they are traditional stories and not informational books, they are not included in this list of topics. Topics in this classification are varied and numerous. In alphabetical order they include child abuse, civil rights, environment, etiquette, fast food industry, gangs, holidays, homelessness, immigrant stories, law, murder, prison, rape, sexual abuse, slavery, spies, substance abuse, teen rights, vampire myths, and weapons.

400—Language

This class is another small and narrowly focused one. It contains English language and foreign language dictionaries plus a few topics related to language. Books about sign language are especially popular with young adults. Lottie L. Riekehof's *The Joy of Signing* offers a history, terminology, and description of signing before presenting drawings of words divided by categories, such as family relationships, sports and recreation, and religion. An index of words makes it easy for readers to find directions for the particular words they want to learn.

500—Natural Sciences and Mathematics

Topics in this class are more predictable than in the 300s. As you might expect, books about animals are particularly popular for leisure reading and for research projects. Topics include books about all animals and insects, astronomy, dinosaurs, earthquakes, mathematics, physics, time travel, veterinarians, and volcanoes. In Sy Montgomery's *The Tarantula Scientist*, Sam Marshall, a spider scientist, observes tarantulas in French Guiana at close range. In-your-face photographs taken by Nic Bishop add fascinating details of the hairy spiders (Sibert Honor 2005). Montgomery and Bishop also form a partnership to study an elusive, rare creature in *Quest for The Tree Kangaroo: An Expedition to the Cloud Forest of New Guinea* (Orbis Pictus Medal 2007; Sibert Honor Book 2007). Phillip Hoose's *The Race to Save the Lord God Bird* chronicles a search in the United States for an Ivory-billed Woodpecker, an endangered bird of glorious beauty (2005 Orbis Pictus Honor Book). Always inspirational and informative when she writes about chimpanzees, Jane Goodall makes a plea for the environment in *The Chimpanzees I Love: Saving Their World and Ours*.

600—Technology (Applied Sciences)

In Catherine Thimmesh's *Team Moon: How 400,000 People Landed Apollo 11 on the Moon*, readers are privy to seven challenges faced by astronauts Neil Armstrong, Buzz Aldrin, and Michael Collins and all the people who made a moon landing possible. Stunning photographs of the moon and the Earth and meticulous research garnered this large format book the 2007 Sibert Medal and a 2007 Orbis Pictus Honor. *Castle*, a classic work by David Macaulay, details through text and pen-and-ink illustration, the construction of a thirteenth-century castle in Wales (Caldecott Honor 1978). Other similarly rendered books of his are *Cathedral, City, Pyramid*, and *Underground*. In *It's Perfectly Normal: Changing Bodies, Growing Up, Sex & Sexual Health*, Robie Harris presents a frank but lighthearted view of sex, complete with informative drawings by Michael Emberley.

This class contains a surprisingly diverse number of topics. The alphabetical list that follows reflects that variety: astronauts, automobiles, babysitting, beautiful bodies, cooking, depression, diseases, eating disorders, inventions, modeling, obesity, pets, plagues, pregnancy, sexuality, suicide, and vegetarians.

700—The Arts, Fine and Decorative Arts

In Jon Krakauer's *Into Thin Air: A Personal Account of the Mount Everest Disaster*, Krakauer, a journalist, witnesses the 1996 tragedy when climbers are caught in a blizzard. He wrote this account for adults, although it has great appeal to young adults as well. Gary Paulsen's *How Angel Peterson Got His Name and Other Outrageous Tales about Extreme Sports* is an easy to read, laugh-out-loud experience, perfect for reading aloud. *Whatcha Mean, What's a Zine? The Art of Making Zines and Mini-comics* by Mark Todd and Esther Pearl Watson was described in a previous chapter.

Books in the 700s address all games, all sports, mountain climbing, skateboarding, architecture, all kinds of art, calligraphy, dance, drawing manga, knitting, music, photography, tattooing, and much more.

800—Literature (Belles Lettres) and Rhetoric

This classification was the primary location for fiction before librarians decided to create a special section. Now it's a prime location for poetry and, in some libraries, for story collections. Poetry is considered nonfiction but not informational. Books on the following topics may be found in a young adult collection: comedy, fantasy worlds and characters, books about the Harry Potter collection, literary criticism, biographies of poets and other writers, and essays written by teens.

900—History, Geography, and Auxiliary Disciplines

In this large section of the library, the Holocaust is a topic about which young adults are curious. In *Hitler Youth: Growing Up in Hitler's Shadow*, Susan Campbell Bartoletti chronicles Hitler's rise to power in relation to the young people of Hitler's youth organization. Stories of the complete dedication of individual young people who followed Hitler and what the organization demanded of them are chilling (2005 Newbery Honor Book; 2005 Sibert Honor Book). In James M. Deem's *Bodies from the Ash: Life and Death in Ancient Pompeii*, a brief history of the eruption of Mount Vesuvius in AD 79 is combined with excavation efforts and results. Photos of skeletons and plaster bodies are riveting reminders of the loss of human lives in the aftermath.

As you would expect, books in the 900s are about countries and histories of the world, Holocaust survivors and the history of the Holocaust, real adventure/survival stories, travel, and war stories.

LIBRARIANS IN ACTION: BOOKTALKING INFORMATIONAL BOOKS

Booktalking informational books is not significantly different from booktalking fiction. Let's test this theory using *Chew on This!*

1. Grab students' attention with a great opening from a book:

   "The Golden Arches are now more widely recognized than the Christian cross" (Schlosser and Wilson 2006, 8).

   "Overweight teenagers today are having surgery to make their stomachs smaller. They are also having heart attacks" (dust jacket).

2. Give some background. The authors, Eric Schlosser and Charles Wilson, give us a brief history of the fast food industry along with vivid tours of feedlots in Greeley, Colorado (read pages 165–166) and a tour of a poultry farm in West Virginia that supplies McDonald's with chicken (read pages 175–176).

   There's much more to learn from this book and, as you can tell, much of it is not pleasant! It's clear that the authors are on a mission, but their information is carefully documented.

3. Select an interesting person, fact, or event to focus on. See number 2.

4. Use an intriguing ending. Will this book change Americans' minds about fast food? (Listen to a few opinions.) Will the book change your mind about fast food? (Again, listen to a few opinions.) Only McDonald's profits and the improved health of Americans will show us.

5. Potential prop to use: A McDonald's Happy Meal.

6. For research projects and further discussion: At the end of the paperback edition of *Chew on This*, read the "Discussion Questions and Action Steps" for some great ideas for collaboration with a classroom teacher.

This works! These are the basic elements of a booktalk and can be adapted to promote any book. If you meet with students who are looking for research topics, choose a few intriguing informational books and booktalk them to help students choose interesting topics.

INFORMATION LITERACY STANDARDS FOR 21ST-CENTURY LEARNERS

It seems appropriate to close a chapter about informational books with information literacy standards. In 2007, Standards for the 21st-Century Learner were unveiled in Reno, Nevada at the American Association of School Librarians annual conference. The new standards promote the following actions for students:

1. Inquire, think critically, and gain knowledge.
2. Draw conclusions, make informed decisions, apply knowledge to new situations, and create new knowledge.
3. Share knowledge and participate ethically and productively as members of our democratic society.
4. Pursue personal and aesthetic growth.

These four standards revolve around the ability to read well and to use resources appropriately. Each standard is divided into four areas: Skills, Dispositions in Action, Responsibilities, and Self-Assessment Strategies. For a list of nine common beliefs and for details about the four standards and four areas, download an eight-page full-color pamphlet from the ALA Web site titled "AASL Standards for the 21st-Century Learner" at www.ala.org/ala/aasl/aasl-proftools/learningstandards/standards.cfm.

CONCLUSION

Informational books for young adults are still evolving. Today's books are not a dry explanation of facts as many books in the past were. A few years ago I was weeding a book collection in a middle school in Kansas. My favorite discovery was a book published in 1956 titled, *Fun with Wire for Boys*. It had not been checked out in the last 20 years. Information books have come a long way in the last 50 years. Some are written in a narrative style; some are part biography, part informational. In others, text interacts with archival photographs, high quality photographs, and facsimile photographs. Some informational books that appeal to young adults are universal in their appeal, some appeal to children of all ages, and some books were written and published for adults but captured the young adult audience as well. Such rich offerings in quality, topic, format, and design allow librarians to fill the shelves with informational opportunities.

PROFESSIONAL RESOURCES FOR INFORMATIONAL BOOKS

Besides perusing standard selection tools for reviews of the best informational books and keeping up-to-date with award-winning books, the following titles belong in the arsenal of professional materials for librarians who work with young adults:

The Middle and Junior High Core Collection (formerly The Middle School and Junior High Library Catalog), published by The H. W. Wilson Company.

The Senior High Core Collection (formerly The Senior High Library Catalog), published by The H. W. Wilson Company.

These two core collections contain lists of recommended fiction and nonfiction arranged by Dewey Decimal numbers. This arrangement makes it easy for a librarian to match book collection deficits with appropriate titles. Each title entry cites an excerpt of a review. Available in both print and online formats, *The Senior High Core Collection* contains over 10,000 fiction and nonfiction entries. Each print subscription consists of a hardcover edition, followed by three years of annual supplements. These core collections are essential to collection development, reader's advisory, and curriculum support. For more details visit the company's Web site at http://www.hwwilson.com.

ASSIGNMENTS IN ACTION: INFORMATIONAL BOOKS
FOR DISCUSSION

1. So many informational books today are designed to include photographs, lessening the amount of written material. Does that discourage reading?
2. Informational books written for children may also appeal to young adults. Why is that? Is this a positive trend in literature for youth?
3. Do boys read more informational books or do girls? Does it matter? Why or why not?

Chapter 6

Cultural Diversity

A counselor came to take Sami out of class. She had a worried expression. "You realize that you are the only Arab student in this school at a very difficult time. If anyone gives you any trouble…"

Sami didn't think he could tell her what had already happened.

It would make him seem weak.

If anyone found out he told, they would hate him even more.
                    From "Hum" by Naomi Shihab Nye in *Face Relations: 11 Stories about Seeing Beyond Color* (2004, 75)

School libraries and public libraries have always offered diversity in their book collections: fairy tales and myths from many cultures, histories and geography books of the world, and literature of countries other than the United States. Since the start of those first libraries, we have seen drastic changes in the definition and scope of diversity reflected in books for young adults. For example, stories of women and minorities were either nonexistent or marginalized. Changes in young adult literature relate to societal issues, historical events, the information age, technological advances, views of education, and writing and publishing opportunities. One result of these changes is better writing devoid of stereotyping. In both fiction and informational books, more authors who write about a specific culture are members of that culture. In the United States today people are becoming more aware of the variety of cultures and religions and striving to become more understanding and appreciative of those unique qualities. More and better books are being written every day to help teens understand the world they live in. This chapter explores cultural awareness and understanding through books about major cultural groups: African Americans, Latino/Latina Americans, Asian Americans, Native Americans, and Jewish Americans, as well as international cultures.

CULTURAL AWARENESS AND UNDERSTANDING

Stories are always a kind of collage—made of scraps of things other people have told me, scraps of memories I have, and scraps of things I've made up completely—all the pieces arranged in such a way that I have a hard time remembering, much later, where any given piece originated. In an ideal society, race relations would be like that: all the pieces making a large whole and harmonizing, allowing us to see not only the beauty of the individual pieces, but their differences as well.

Kyoko Mori, author of *Shizuko's Daughter* and *One Bird*.
From *Face Relations: 11 Stories about Seeing Beyond Color*,
ed. by Marilyn Singer (2004, 219)

Literature of a variety of cultures offers young adults three opportunities. First, they can attain a broader view of the world by reading about cultures other than their own. Second, they will be able to better interrupt prejudice and misunderstandings about people of other cultures. Third, minority youth will be able to view themselves in a positive manner (Landt 2006).

A MODEL OF CULTURAL UNDERSTANDING

A comprehensive model of cultural understanding developed by Don C. Locke provides a list of 10 elements to aid understanding of a particular culture. These 10 elements are "racism and prejudice, language and the arts, history of oppression, poverty and economic concerns, acculturation, sociopolitical factors, child-rearing practices, religious practices, family structure and dynamics, and cultural values and attitudes" (Locke 1998, 2). Young adult fiction and non-fiction can contribute to the understanding of one or more of these elements of a particular culture. Librarians and readers today want information about cultures different from their own, and they want and need that information delivered with respect to each culture. When selecting books about a variety of cultures, librarians can depend on two major sources for determining quality of content and design—book reviews and book award winners. Librarians will want to become familiar with trusted writers of books for each culture as well as those authors who write about many cultures.

A multicultural collection consists of the literature of many cultures, including fiction, poetry, biography, informational books, and folk literature. In this chapter, five major ethnic groups will be highlighted: African Americans, Latino/Latina Americans, Asian Americans, Native Americans, and Jewish Americans. The expectations for a multicultural collection should be high. Literature by and about these five major ethnic groups in the United States does not include literature written about these groups in other countries. Books should have the following attributes:

1. Excellence in writing

2. Avoidance of stereotypes

3. Accurate information

4. Respect for the culture

5. Favorable reviews and/or award winners

AFRICAN AMERICANS

I am the granddaughter of a slave.

My grandfather—not my great-great-grandfather or some long-distance relative—was born a slave in the year 1860 on a farm in North Carolina. He did not become free until the end of the Civil War, when he was five years old.

> Opening lines of the Author's Note from *Copper Sun*
> by Sharon Draper, 2006, unpaged

Of all the minority cultures in the United States, African Americans have been written about more thoroughly in young adult literature than any other minority. This success is due primarily to the Coretta Scott King Book Award, whose purpose is "to encourage the artistic expression of the African American experience via literature and the graphic arts, including biographical, historical and social history treatments by African American authors and illustrators," according to the Web site. The first award was given in 1970 to Lillie Patterson for *Martin Luther King, Jr.: Man of Peace.* Currently, the award is presented annually by the Coretta Scott King Committee of the American Library Association's (ALA) Ethnic Multicultural Information Exchange Round Table (EMIERT).

Criteria for the Selection
of Coretta Scott King Awards

Criteria for the award listed on the Web site are the following:

a. Must portray some aspect of the African American experience, past, present, or future.

b. Must be written/illustrated by an African American.

c. Must be published in the U.S. in the year preceding presentation of the Award.

d. Must be original work.

e. Must be written for a youth audience in one of the three categories: Preschool–grade 4, Grades 5–8, Grades 9–12.

f. Must meet established standards of quality writing for youth which include:

Clear plot, well-drawn characters which portray growth and development during the course of the story, writing style which is consistent with and suitable to the age intended, and accuracy.

g. Particular attention will be paid to titles that seek to motivate readers to develop their own attitudes and behaviors as well as comprehend their personal duty and responsibility as citizens in a pluralistic society.

h. Illustrations should reflect established qualitative standards and "heighten and extend the reader's awareness of the world around him. They should lead him to an appreciation of beauty. The style and content of the illustrations should be...neither coy nor condescending...Storytelling qualities should enlarge upon the story elements that were hinted at in the text and should include details that will awaken and strengthen the imagination of the reader and permit him to interpret the works and pictures in a manner unique to him" (Cianciolo1972, 24–25).

More details about the Coretta Scott King Book Awards, including its history, are available on the ALA Web site at www.ala.org/ala/emiert/corettascottking-bookaward/corettascott/cfm.

Awards that heighten the visibility of minority writers and of the minorities themselves in a positive manner are invaluable in providing role models and for encouraging and increasing book contributions. Without the Coretta Scott King Book Awards, and other ethnic specific awards, it's doubtful that we would have the quality contributions we have today.

10 Elements of Cultural Understanding

Outstanding books about African Americans lead African American young adults to better understand their own history and culture and to view themselves and their heritage with pride. Following 10 elements of Locke's model for cultural understanding, we can sample a range of quality titles appropriate for grades 6–12. Of course, most titles incorporate several of the elements, such as "racism and prejudice" and "acculturation." Theme, plot, setting, style, character, viewpoint, and tone—all literary elements merge to support the elements of multicultural understanding. For each element below there are one or more recommended books, either fiction or nonfiction or both, that will give young adults a worthwhile view of African Americans and their culture.

Racism and Prejudice

The Legend of Buddy Bush (2004) by Shelia P. Moses was a National Book Award Finalist for Young People and a Coretta Scott King Award Honor Book. In 1947 Buddy Bush is accused of attempted rape of a white woman after a brief encounter on a sidewalk one evening. This fictionalized account is told by 12-year-old Pattie Mae, Buddy's niece, as she witnesses the results of racism and prejudice in North Carolina. *The True and Dramatic Story of Prudence Crandall and Her Students* by Suzanne Jurmain, an Orbis Pictus Honor Book, is a nonfiction account of Crandall's determination to teach girls of color in the school she establishes in 1831 in Connecticut. After a savage attack on the school building, Crandall gives up and puts the school up for sale.

Language and the Arts

Her Stories: African American Folktales, Fairy Tales, and True Tales by Virginia Hamilton, illustrated by Leo and Diane Dillon, won the 1996 Coretta

Scott King Author Award and a Coretta Scott King Honor Book for illustration. Hamilton selected African American tales about women, and she retells them in her own colloquial style. These tales are entertaining, brief, and perfect to read aloud to audiences in upper elementary school through middle school. Each tale is enhanced with one full-page illustration rendered beautifully in acrylics. Comments after each tale inform readers of the source of the tale and how the tale fits into Hamilton's knowledge of traditional literature and African American culture. *Her Stories* incorporates transformed language and the art of storytelling.

History of Oppression

Sharon Draper's *Copper Sun*, winner of the 2007 Coretta Scott King Author Award, is a fictional account of Amari, a 15-year-old girl, taken from her African village and transported on a slave ship to Florida. Fast-paced and horridly fascinating, readers suffer with Amari as she witnesses her family murdered by white men and Ashanti men. Throughout the ordeal of her capture, transport across the Atlantic Ocean, and sale to a plantation owner, she is beaten and raped. With a white, indentured servant girl who has become her friend, Amari escapes and gains her freedom. Patricia C. and Fredrick L. McKissack's *Days of Jubilee: The End of Slavery in the United States* won a 2004 Coretta Scott King Author Honor and offers readers a nonfiction account of the events that contributed to the end of slavery, the people who supported its end, and those who obtained their freedom, their "day of jubilee." Sepia photographs, diaries, and slave narratives add to the authenticity and human touch of this account.

Poverty and Economic Concerns

The following titles put faces on those African American teens who endure special challenges as a result of their family's poverty. In Janet McDonald's *Spellbound*, 16-year-old Raven thinks she has lost her chance to attend college when she has a baby after her first sexual experience. Her older sister, Dell, encourages her to compete in a spelling bee that awards the winner a college scholarship. Humorous give-and-take between Raven and her best friend, Aisha, rescues Raven's story from being depressing. In Sharon G. Flake's *Money Hungry*, 13-year-old Raspberry is obsessed with making and keeping money so that she and her mother will never be homeless again. Coe Booth's *Tyrell* shifts to the plight of 15-year-old Tyrell, whose father is in jail and whose mother refuses to work. Desperately trying to keep his younger brother in school and trying to keep them both alive, Tyrell shows courage and ingenuity as he fights the threat of homelessness in New York City's South Bronx. Raw language and Tyrell's plight told in first person firmly set this novel in the neighborhood of city projects.

Acculturation

Many books in this ethnic group indicate the blending of cultures. African Americans' beliefs and values either assimilate into or blend with the beliefs and values of white Americans and even result in a bicultural community for African Americans (Locke 1998). Acculturation can be witnessed in two of Jacqueline Woodson's novels in which black protagonists live professionally and economically successful lives: *If You Come Softly* and *Hush*. In *If You Come Softly*, Miah, black, and Ellie, white, experience stares and whispers when they hold hands. They are subjected to bigotry as a mixed-race couple, but Miah's parents are accepting of Ellie while Ellie waits to tell her parents. Then when she does, it's too late. Ellie says, "Once I asked Miah if he ever forgot he was black. *No. I never forget,* he said. *But sometimes it doesn't matter—like I just am*" (Woodson 1998, 174). In *Hush*, 12-year-old Evie and her family are rushed into the Witness Protection Program after her policeman father testifies against those involved in a racially motivated shooting. Evie's previous life is gone but she must try to look forward to a life of her own creation. Marilyn Nelson's *Carver: A Life in Poems*, a brief biography, reflects the respect given to a man who began life as a slave and emerged to be a respected scientist, teacher, and man. Her lyrical poetry speaks of racism, hard work, education, and Carver's friends, black and white, young and old. Mildred D. Taylor's *The Land* is a prequel to *Roll of Thunder, Hear My Cry*, the 1977 Newbery Medal winner. Hard-earned acculturation is found in the acquisition of land that Paul-Edwards earns and pays for after years of back-breaking work. This rich historical novel is a credit to Taylor's writing skill.

Sociopolitical Factors

In Han Nolan's *Summer of Kings*, the year is 1963, and it's a pivotal year for 14-year-old Esther. She's living in her family's Westchester mansion when 18-year-old King-Ray Johnson comes to stay with her family, temporarily escaping from southern racial violence. He becomes obsessed with the teachings of Malcolm X. Esther is fascinated with him and his views, and gradually her life is changed, even convincing her family to join her in the historic march for civil rights in Washington, DC. Meanwhile, back in Alabama, King-Ray's life ends tragically. Biographies of Malcolm X and other African American political leaders can add value to this category.

Child-Rearing Practices

The First Part Last by Angela Johnson won the 2004 Michael L. Printz Award and the 2004 Coretta Scott King Author Award. In this brief novel of 131 pages, the reader is treated to a unique viewpoint in young adult literature—an unwed teen father taking care of his baby daughter. This intimate view of fatherhood and what Bobby gains and what he loses as he takes care of Feather by himself is heart-warming and heart-breaking all at the same time.

Religious Practices

Tonya Bolden's *Rock of Ages: A Tribute to the Black Church*, illustrated by R. Gregory Christie, traces the emergence of black churches during slavery through the present. An illustrated prose poem conveys "the history, music, biographies, events, deeds, locations, and inspiration of the church" (Brown and Stephens 2003, 224).

Family Structures and Dynamics

Miracle's Boys and *Heaven* don't necessarily represent typical African American families. In the news much is discussed about single-parent families headed by a mother or children who are being raised by grandparents. In Jacqueline Woodson's *Miracle's Boys*, a winner of the 2001 Coretta Scott King Author Award, three brothers struggle to be a family after their mother dies of diabetes, their father already dead from hypothermia after rescuing a drowning woman. In Angela Johnson's *Heaven*, also a Coretta Scott King Author Award, Marley discovers at 14 years old that she is adopted. It's a complete shock to her and one that makes her question the nature of a family.

Cultural Values and Attitudes

For urban views of values and attitudes within the African American culture, two short story collections by Walter Dean Myers and one by Sharon Flake supply a variety of scenarios and themes. Walter Dean Myers's *What They Found: Love on 145th Street* consists of 15 interrelated stories with characters that are tied in some way to Harlem. Some characters from Meyers's *145th Street: Short Stories* make appearances in this latest volume. Sharon G. Flake's *Who Am I Without Him? Short Stories about Girls and the Boys in Their Lives*, a Coretta Scott King Honor Book, offers readers eight stories told from girls' viewpoints and two told from boys' viewpoints.

Authors in Action: Distinguished African Americans

A distinguished group of African Americans has consistently published high quality literature for young adults. They have received many accolades for their work, for their sensitivity to societal issues, and for their unique insights into the lives of African Americans. Consult their Web sites, individual biographies, and biographical reference works for more information about them.

Christopher Paul Curtis won a Newbery Honor and the Coretta Scott King Author Award in 1996 for his first book, *The Watsons Go to Birmingham—1963*, an immensely humorous yet tragically realistic historical novel. His second book, *Bud, Not Buddy*, won the 2000 Newbery Medal and the 2000 Coretta Scott King Author Award. In 2008, his fourth novel, *Elijah of Buxton*, won the Coretta Scott King Author Award and a Newbery Honor. As a writer, Curtis's strengths are his strong, precise voice and sense of family and his ability to see humor in life, no matter the circumstances. Visit his Web site at www.randomhouse.com/features/christopherpaulcurtis/ to learn more about him and his writing.

Sharon Draper has a loyal following of African American young adults who are drawn to her and her books as both she and her books speak directly to teens. Besides *Copper Sun*, mentioned previously, Draper's other books are *Tears of a Tiger, Forged by Fire, Romiette and Julio, Darkness Before Dawn, The Battle of Jericho, November Blues*, and *Fire from the Rock*. Her books have won combinations of Coretta Scott King Awards, Quick Picks for Reluctant Readers, Best Books for Young Adults, and Young Adults' Choices. Visit her Web site at www.sharondraper.com for more details about her.

Sharon G. Flake is a relatively new writer for young adults. Her first published book, *The Skin I'm In*, won a John Steptoe New Talent Award and a Coretta Scott King Author Award. Four books that followed are *Money Hungry, Begging for Change, Who Am I Without Him*, and *Bang*. She writes realistic fiction about the lives of African American young adults. Visit her Web site at www.sharongflake. com for a list of awards.

Angela Johnson won the 2004 Michael L Printz Award and the 2004 Coretta Scott King Author Award for *The First Part Last*, the story of an unwed teen-aged African American father who accepts the responsibility for taking care of his baby daughter. Two of her previous books won Coretta Scott King Book Awards also: *Heaven* and *Toning the Sweep*. *The Other Side: Shorter Poems*, about growing up in Shorter, Alabama, physically and emotionally takes readers to her home, although she now lives in Kent, Ohio.

Walter Dean Myers grew up in Harlem and is the father of Christopher Myers, an author and illustrator of children's books. Walter Dean Myers's *Monster* was the first winner of the Michael L. Printz Award, and Myers was selected as the winner of the Margaret Edwards Award in 1994, especially recognized for *Hoops, Motown and Didi, Fallen Angels*, and *Scorpions*. His books have been honored with many other awards, too numerous to mention here. His more recent titles include *Bad Boy: A Memoir, The Greatest: Muhammed Ali, Shooter, Here in Harlem Poems in Many Voices, Autobiography of My Dead Brother*, and *What They Found: Love on 145th Street*. Myers's varied interests and versatility as a writer allow him to create fiction, poetry, biography, and informational books about African Americans. For a complete list of books Myers has written visit his Web site at www.walterdeanmyers.net.

Mildred Taylor won the 1977 Newbery Medal for *Roll of Thunder, Hear My Cry*, the powerful Depression-era story of 13-year-old Cassie Logan and her family trying to survive in Mississippi. Two sequels of the Logan saga are *Let the Circle Be Unbroken* and *The Road to Memphis*. *The Land*, a prequel to the first Logan book and mentioned previously, won the 2002 Scott O'Dell Award for historical fiction and the 2002 Coretta Scott King Author Award. Born in Jackson, Mississippi, Taylor makes her home in Colorado.

Rita Williams-Garcia has written five significant novels about youth of color: *Blue Tights, Like Sisters on the Homefront, Fast Talk on a Slow Track, Every Time a Rainbow Dies*, and *No Laughter Here*. Visit her Web site at www.ritawg.com.

Jacqueline Woodson was awarded the 2007 Margaret Edwards Award for her lifetime contribution to young adult literature and specifically for five novels: *I Hadn't Meant to Tell You This, Lena, From the Notebooks of Melanin Sun, If You Come Softly*, and *Miracle's Boys*. Her novels have won Coretta Scott King Book Awards and state awards and have been named to Quick Picks for Reluctant Readers and Best Books for Young Adults. For biographical information and a list of all of her books, visit her Web site at www.jacquelinewoodson.com.

History in Action: First Minority Authors to Win John Newbery Awards

Books written specifically for young adults and about cultures from countries other than the United States have improved significantly during the past

20 years. Stereotypical characters and settings are minimized or absent in more recent publications, and books about minorities are winning awards.

In 1975 Virginia Hamilton was the first minority author to win a John Newbery Medal. She won for *M. C. Higgins, the Great*, a realistic story of Mayo Cornelius Higgins, who dreams of escaping his home on the Ohio hills at the edge of a strip mining operation. Hamilton continued to publish novels about African Americans for youth until her death in 2002. In 1976 Laurence Yep won a Newbery Honor for his historical novel, *Dragonwings*, the story of Moon Shadow Lee, a young boy who immigrates to San Francisco in the early twentieth century. Yep was the first Chinese American to win a Newbery Honor, and he continues to publish fiction for upper elementary and middle school students.

LATINO/LATINA AMERICANS

What can be funny about having to stand up in front of everyone you know, in a ruffly dress the color of Pepto Bismol, and proclaim your womanhood? Nothing. *Nada.* Zip. Not when you're fifteen—too young to drive, win the lottery, or vote for a president who might lower the driving and gambling ages. Nothing funny at all. At least that's what I thought in September.
Opening lines from *Cuba 15* by Nancy Osa (2003, 1)

Latino/Latina Americans increasingly are being featured in books written for young adults. Included in this diverse population are Puerto Ricans, Cubans, Mexican Americans, Chicanos, and other immigrants from 20 different countries, although primarily from Mexico and Central America. Although each minority group shares similarities based on the Spanish language, each varies in customs and language.

Pura Belpré Award

Similar to the Coretta Scott King Award, special awards for Latino/Latina American literature provide role models and encourage the writing and publishing of quality literature for young adults. The Pura Belpré Award is one of the best-known awards. According to the Web site, the award,

established in 1996, is presented to a Latino/Latina writer and illustrator whose work best portrays, affirms, and celebrates the Latino cultural experience in an outstanding work of literature for children and youth. It is co-sponsored by the Association for Library Service to Children (ALSC), a division of the American Library Association (ALA), and the National Association to Promote Library and Information Services to Latinos and the Spanish-Speaking (REFORMA), an ALA affiliate. The award is named after Pura Belpré, the first Latina librarian from the New York Public Library. As a children's librarian, storyteller, and author, she enriched the lives of Puerto Rican children in the U.S.A. through her pioneering work of preserving and disseminating Puerto Rican folklore.

Two awards are given biennially, one for narrative and one for illustration. Honor Books may also be named. The winners include books for children and young adults. For more details consult Awards and Scholarships at www.ala.org/ala/alsc/.

Tomás Rivera Mexican American Children's Book Award

Most states in the United States offer children's and young adult book awards. They are termed *state awards* because an organization in the state administers the details of the award. In some states the awards are limited to authors who live in that state. For awards in the State of Texas, the eligibility of an author's work depends on a book's appropriateness for particular ages, not on a residency requirement of the author. For example, if books are to be considered for the Texas Lone Star List, they must be appropriate for grades 6–8. For books to be eligible for a second young adult book list, The Texas Tayshas Reading List, books must be appropriate for high school readers. Typically, state awards and the winning authors, books, and lists are heavily promoted and supported within schools and public libraries in order to encourage reading.

A lesser known award than the Pura Belpré Award is the Tomás Rivera Mexican American Children's Book Award, named in honor of Tomás Rivera, a native of Crystal City, Texas. He was the first Mexican American to be selected as Distinguished Alumnus at Texas State University in San Marcos. According to the Web site, "The creation of this Tomás Rivera Mexican American Children's Book Award in his honor goes a long way towards keeping alive the prophesy he saw as part of our legacy as members of a healthy and responsible community. This children's book award will also work towards sustaining the vision he saw for the education of Mexican Americans in the Southwest and the great United States. It is therefore unquestionably right and proper that this award be given in his name, his honor, his prophesy to encourage authors, illustrators and publishers of books that authentically reflect the lives of Mexican American children and young adults in the United States." The first Tomás Rivera Award was given in 1995 to *Chato's Kitchen*, a picture book written by Gary Soto and illustrated by Susan Guevara. Three titles appropriate for young adults have won the award: *Breaking Through* by Francisco Jimenez in 2001, *Becoming Naomi León* by Pam Muñoz Ryan in 2004, and *Downtown Boy* by Juan Felipé Herrera in 2006. For further information consult www.educa tiontxstate.edu/subpages/tomasrivera.

Américas Book Award for Children's and Young Adult Literature

A third award honoring children's and young adult books about Latino/ Latina Americans is the annual Américas Book Award for Children's and Young Adult Literature, given for books published "in English or Spanish that authentically and engagingly portray Latin America, the Caribbean, or Latinos in the United States. By combining both and linking the Americas, the award reaches beyond geographic borders, as well as multicultural-international boundaries, focusing instead upon cultural heritages within the hemisphere," according to the Web site. The award names Honorable Mentions and Commended Titles as well as Award Winners. The first award was given in 1993, and the award is sponsored by the national Consortium of Latin American Studies Programs

(CLASP) at the University of Wisconsin–Milwaukee. For more information about the award visit www.uwm.edu/Dept/CLACS/outreach/americas.html.

Award-Winning Books about Latino/Latina Americans

Viewing literature through these three awards presents the opportunity to encompass the variety of cultures within a larger Spanish-speaking and English-speaking culture. A sampling of award-winning books about Latino/Latina Americans includes fiction, poetry, a memoir, and interviews.

The Afterlife by Gary Soto. The story begins after 17-year-old Chuy is stabbed to death in a men's room. While in death Chuy becomes a complex character observing his family and friends after he has died, looking for the man who killed him, and illogically finding a girlfriend. Chuy has a limited amount of time before he fades away forever.

Before We Were Free by Julia Alvarez (2004 Pura Belpré Award and 2002 Américas Award). Anita de la Torre is a 12-year-old girl in the Dominican Republic when her father and others in her family attempt to assassinate their dictator in 1960. Her family is terrorized until finally Anita must leave her country to seek asylum in the United States. It's a confusing time for her, experiencing adolescence, the break-up of her large supportive family, the terror of the political situation, and the adjustment to becoming an immigrant.

Breaking Through by Francisco Jiménez (2002 Pura Belpré Honor Book). In this fictionalized autobiography and sequel to *The Circuit: Stories from the Life of a Migrant Child*, Frankie experiences casual prejudice and the despair of his parents as he tries to survive a high school education. In *The Circuit*, a memoir, the Jiménez family emigrates from Mexico and works in the strawberry fields of California.

Cool Salsa: Bilingual Poems on Growing Up Latino in the United States edited by Lori M. Carlson. Teen views of Latino life sparkle in this mix of diverse poems from many poets. Poems are divided into topics: school days, home and homeland, memories, hard times, time to party, and a promising future. Some poems are written in both Spanish and English; some are a combo of the two languages.

Crossing the Wire by Will Hobbs (2006 Américas Award Commended Title). Known for his fictional adventure/survival stories, Hobbs tackles the topic of illegal border crossings. Leaving his mother and siblings, 15-year-old Rico makes the trek to northern Mexico in an attempt to reach El Norte and look for work. His dangerous journey is realistic, and readers will be propelled along with Rico as he's driven to reach his goal.

Cuba 15 by Nancy Osa (2004 Pura Belpré Honor Book). Violet Paz, who lives in Chicago and is half Polish and half Cuban, is surprised and reluctant to become involved in her own quinceañera, a traditional ceremony acknowledging her womanhood during her 15th year. A candid and humorous look at her family, friends, and herself add up to a refreshing story about growing up.

Esperanza Rising by Pam Muñoz Ryan (2002 Pura Belpré Award). Esperanza's life changes drastically as she's forced to leave her privileged Mexican ranch and work in company-owned fields in California. It's a shock to her and her family, but gradually she adjusts and emerges a more mature, more aware young person who has hope for her future.

My Own True Name: New and Selected Poems for Young Adults by Pat Mora. For mature teens, Mora's collection represents universal and bicultural experiences, including her own as a Latina in the Southwest. Using the cactus plant as a metaphor, she divides these sixty poems into three sections: Blooms, thorns, and roots.

The Tequila Worm by Viola Canales (2006 Pura Belpré Award). Growing up in Mc-
Allen, Texas, Sofia's story reveals both the joy and pain of her community
as she strives to win a scholarship to an elite Austin school. Each chapter
ties to the narrative through a custom in her life, such as cleaning beans,
freezing tamales, and respecting the saints at Saint Luke's.

Voices from the Fields: Children of Migrant Farmworkers Tell Their Stories, interviews and photographs by S. Beth Atkin. Nine children tell what it is like to
live as Latino/Latina American migrant workers. They are frank about the
hardships and prejudice but also about progress and their pride in their
heritage. Black-and-white photographs effectively complement their stories.

As with African American literature, Locke's 10 elements of multicultural understanding are evident in Latino/Latina American literature. The major focus
of these books is immigration to the United States, how it affects individual
lives, and how Latinos/Latinas experience acculturation.

ASIAN AMERICANS

"Listen," he said. "This is important. I'll teach you about science, math,
geography, or law, if you like, because that's why I'm here. But what I *want*
to teach you, more than anything else, is how to be intelligent, alert, aware,
and contributing members of the world around you. What I can't accept is to
see any of you wandering aimlessly through life, turning whichever way the
wind blows and adding nothing to the good in the world. I want your eyes
open and your hearts and minds engaged, does that make sense to you?"
From *House of the Red Fish* by Graham Salisbury (2006, 82)

Traditionally, the term "Asian Americans" refers to people from eastern Asia
(China, Japan, Korea, and Mongolia), southeastern Asia (Singapore, Indonesia,
Vietnam, Thailand, and Cambodia), and Pacific Islanders, including Americans
from Hawaii and Guam. An Asian Pacific American Heritage Month in May celebrates the people and cultures of Asia and the Pacific Islands.

The Asian/Pacific American Award for Literature (APAAL) is a recent award
established "to honor and recognize individual work about Asian/Pacific
Americans and their heritage, based on literary and artistic merit," according
to the Web site. Eligible works must be originally written in English by a U.S.
citizen or permanent resident. Adult, children's, and young adult categories
are included in this annual award. Two Newbery Medal winners have also won
an APAAL Award: *Kira-Kira* by Cynthia Kadohata and *A Step from Heaven* by
An Na (winner of the 2002 Michael L. Printz Award). For more information visit
www.apalaweb.org/awards/awards.htm.

Recommended Books about Asian Americans

Books written for children and young adults about Asian Americans focus
on immigration, acculturation, and the Japanese internment camps after the
attack on Pearl Harbor.

April and the Dragon Lady by Lensey Namioka. April Chen, a Chinese American
teenager prepares to leave for college but finds herself in charge of her

aging grandmother. April is torn between her duty and her desire for self-fulfillment.

Farewell to Manzanar by Jeanne Wakatsuki Houston and James D. Houston. In this classic memoir of life in an internment camp in California, the Houstons write about her experiences as a seven-year-old child.

Ties That Bind, Ties That Break by Lensey Namioka. Ailin rebels against the Chinese tradition of binding a young girl's feet. Her family is shocked when she chooses to immigrate to San Francisco. In Namioka's *A Step from Heaven*, Young Lin faces a language barrier and other difficulties after emigrating from Korea.

Under the Blood-Red Sun by Graham Salisbury. A descendent of some of the first missionaries to arrive on the Hawaiian Islands, Salisbury has written three novels related to World War II and the attacks on Pearl Harbor. In *Under the Blood-Red Sun*, on December 7, 1941, Tomi is playing with a friend when Pearl Harbor is attacked. Shortly afterward, his father and grandfather are arrested in a round-up of Japanese men. In *House of the Red Fish*, Tomi's story picks up in 1943 in Honolulu when Tomi is determined to raise his papa's fishing boat from the canal where it was sunk in 1941. In *Eyes of the Emperor* Eddy Okubo joins the army with his two best friends in 1941. After Pearl Harbor is attacked, he and his friends are sent to Mississippi on a secret mission to see if dogs can be trained to find enemy Japanese. The three young men experience heart-breaking prejudice and suspicion as they try to contribute to the war effort.

Weedflower by Cynthia Kadahota. Twelve-year-old Sumiko narrates her story of life before and after Pearl Harbor. She and her family are shipped to an internment camp in Arizona where she befriends a Mohave boy.

NATIVE AMERICANS

The philosophy I grew up with taught me to regard all things as having a purpose, as having a spirit—and to treat them accordingly. All things are connected in the great cycle, and nothing can be independent of any part of it. Everything in nature is related. We are all but a small part in this great collection.

The teachings of my elders make it very clear that this land is sacred and that *we* belong to *it*. To desecrate this place in any manner is not acceptable.

I live in a dual society like many in my generation of Navajo. We extract from the past to maintain harmony within. We acknowledge the present and the high-tech world we have been thrust into.

From the Introduction to *Navajo: Visions and Voices Across the Mesa* by Shonto Begay (1995, 7)

Native Americans are a special minority in the United States. They did not emigrate as did Asian Americans and other groups. To state the obvious: They were here first. To respect Native Americans as a people and as a culture means acknowledging individual tribes, being willing to learn about their heritage, understanding their reverence for nature, and knowing that they live in a dual society of ancient beliefs and modern day challenges.

Many young adult books meet these requirements through poetry, nonfiction, and fiction. Through his poetry and art in *Navajo: Visions and Voices Across the Mesa*, Shonto Begay shares Navajo experiences with readers: creation stories, the beauty of nature, his grandmother's strength, a solar eclipse, his mother's kitchen, and much more, complemented by full-page artwork in acrylics or watercolor and pencil. In Russell Freedman's *Indian Chiefs*, six Western Indian chiefs are featured: Red Cloud of the Oglala Sioux, Santanta of the Kiowas, Quanah Parker of the Comanches, Washakie of the Shoshonis, Joseph of the Nez Perces, and Sitting Bull of the Hunkpapa Sioux. Their brief biographies reveal moments of crisis as white pioneers encroach on their land in a western movement across the United States. In *Pocahontas* by Joseph Bruchac, readers gain insight into the settling of Jamestown, Virginia, told in alternating viewpoints by Pocahontas and John Smith. According to Bruchac, in 1607 neither the British settlers nor the people of the Powhatan Nation comprehended each other's strange ways. For a very different view of Navajo men, Nathan Aaseng's *Navajo Code Talkers* takes readers into the Pacific in World War II. The complex Navajo language proved to be the basis of an unbreakable code that saved lives and contributed to the American forces' defeat of Japan.

Realistic Fiction about Native Americans

Both historical and modern realistic fiction has been written about Native Americans, some by Native Americans and more by white writers. Two historical novels reveal the day-to-day details of life in the People's villages. In Jan Hudson's *Sweetgrass*, a 15-year-old Blackfoot girl yearns to prove she's mature enough to marry Eagle-Sun, a handsome young warrior. In Carolyn Meyer's *Where the Broken Heart Still Beats: The Story of Cynthia Ann Parker*, a nine-year-old girl is kidnapped from her West Texas home by raiding Comanche warriors. Twenty-five years later she tries to make white settlers understand that she must return to her Comanche family.

In modern realistic fiction, Native American teenagers face racial prejudice and the angst of acculturation. Robert Lipsyte's series, beginning with *The Contender*, focuses on the challenges of boxing and a young man's drive to succeed. In Harlem, Alfred Brooks, a young black man, struggles to overcome problems while Mr. Donatelli coaches him. *The Contender* is a powerful book that sets the stage for the Native American protagonists featured in the subsequent companion books. The next three novels take readers into the divided world of Sonny Bear, a Moscondaga filled with anger at the unfairness of his position between the white world and his Native American world in *The Brave, The Chief,* and *Warrior Angel*. In Rob MacGregor's *Prophecy Rock*, a Young Adults' Choices book, Will Lansa travels to the Hopi reservation in Arizona to visit his police chief father and becomes involved in a murder mystery. Cynthia Leitich Smith's *Rain Is Not My Indian Name* follows Cassidy Rain Berghoff and her camera as Cass tries to recover from the grief over her best friend's death and her ambivalence about becoming involved in her Aunt Georgia's summer Indian Camp. Smith is a mixed blood, enrolled member of the Muscogee (Creek) Nation. More information can be found about her at www.cynthialeitichsmith.com.

To access more information about Native American tribes and literature for young adults, visit Debbie Reese's Web site at www.nah.uluc.edu/faculty-Reese.htm. Reese is an assistant professor of American Indian Studies at the University of Illinois at Urbana-Champaign and an enrolled member of the

Nambe Pueblo Tribe. At her Web site click on Resources for a lengthy bibliography of books for youth about Native Americans.

One Book in Action: *The Absolutely True Diary of a Part-Time Indian* by Sherman Alexie

Sherman Alexie won the 2007 National Book Award for Young People for his autobiographical novel, *The Absolutely True Diary of a Part-Time Indian*, art by Ellen Forney. Arnold Spirit, Jr., the protagonist, demonstrates the frustration of trying to remain loyal to one's Native American heritage while desiring to break from a cycle of poverty and isolation. With wit and humor, Alexie, a member of the Coeur d'Alene tribe in Spokane, Washington, chronicles Junior's experiences at an all-white high school. Junior travels 22 miles each way from the Spokane Indian reservation, where he and his parents live, to the front steps of Reardan High School.

For possible teacher–librarian collaboration, this novel offers numerous possibilities as the center of research projects. Once a librarian has booktalked the novel and students have read it, a teacher and a librarian can explore topical ideas with the students based on the characters and events in the novel. Students can take advantage of information available on Web sites, in databases, in reference books, and in nonfiction books. They might ask themselves: What is the real story behind Junior's challenges?

1. Spokane tribes (visit www.spokanetribe.com). Junior has lived on the reservation all of his life. What are the customs and beliefs of the tribes?
2. Spokane Indian reservation. Inhabitants live in poverty despite the presence of a casino. Why? How common is poverty on Indian reservations in the United States?
3. Medical problems. Junior was born brain-damaged and has seizures and lisps and stutters as a result. What happens to the brain when it's damaged? How can brain damage affect the body?
4. Death and grief. During the novel, Junior's dad's best friend, his grandmother, and his sister die violent deaths. What are the stages of grief? What customs do Spokane tribes follow?
5. Alcoholism. Junior's parents are drunks. What does alcohol do to the body? Is alcoholism more prevalent on Indian reservations than in mainstream society?
6. Bullying. Due to Junior's small size and frail appearance, he is bullied throughout his childhood. What can parents and schools do to minimize or prevent bullying?

Other topics that could be explored based on this novel are friendship, romance, basketball, sportsmanship, and controlling one's future. For a quick guide to collaborative planning and collaborative units, consult David V. Loertscher's *Reinvent Your School's Library in the Age of Technology: A Guide for Principals and Superintendents*, available from http://www.lmcsource.com.

JEWISH AMERICANS

Danny and I probably would never have met—or we would have met under altogether different circumstances—had it not been for America's entry into the Second World War and the desire this bred on the part of some English teachers in the Jewish parochial schools to show the gentile world that yeshiva students were as physically fit, despite their long hours of study, as any other American student. They went about proving this by organizing the Jewish parochial schools in and around our area against one another in a variety of sports. I became a member of my school's varsity softball team.

From *The Chosen* by Chaim Potok (1967, 2)

As with other ethnic groups, Jewish Americans share problems associated with immigration, oppression, racism, and acculturation. As would be expected, religion, ancestry, and the Holocaust loom large in both personal and group experiences and stories, in both fiction and nonfiction.

Association of Jewish Libraries—Book Awards

The Association of Jewish Libraries (AJL) established a children's book award in 1968, later named the Sydney Taylor Book Award after the author of *All-of-a-Kind Family*, Taylor's family stories of growing up on the Lower East Side of New York City with four sisters. According to guidelines for the award on the Web site, the purpose "is to encourage the publication of outstanding books of Jewish content for children, books that exemplify the highest literary standards while authentically portraying the Jewish experience. We hope that official recognition of such books will inspire authors, encourage publishers, inform parents and teachers, and intrigue young readers. We also hope that by educating readers about the Jewish experience, we can engender pride in Jewish readers while building bridges to readers of other backgrounds." The award includes books written about Jews, no matter their geographical location, as well as the experiences of Jewish Americans. The award was expanded to include books for teens, named the Sydney Taylor Book Award for Teen Readers instead of the Taylor Book Award. Books about Jews in locations other than the United States can be found in a sampling of international literature in the International Cultures section. For more information visit www.SydneyTaylorBookAward.org.

Award-Winning Novels about Jewish Americans

Trials, tribulations, and joys of being Jewish in America are revealed in five award-winning young adult novels. Chaim Potok's *The Chosen* is a classic growing-up story of two boys, Danny and Reuven. In Brooklyn, New York, Reuven, a Modern Orthodox Jew, and Danny, the son of a Hasidic rabbe, meet during a softball game and become friends. In another classic story, Bette Greene's *Summer of My German Soldier*, 12-year-old Patty Bergen helps a prisoner of war escape as she wages a war with her abusive father and encounters prejudice in the community. Carolyn Meyer's *Drummers of Jericho* won a 1995 Taylor Honor Award for Older Readers with the story of Pazit, a high school girl who protests the marching band's formation of a cross. Her protest reaches beyond the school community to involve the ACLU and to pit Jews against Christians. More recently, Dana Reinhardt's *A Brief Chapter in My Impossible Life* won a 2007 Association of Jewish Libraries Honor Award for Teens. Simone has always known that she is adopted, but during her junior year in high school her parents press her to accept contact with her birth mother, Rivka, a Hasidic Jew. In another case of the young connecting with an older adult, Jordan Sonnenblick's *Notes from the Midnight Driver* takes 16-year-old Alex Gregory from a foolish accident involving vodka and his mom's car to 100 hours of community service. Alex is supposed to help Solomon Lewis, a disagreeable old man with emphysema and a penchant for Yiddish phrases. Sonnenblick's sense of humor lightens the story and results in a shaky friendship between the two. The novel was chosen a 2007 AJL Notable Book for Teens.

RECOMMENDED COLLECTIONS
OF MULTIETHNIC STORT STORIES

Bode, Janet. *New Kids in Town: Oral Histories of Immigrant Teens.* Nonfiction.
Cofer, Judith Ortiz. *An Island Like You: Stories of the Barrio.* Fiction.
Gallo, Donald R., ed. *Join In: Multiethnic Short Stories by Outstanding Writers for Young Adults.* Fiction.
Meyer, Carolyn. *Rio Grande Stories.* Fiction—New Mexico.
Singer, Marilyn, ed. *Face Relations: 11 Stories about Seeing beyond Color.* Fiction.

INTERNATIONAL CULTURES

I have learned this about life: I know, as my neighbors in Bitlis tried to tell me, that there is pain and disillusion in the heart of it. I know as my father knew, that character and discipline are the steel that fortify it, and that somewhere, beyond pain and disillusion, great blessings are made.
From *Forgotten Fire* by Adam Bagdasarian (2000, 271)

International cultures can be found within the covers of books published in the United States and those published in other countries, both English-speaking and non–English-speaking. In learning about cultures outside the United States, young adults have a large body of literature available to them.

International literature is usually defined as literature published in other countries in the English language or in the language of the country. If the literature is published in a language other than English, it may be translated to make it accessible to English language speakers.

Books written for young adults about individual international cultures set in foreign countries are written about history, wars, geography, and customs of the country. There will be biographies of world leaders and of people who have made an impact in a particular country. There will be stories of ordinary people living ordinary lives within their culture. There will be poetry, folktales, and fiction. Books about countries of the world are expected to have universal themes of the human condition and express, at least minimally, some of the geography or history or heritage of that particular country.

Mildred L. Batchelder Award

One unique award for youth literature makes international literature particularly accessible. The Mildred L. Batchelder Award brings attention to countries where English is not the first language. The award is given to a U.S. publisher for the translation of an outstanding book for youth originally published in a foreign country and translated into English. The annual award was first given in 1966 and honors a former executive director of the Association for Library Service to Children. According to the Web site, Mildred Batchelder's life's work was "to eliminate barriers to understanding between people of different cultures, races, nations, and languages." In the last 10 years, winning books have been translated from Italian, German, French, Danish, Hebrew, Swedish, Dutch, and Japanese. Anne-Laure Bondoux's *The Killer's Tears*, winner of the 2007 Batchelder Award, is a brief novel set on the desolate tip of Chile and tells a shocking story. A man suddenly appears at the poor farmhouse of 10-year-old Paolo and his parents. The man kills the farmer and his wife but spares their son. Another man joins them and the trio lives together until tragedy once again strikes. This thought-provoking novel of innocence, guilt, and love is recommended for grades 9–12. Two Honor Books were awarded in 2007 for Jean-Claude Mourlevat's *The Pull of the Ocean* (translated from French) and Silvana de Mari's *The Last Dragon*, translated from Italian. For more information about the Batchelder Award, visit www.ala.org/ala/alsc/awardsscholarship/literaryawds/batchelderaward/batchelderaward/cfm.

Recommended Fiction and Nonfiction
from International Cultures

Al-Windawi, Thura. *Thura's Diary: My Life in Wartime Iraq*. Nonfiction. Iraq.
Bagdasarian, Adam. Forgotten Fire: A Novel. Fiction. Turkey—Armenian Holocaust.
Bartoletti, Susan Campbell. *Black Potatoes: The Story of the Great Irish Famine, 1845–1850*. Nonfiction. Ireland.
Greenberg, Jan and Sandra Jordan. *Vincent van Gogh: Portrait of an Artist*. Nonfiction. Netherlands.
Hamanaka, Sheila. *Treasures of Japan*. Nonfiction. Japan.
McCormick, Patricia. *Sold*. Fiction. India.
Meltzer, Milton. *Never to Forget: The Jews of the Holocaust*. Nonfiction. Europe.
Nye, Naomi Shihab. *Habibi*. Fiction. Jerusalem.
Nye, Naomi Shihab. *19 Varieties of Gazelle: Poems of the Middle East*.
Rodriguez, Deborah. *Kabul Beauty School: An American Woman Goes Behind the Veil*. Nonfiction. Afghanistan.
Satrapi, Marjane. *Persepolis*. Nonfiction graphic novel. Iran.
Sis, Peter. *The Wall: Growing Up Behind the Iron Curtain*. Nonfiction. Czechoslavakia.
Smith, Roland. *Elephant Run*. Fiction. Burma, India.
Spinelli, Jerry. *Milkweed*. Fiction. Poland—Holocaust.
Stanley, Diane. *Saladin: Noble Prince of Islam*. Nonfiction. Middle East, Crusades.

Staples, Suzanne Fisher. *Shabanu: Daughter-of-the-Wind*. Fiction. Cholistan Desert (Pakistan).

Stewart, Whitney. *The 14th Dalai Lama: Spiritual Leader of Tibet*. Nonfiction. Tibet.

Warren, Andrea. *Surviving Hitler: A Boy in the Nazi Death Camps*. Nonfiction. Poland.

Whelan, Gloria. *Homeless Bird*. Fiction. India.

Zusak, Markus. *The Book Thief*. Fiction. Germany—Holocaust.

LIBRARIANS IN ACTION: PODCASTING AND READER'S ADVISORY

Incorporate podcasting into your library program as a great way to share booktalks performed by teens. The word "podcasting" is a combination of the words "iPod" and "broadcast." Its purpose is to share audio with a large audience. For example, students (or a librarian) could record brief booktalks and make them available on the library's Web site for patrons (or anyone) to hear. It's a way to encourage reading by recommending books through the drama of booktalking. For how-to's, planning suggestions, and projects, read "Podcasting in the School Library, Part 2: Creating Powerful Podcasts with Your Students" by Annette Lamb and Larry Johnson in *Teacher Librarian: The Journal for School Library Professionals*.

Reader's advisory is a method of talking with young adults to help them find the books they want to read for entertainment or for information. (Sometimes those are the same!) Participating in reader's advisory is one of the pleasures of working as a librarian. For advice about how to prepare to advise teens about books, read the first two chapters in part 1 of RoseMary Honnold's *The Teen Reader's Advisor:* "Practice a 'YA Attitude' Toward Teens" and "Develop Useful Teen Reader's Advisory Practices." Then peruse the annotated bibliographies in part 2 on a wide range of topics.

CONCLUSION

With the cultural population of the United States growing every day, it's increasingly important to respect cultural diversity. Books written for young adults and read by young adults can aid with the understanding of ethnicity in the United States and in other countries. Those same books can help young adults from a particular ethnic group feel pride in their own culture.

PROFESSIONAL RESOURCES ABOUT CULTURAL DIVERSITY

Brown, Jean, and Elaine C. Stephens, eds. 2003. *Your Reading: An Annotated Booklist for Middle School and Junior High*. 11th ed. Urbana, Illinois: National Council of Teachers of English.

> Of particular relevance to multiculturalism is one chapter entitled "Challenges of Today's World," a listing of books about diversity, problems and issues, and geography and cultures.

Herald, Diana Tixier. 2003. *Teen Genreflecting: A Guide to Reading Interests*. 2nd ed. Westport, CT: Libraries Unlimited.

> Includes one chapter titled "Multicultural Fiction" with brief annotated lists about major ethnic groups, plus "Cultures around the World."

Honnold, RoseMary. 2006. *The Teen Reader's Advisor*. New York: Neal-Schuman.

> Note annotated bibliographies titled "Multicultural" and "Religion and Spirituality."

Locke, Don C. 1998. *Increasing Multicultural Understanding: A Comprehensive Model*. 2nd ed. Thousand Oaks, CA: Sage.

> An analysis of minorities in the United States.

Rochman, Hazel. 1993. *Against Borders: Promoting Books for a Multicultural World*. Chicago: American Library Association.

> Excellent perspective on the topic of multiculturalism and includes annotated lists of fiction and nonfiction for young adults.

"This Small World: A Glimpse of Many Cultures." YALSA's Popular Paperbacks for Young Adults, 2003. http://www.ala.org/yalsa/booklists/poppaper.

> A list of briefly annotated books available online.

ASSIGNMENTS IN ACTION: CULTURAL DIVERSITY FOR DISCUSSION

1. Does it matter if a book written about Native Americans is not written by a Native American author? (This could be asked about any cultural group.) Why or why not? Check for articles written on this intriguing topic.

2. Besides offering a quality multicultural collection of books, what else can librarians do to promote awareness and understanding about ethnic groups in the United States?

3. How are the coming-of-age struggles of adolescents similar to those of immigrants to the United States? Read Betty Carter's article, "The Outsiders," in *Voices from the Middle*, December 2001.

7

The Freedom to Read

I realized then a very weird but simple truth: although books were as much a part of my life as anything had ever been, as much a part of me as the air I breathe or the blood that runs through my veins, nothing I had ever read in a book had in itself caused me to be really, truly unhappy. Real low-down, rank, grotty unhappiness does not come from books. It comes from life.

From Kathryn Lasky's *Memoirs of a Bookbat* (1994, 72–73)

The freedom to read is a right granted to citizens of the United States through the freedoms of the First Amendment to the Constitution. That freedom is granted to children and teenagers, articulated in "Students' Right to Read" by the National Council of Teachers of English and in "Library Bill of Rights," adopted by the American Library Association. In this chapter, information about intellectual freedom and the right to read is centered on basic definitions of intellectual freedom, major stages for handling book challenges, and ideas for celebrating banned books.

DEFINITIONS OF INTELLECTUAL FREEDOM TERMS

Before delving into freedom to read issues especially related to young adults and their reading, definitions of basic actions should help set the stage.

Intellectual Freedom. According to the *Intellectual Freedom Manual*:

In basic terms, intellectual freedom requires the fulfillment of two essential conditions: first, that all individuals have the right to hold any belief on any subject and to convey ideas in any form the individual deems appropriate; second, that society makes an equal commitment to the right of unrestricted access to information and ideas regardless of the communication medium used, the content of the work, and the viewpoints of both the author and receiver of information. Without the ability of all people to have access to information without restriction, the freedom to express oneself through a chosen mode of communication becomes virtually meaningless. The right of intellectual freedom implies a circle, and that circle is broken if either freedom of expression or access to ideas is stifled. (Office for Intellectual Freedom of the American Library Association 1992, ix)

Think of the term "intellectual freedom" as a large umbrella. Underneath that umbrella we find both negative actions (censoring, banning, challenging, labeling) and positive actions (reconsideration, selecting, reading freely). Each of these actions has a direct relationship to books published, written, and read by young adults. Each action is defined in terms relating to a librarian who works with young adults.

Censoring a book or other library materials means a person or group of people (censors) intend to remove or have removed specific materials from library shelves. It's an all-encompassing term.

Banning a book or other library materials means a person or group of people (censors) are keeping one or more items from being circulated to anyone who attends a particular school or patronizes a particular public library.

Challenging a book or other library materials means a potential censor has complained about the contents of an item available in a particular library. It may mean that the person wants the book removed from the library shelves or it may mean that the person simply wants to talk with the librarian about its suitability for students or patrons. This could be a verbal or written challenge (complaint).

Labeling a book or other library materials is an attempt to restrict particular items from use. For instance, librarians in a school might house books about sex education on a shelf behind the circulation desk and require students to bring a note from a parent to gain permission to check out one of the books. This is considered "labeling" because it prevents the free circulation of materials.

Reconsidering can be a positive action, reinforcing selection procedures and allowing for the voices of tax payers to be heard. Once a formal complaint is made to a school district or library system, a committee examines the selection process to determine if the book being challenged was selected according to a materials selection policy.

Selecting is a positive, inclusive action. Books, movies, audios, and other library materials are purchased because they have something positive to contribute to patrons and students.

Reading freely allows young adults to read (or listen to) any books in their school libraries (or classrooms) or public libraries without restrictions on age, according to "The Library Bill of Rights."

HISTORY IN ACTION: CLASSIC CHALLENGES

Challenges to books that young adults read is not a new phenomenon, nor is it limited to recently published books. In the Office of Intellectual Freedom's list of "The Most Frequently Challenged Books of 1990–2000," titles are listed numerically, with 1 being the most challenged and 100 the least. In 1967, S. E. Hinton's *The Outsiders* was published. Her book is considered the first book of modern young adult literature. Paul Zindel's *The Pigman* was published the next year. In recognition of these two significant young adult novels, titles published more than 40 years ago were selected for a historical list of challenged books, including books published for adults as well as those published for young adults.

5. *The Adventures of Huckleberry Finn* by Mark Twain (1884)
6. *Of Mice and Men* by John Steinbeck (1965)
13. *The Catcher in the Rye* by J. D. Salinger (1951)
22. *A Wrinkle in Time* by Madeleine L'Engle (1962)
41. *To Kill a Mockingbird* by Harper Lee (1960)
43. *The Outsiders* by S. E. Hinton (1967)
44. *The Pigman* by Paul Zindel (1968)
47. *Flowers for Algernon* by Daniel Keyes (1966)
52. *Brave New World* by Aldous Huxley (1932)
70. *Lord of the Flies* by William Golding (1954)
71. *Native Son* by Richard Wright (1940)
84. *The Adventures of Tom Sawyer* by Mark Twain (1894)

MAJOR STAGES IN HANDLING BOOK CHALLENGES

There are four major actions to take in handling book challenges in libraries: be informed, be prepared, understand the levels of complaints, and inform the learning community.

Be Informed

Before materials in your library are challenged, take steps to be informed about intellectual freedom. First, keeping a copy of the most recent edition of the *Intellectual Freedom Manual* in your professional collection and another copy in your student book collection is a great start to being informed. The seventh edition of the publication of ALA's Office for Intellectual Freedom contains the following six parts:

Part 1: Intellectual Freedom and Libraries: An Overview
Part 2: Library Bill of Rights (interpretations and history)
Part 3: Protecting the Freedom to Read (policy statements, history, and guidelines)
Part 4: Intellectual Freedom and the Law
Part 5: Preparing to Preserve and Protect Intellectual Freedom
Part 6: Working for Intellectual Freedom

The work contains interpretations that are particularly relevant to youth:

"Access for Children and Young People to Nonprint Formats"

"Access to Resources and Services in the School Library Media Program"

"Free Access to Libraries for Minors"

"Minors' First Amendment Rights to Access Information"

Second, for unique perspectives on school libraries and censorship, read Nancy Kravitz's *Censorship and the School Library Media Center* (2002), or at least have a copy on hand. Chapters include "Who and Why" (of challenges), "Historical Perspectives," "Cases in Law," "Challenged Material," "Policies and Procedures," "Today's Issues," and "In Defense of Intellectual Freedom." Appendices include basic documents: The Library Bill of Rights and the following interpretations:

Access to Resources and Services in the School Library Media Program

Free Access to Libraries for Minors

Restricted Access to Library Materials

Access for Children and Young People to Videotapes and Other Non Print Formats

Challenged Materials

Statement on Intellectual Freedom

National Council of Teachers of English Students' Right to Read

Third, use an essential source of information, ALA's Office of Intellectual Freedom (OIF), accessible online at www.ala.org/alaorg/oif. According to the Web site, the Office for Intellectual Freedom "is charged with implementing ALA policies concerning the concept of intellectual freedom as embodied in the Library Bill of Rights, the Association's basic policy on free access to libraries and library materials. The goal of the office is to educate librarians and the general public about the nature and importance of intellectual freedom in libraries." Take time to explore the Web site for basic information as well as up-to-the-minute news about challenges and current issues. This is a site to visit repeatedly to view recent headlines and to take advantage of the OIF Blog. Major topics on the Web site are:

Basics

First Amendment

Statements and Policies

Intellectual Freedom Toolkits

Intellectual Freedom Issues

Banned Books Week

For Young People

Intellectual Freedom Groups and Committees

Awards, Institutes, Programs, and Publications

About Us

Two notable offerings on the OIF Web site are Banned Books Week and For Young People. Under the topic of Banned Books Week are suggestions for informing students and patrons about intellectual freedom and challenged materials; activities appropriate for children, young adults, and adults; and lists of the most frequently challenged books. For instance, for the 25th anniversary of Banned Books Week (2006), ALA compiled the top most challenged books from 2000–2005. Of the 10 books, 6 are considered young adult books, and 9 of the 10 are appropriate for high school library collections. Only one series of books on the list is most appropriate for elementary level students: Dav Pilkey's Captain Underpants series. Two books are adult books but commonly found in high school libraries: John Steinbeck's *Of Mice and Men* and Maya Angelou's *I Know Why the Caged Bird Sings*. It's no surprise that the Harry Potter books are at the top of the list. The top 10 challenges of 2006 include one children's picture book, *And Tango Makes Three* by Justin Richardson and Peter Parnell, and two adult books, Toni Morrison's *The Bluest Eye* and *Beloved*, books that are likely to be included in high school collections. Books on the 2006 list specifically published for young adults are the Gossip Girls series by Cecily Von Ziegesar; the Alice series by Phyllis Reynolds Naylor; *The Earth, My Butt, and Other Big Round Things* by Carolyn Mackler; *Athletic Shorts* by Chris Crutcher; *The Perks of Being a Wallflower* by Stephen Chbosky; and *The Chocolate War* by Robert Cormier.

Fourth, take time for a quick search online for articles, editorials, and news items that discuss intellectual freedom for young adults. This strategy will keep you up-to-date on what's being challenged and why, and may provide you with information you can use immediately in your library. For instance, Doug Johnson's article titled "Don't Defend That Book" reminds librarians that their job is to "know your selection policy, select from authoritative reviews, insist on due process if a book is challenged, and make children responsible for their own choices" (Johnson 2007, 98). That last one about making children responsible for their own choices means that professional librarians "cannot act in place of parents (in loco parentis) to restrict access to materials to individuals" (Johnson 2007, 98).

Being informed about which young adult books are being challenged is not an invitation to avoid including these books in a library collection but rather an opportunity to be aware of what is controversial and to read and collect professional reviews of the books in the event that there is a complaint. *Hit List for Young Adults 2: Frequently Challenged Books* (Lesesne and Chance 2002), an ALA publication, can help you understand the process of being informed about specific controversial books, the reasons for complaints and challenges against particular books, and where you can locate resources about 20 authors and their work. Authors included are Marion Dane Bauer, Nancy Garden, Chris Crutcher, Francesca Lia Block, J. D. Salinger, Robert Cormier, Robert Newton Peck, Bette Greene, Walter Dean Myers, Judy Blume, Janet Bode and Stan Mack, Maya Angelou, Lois Duncan, S. E. Hinton, Stephen Chbosky, Paul Zindel, Garth Nix, Laurie Halse Anderson, and Caroline Cooney.

Be Prepared

Once you have accumulated tools to inform you about intellectual freedom, you are ready to ask this vital question: Is there an approved materials selection policy available in the school district or library district? If your answer is "yes," you are fortunate and will need to familiarize yourself with the policy. In schools, the policy should be approved by the school board and included with other board policies. In public libraries, the policy should be approved by the library board. Keep at least one copy in the library for your reference and for parents and other patrons who want information about the library's selection process.

- If there isn't a materials selection policy for the library (or the school), begin researching the possibilities right away! A materials selection policy is a guide to the process of selecting books and other materials for young adults. It should contain the following:

  - District's philosophy of the library
  - Selection objectives
  - Responsibility for selection
  - Criteria for selection
  - Criteria for gifts and unsolicited materials
  - Procedures for selection
  - Position on intellectual freedom
  - Policy and procedures for handling challenged material (Kravitz 2002, 192–195)

Kravitz's *Censorship and the School Library Media Center* describes a materials selection policy and provides an example of one used in the School District of Philadelphia.

Understand the Levels of Complaints and Challenges

One way to understand the process of complaints and challenges is through hypothetical scenarios based on real experiences. To understand the possibilities, three scenarios are presented based on school library situations: a casual inquiry, a complaint, and a formal challenge.

A Casual Inquiry

It's Wednesday morning in a middle school, and classes have begun with announcements. You, the librarian, are at your desk reviewing your schedule of activities for the day. As soon as announcements end, an eighth-grade English class will enter the library for a booktalking session on new books. A woman appears at the door of your office and asks if you are the librarian. She identifies herself as Mrs. Smith, the mom of an eighth-grade boy. You recognize his name but can't match a face to the name. She asks if she can visit with you a minute about a book he checked out. At first you think that the student has lost a book, and his mother has come to pay for it. Then she says, "He checked out *Fallen Angels*, and his father and I don't talk like that." Of course, you are familiar with Walter Dean Myers's wonderful historical fiction about the Vietnam War. Because the book has become a classic, you know it well. It does contain profanity. That's what disturbs this boy's parents.

Here's what you do:

- Listen politely to what this concerned mother has to say.
- Share the selection process with her.
- Share a review of the book with her.
- Show her a copy of Herald's *Teen Genreflecting*, a selection tool that notes that *Fallen Angels* won a Coretta Scott King Award, was a Best Book for Young Adults, and is recommended for junior high and senior high students.
- Recommend that she share her concerns about profanity with her son, although she has probably already done that.
- Offer for her to contact you anytime she has a concern about a library book.
- Thank Mrs. Smith for coming to visit you in person.

Fortunately, this mom just wanted to know that someone professional and knowledgeable was in charge of selecting books. She wanted to express her dismay at the language in the book. She didn't want it removed from the shelves, nor did she want you to monitor her son's reading choices in the future. This type of conversation can improve public relations and allow you to get to know students' parents better. Be sure to let your principal know that you have had a friendly visit with a parent about *Fallen Angels*.

A Complaint

You may be surprised to learn that Mrs. Smith's husband made an appointment with your principal shortly after her visit with you. Your principal requests that you attend the meeting and bring reviews of the book and information about your selection process. You assemble three folders with identical information for your principal, Mr. Smith, and yourself. Each folder contains copies of the following documents:

- Reviews of *Fallen Angels*
- A copy of the district's materials selection policy, including the reconsideration process
- A copy of the ALA's Library Bill of Rights
- A copy of Access to Resources and Services in the School Library Media Program: An Interpretation of the Library Bill of Rights
- A copy of NCTE's The Freedom to Read

You could also take copies of review journals and a copy of *Teen Genreflecting* to show examples of selection tools although you don't want to overwhelm Mr. Smith with too much material.

At the meeting in the principal's office you describe the selection process and how *Fallen Angels* fits into the district's policy. You listen to Mr. Smith's concerns about the book, and you answer questions from Mr. Smith.

After all the listening and explaining, Mr. Smith tells you and your principal that *Fallen Angels* is not appropriate for anyone in the eighth grade and should not be available on the library's shelves. At this point your principal says, "Let me be sure I understand what you're saying, Mr. Smith. You don't believe any students in the school should have access to the book; you think it should be removed from the shelves?"

At Mr. Smith's affirmative answer, you remind him of the materials selection policy and the role of the reconsideration form. If he believes the book doesn't belong on the shelves, he must fill out a reconsideration form and return it to the principal or submit it to the superintendent. You remind Mr. Smith that the book continues to circulate until the reconsideration process has concluded. This scenario is a standard one with each person responding politely as the district policy and process is being followed.

A Formal Challenge

Sometimes the reconsideration form is never completed and never returned to the principal or submitted to the superintendent. In this scenario, however, Mr. Smith reads *Fallen Angels*, completes the form, and submits it to the superintendent. If a materials selection policy is in place, a district committee is convened as soon as possible. Ideally, this is a committee that has its membership established each fall in a school district; in public libraries it is a continuing committee with members changing as needed. It's best to have the committee already in place in the fall so that if challenges are filed, there's no scrambling to identify committee members. In a school district, membership consists of school administrators, librarians, teachers, parents, and students. The make-up of the committee is articulated in the reconsideration process approved by the school board. The librarian and principal where the challenge is initiated should not be on the committee. This helps avoid involving school personalities at a particular campus. While the committee meets, *Fallen Angels*, the book in question, remains in circulation. Once the committee makes a decision, the school board and the superintendent are notified. They can decide to uphold the decision or not. In this scenario, *Fallen Angels* remained on the shelves in all middle schools and high schools in the district, and that was the end of the challenge. The reconsideration committee, the school board, and the superintendent agreed it was an appropriate selection according to the school district's selection policy.

Inform Students, Teachers, Administrators, and Parents (the Learning Community)

A task of the school librarian is to inform students and other members of the learning community about intellectual freedom and what it means. For teachers and administrators this can be handled through staff development sessions lead by the librarian or invited guests with expertise in intellectual freedom. For students lessons, displays and activities should be

offered as part of the annual library programming or by coll
history and English teachers. Banned Books Week, celebrat
the fall and promoted by the OIF, is an excellent device for
tant questions about the freedom to read. A parent–student ⟩
a forum highlighting intellectual freedom can inform parent
selection process and build positive community relationship⟨
time.

LIBRARIANS IN ACTION: AN ALA PRESIDENT SPEAKS OUT

The release of a movie version of Philip Pullman's *The Golden Compass* triggered boycotts of the book and movie. Conservative religious organizations believed that the book and movie were an attack on Christianity and the Catholic Church. *The Golden Compass* is the first book in a trilogy of fantasies with 11-year-old orphan Lyra Belacqua as the main character. In her world, a person's soul manifests itself as an animal, referred to as a daemon. Lyra leaves the safety of Jordan College at Oxford, England on a quest to save missing children from being separated from their daemons. She encounters scheming scientists, armored bears, gypsies, witch clans, and plenty of danger as she journeys to the frozen north.

In an ALA/OIF blog posted on December 4, 2007, Loriene Roy, ALA president, responded to the attempts to remove *The Golden Compass* and its sequels from libraries and schools:

> It is one thing to disagree with the content of a book or the viewpoint of an author; it is quite another thing to block access to that material because of that disagreement. Removing a book from a school or library because the author is an atheist, or because a religious group disagrees with the book's viewpoint, is censorship that runs counter to our most cherished freedoms and our history as a nation that celebrates and protects religious diversity.
>
> We realize, of course that not every book is for everyone. Parents know their children best and should guide their children's reading. If parents think a particular book is not suitable for their child, they should guide their child to other books. But they should not impose their beliefs on other people's children.
>
> By resisting the call to censor and boycott *The Golden Compass*, we send the message to young people that in this country they have the right to choose what they will read and that they will be expected to develop the ability to think critically about what they read, rather than allowing others to do their thinking for them. (Roy 2007)

Ironically, as often happens with a controversial book that stirs public reaction, more media attention is brought to the movie and the books, increasing their popularity. This is happening with *The Golden Compass*, much as it did with the Harry Potter books.

A Discussion Guide to the movie and book is available from Random House Children's Books. Young adults intrigued by this fantasy can learn more about Philip Pullman at www.hisdarkmaterials.com and can find their own daemon at www.goldencompassmovie.com by using the "Demon Generator."

ONE BOOK IN ACTION: *The Earth, My Butt, and Other Big Round Things* BY CAROLYN MACKLER

Carolyn Mackler is the author of *The Earth, My Butt, and Other Big Round Things* (a 2004 Printz Honor Book and a 2005 Young Adults' Choices selection), listed number 4 of the OIF's most frequent challenges of 2006. According to the OIF Web site, complaints about the novel are "sexual content, anti-family, offensive language, and unsuitable to age group." Mackler responds that her novel is "about self-esteem, feeling good about yourself as you are. I write about normal teenage girls who have many facets to their personalities and lives. I really try to reflect the teenage world as it is. I don't gloss over things; I don't ignore the ugly stuff" (Bronson 2007). Virginia Shreves, the novel's 15-year-old protagonist, struggles to lose weight and to comprehend why her older brother commits date rape. Mackler writes with insight and humor and leaves readers with a hopeful ending. Mackler's other novels are *Love Is a Four-Letter Word*, *Vegan Virgin Valentine*, and *Guyaholic*. Her novels have special appeal to teen girls.

To get to know Mackler better, teens can visit her Web site (at www.carolynmackler.com), where they can send her messages, find out how to start a book club, read interesting questions about *The Earth, My Butt, and Other Big Round Things*, and, through her blog, follow her life as an author. She lives in New York City and is friends with Judy Blume.

LITERATURE IN ACTION: CELEBRATING BANNED BOOKS!

To some educators it may seem odd to celebrate books that are controversial, but the idea is to celebrate young adults' freedom to read. By focusing on books that have been challenged or have been banned from school or public libraries, we encourage the defense of young adults' right to read. Challenged books are controversial for a wide range of reasons. Challenged books may include profanity, sexual references, drug abuse, violence, antireligious messages, and controversial ideas. Books published for young adults contain elements to offend everyone.

Every three years, ALA publishes *Banned Books Resource Guide* (see, for example, Doyle 2007) for use during Banned Books Week (and throughout the year). Typically, the guide provides a list of banned books, information on the First Amendment, and an action guide with suggested activities for celebrating Banned Books Week plus suggestions and help for dealing with complaints and challenges. You can also visit the Banned Books Web site at www.ala.org/bbooks.

My observation has been that high school students in particular get excited learning about banned books. Sometimes it's the first time they have heard or really understood that in America books can be taken off of library shelves by censors. In a high school in Kansas after hearing booktalks on banned books, a group of students vowed to read every one of the titles on the list available in their school library, not because they wanted to read four-letter words, but because they wanted to understand why these books were considered dangerous.

The following activities can increase awareness of censorship and can actually encourage young adults to read:

Booktalk a dozen frequently challenged books.

Design bookmarks to distribute during Banned Books Week.

Display challenged books using provocative wording, such as "Dangerous Books!" "Don't read these books!" "Censored!"

Use ALA slogans developed for bookmarks and posters from previous Banned Books Weeks for designing your own promotional materials:

2007—Get Hooked on a Banned Book: Banned Books Ahoy! Treasure Your Freedom to Read

2006—Celebrate the 25th Anniversary of Banned Books Week

2005—Read Banned Books: They're Your Ticket to Freedom

2004—Campaign for the Freedom to Read: Elect to Read a Banned Book

2003—Can the Ban on Books!

2002—Let Freedom Read: Read a Banned Book

2001—Develop Yourself: Explore Your Mind to a Banned Book

2000—Fish in the River of Knowledge: Celebrate Your Freedom to Read

Distribute ALA's current list of frequently challenged books, including titles for children, young adults, and adults.

Post quotes on the First Amendment throughout the library.

Collaborate with a history teacher for a discussion on First Amendment rights.

Collaborate with an English teacher for a class reading of a banned or challenged book.

Invite an author whose books have been challenged to speak about the experience.

Web-Accessible Intellectual Freedom Documents

Code of Ethics for Librarians
  www.ala.org/ala/oif/statementspols/cdeofethics/codeethics.htm

First Amendment of the Bill of Rights of the U.S. Constitution
  www.ala.org/ala/oif/firstamendment/firstamendment.htm

Interpretations to the Library Bill of Rights
  www.ala.org/ala/oif/statmentspols/statementsif/ulirarybillrights.htm.

Notable First Amendment Court Cases
  www.ala.org/ala/oif/firstamendment/courtcases/courtcases.htm

CONCLUSION

Librarians who work with young adults have the privilege of protecting their freedom to read freely. By following a materials selection policy and being knowledgeable about intellectual freedom, librarians will be ready to handle complaints and challenges to specific titles. Celebrating the freedom to read and teaching the learning community about intellectual freedom can result in a stronger community.

PROFESSIONAL RESOURCES ABOUT INTELLECTUAL FREEDOM

Adams, Helen R. 2007a. "Intellectual Freedom 101." *Knowledge Quest* 36, no. 2 (November/December): 12–15.

Adams, Helen R. 2007b. "What I Learned: An Interview with Cassandra Barnett." *Knowledge Quest* 36, no. 2 (November/December): 16–20.

Asheim, Lester. 1928. *Not Censorship but Selection.* http://www.ala.org/ala/oif/basics/notcensorship.htm (accessed January 24, 2008).

Dickinson, Gail. 2007. "Tough Choices: The Question. . .What Should I Do If My Principal Orders Me to Remove an Unchallenged Book?" *Knowledge Quest* 36, no. 2 (November/December): 70–71.

Doyle, Robert P. 2007. *2007 Banned Books Resource Guide.* Chicago: American Library Association.

Garden, Nancy. 1996. "Annie on Trial: How It Feels to Be the Author of a Challenged Book." *Voice of Youth Advocates* 19 (June): 79–82, 84.

Johnson, Doug. 2007. "Don't Defend That Book." *Library Media Connection* 26 (August/September): 98.

Kelsey, Marie. 2007. "Are We Lucky for the First Amendment? A Brief History of Students' Right to Read." *Knowledge Quest* 36, no. 2 (November/December): 26–29.

Kravitz, Nancy. 2002. *Censorship and the School Library Media Center.* Westport, CT: Libraries Unlimited.

Lehr, Susan, ed. 1995. *Battling Dragons: Issues and Controversy in Children's Literature.* Portsmouth, NH: Heinemann.

Lesesne, Teri, and Rosemary Chance. 2002. *Hit List for Young Adults 2: Frequently Challenged Books.* Chicago: American Library Association.

Office for Intellectual Freedom of the American Library Association. 2006. *Intellectual Freedom Manual.* 7th ed. Chicago: American Library Association.

Peck, Richard. 1986. "The Genteel Unshelving of a Book." *School Library Journal* 32 (May): 37–39.

ASSIGNMENTS IN ACTION: THE FREEDOM TO READ FOR DISCUSSION

1. Do librarians self-censor? "Essentially the goal of censorship is to remove or eliminate particular materials whereas the goal of professional guidelines is to provide criteria for selection, using both standards for literary quality and knowledge of child development" (McClure 1995, 19). When librarians read reviews and realize a book

contains controversial topics, do they tend to avoid purchasing those titles? If so, this is self-censorship. Do you know librarians who regularly self-censor? The National Council of Teachers of English (NCTE) helps clarify differences between censorship and selection through a five-level chart found on the NCTE Web site. Based on the NCTE chart, below are four examples of titles that might be censored but should be selected by a librarian.

- Exclusion of specific materials. Robert Cormier's *Chocolate War* might be censored for its unhappy ending, but it should be *selected* for providing a realistic view of life.
- Negative elements versus positive elements. Sherman Alexie's *The Absolutely True Story of a Part-time Indian* could be challenged for its stereotypical view of Native Americans, but it should be *selected* for its honest portrayal of the contemporary dilemmas of Native Americans.
- Limited access to ideas and information. Robie Harris's *It's Perfectly Normal* could be challenged for its graphic and frank depiction of sex, but it should be *selected* for its honest and clearly presented information.
- Isolated parts of a work. Walter Dean Myers's *Fallen Angels* might be censored for its profanity, but it should be *selected* for its accurate portrayal of soldiers under the stress of war.

For further exploration of censorship versus selection by librarians, read Lester Asheim's classic 1953 article titled "Not Censorship But Selection," available at www.ala.org/ala/oif/basics/notcensorship.htm. What YA books that you have read might be tempting for librarians to self-censor?

2. Sometimes reading novels about book burnings and censoring can help young adults understand the impact of censorship better than a "lesson" about censorship. These novels tend to be didactic, carrying a heavy message from the author about the dangers of censoring books. Still, they can provoke spirited discussions and can lead to research about the history of banning books. Read one of these novels and speculate on its potential impact on a teen. How might it help the understanding of a student's right to read?

The Book Thief by Markus Zusak

> Death narrates this World War II-era Holocaust story of Liesel, a young girl who loves books and steals them from the mayor's wife.

The Day They Came to Arrest the Book by Nat Hentoff

> Teaching Mark Twain's *The Adventures of Huckleberry Finn* causes a furor at George Mason High School. Some students and parents think the novel is racist, sexist, and immoral. Can its censorship be stopped?

Fahrenheit 451 by Ray Bradbury

> In this classic adult novel, firemen burn books, but one fireman hides books and is turned in by his wife. He flees and joins a group of outlaw scholars who hold the contents of books in their heads.

The Last Book in the Universe by Rodman Philbrick

> In this dystopian novel, an orphan boy struggles to survive in a chaotic world, accompanied by an old man who is writing a book for whom there are no readers.

The Last Safe Place on Earth by Richard Peck

Using a dysfunctional family, Peck dramatizes the dangers of censorship in a story that's at once didactic and witty.

Memoirs of a Bookbat by Kathryn Lasky

Harper, an intelligent teen who loves to read, leaves her Christian fundamentalist family and escapes to her grandmother's home where she has freedom to read what she wants.

Sledding Hill by Chris Crutcher

Heavy lessons about book banning and a protagonist who speaks from the afterlife take aim at censors in this odd but enjoyable novel.

The Year They Burned the Books by Nancy Garden

Outrage involving sexual orientation, censorship, and prejudice is interwoven with the lives of high school students.

3. Interview a group of young adults about intellectual freedom. How do middle school and high school students respond to the following questions?

- Are you old enough or mature enough to have access to the same information available to adults?
- Are there information or images that you think people your age should not be allowed to access? What about young people five years younger than you?
- Who do you think should decide what information you have access to?
- Do your parents have the right to know what you are reading or viewing online?

Professional References

AASL Standards for the 21st-Century Learner. American Library Association, November 8, 2006. http://www.ala.org/ala/aasl/aaslproftools/learningstandards/standards.cfm (accessed March 26, 2008).

Adams, Helen R. 2007a. Intellectual freedom 101. *Knowledge Quest* 36, no. 2 (November/December): 12–15.

Adams, Helen R. 2007b. What I learned: An interview with Cassandra Barnett. *Knowledge Quest* 36, no. 2 (November/December): 16–20.

Adams, Lauren. 2004. Chick lit and chick flicks: Secret power or flat formula? *The Horn Book Magazine* 80, no. 6 (November/December): 669–677.

Alderdice, Kit. 2004. Chick lit for teens and tweens. *Publishers Weekly* 251, no. 46 (November 15): 24.

Alessio, Amy J., and Kimberly A. Patton. 2007. *A year of programs for teens.* Chicago: American Library Association.

Alex Award. Young Adult Library Services Association. http://www.ala.org/yalsa/booklists/alex (accessed June 28, 2008).

Amazing Audiobooks for Young Adults. Young Adult Library Services Association. http://www.ala.org/ala/yalsa/booklistsawards/selectedaudio/audiobooks/cfm (accessed July 1, 2008).

Américas Book Award for Children's and Young Adult Literature. http://www.uwm.edu/Dept/CLACS/outreach/americas.html (accessed October 27, 2007).

Anderson, Sheila B. 2004. *Serving older teens.* Westport, CT: Libraries Unlimited.

Anderson, Sheila B. 2005. *Extreme teens: Library services to nontraditional young adults.* Westport, CT: Libraries Unlimited.

Anderson, Sheila B., ed. 2006. *Serving young teens and 'tweens.* Westport, CT: Libraries Unlimited.

Asheim, Lester. 1928. *Not Censorship but Selection.* http://www.ala.org/ala/oif/basics/notcensorship.htm (accessed January 24, 2008).

Asian/Pacific American Award for Literature. Asian/Pacific American Librarians Association. http://www.apalaweb.org/awards/awards.htm (accessed November 8, 2007).

Barber, Raymond W., and Patrice Bartell, eds. 2007. *Senior High Core Collection: A Selection Guide.* 17th ed. Bronx, NY: H. W. Wilson.

Bartel, Julie. 2005a. Annotated list of magazines. *School Library Journal* 51, no 7. (July): 37–41.

Bartel, Julie. 2005b. The good, the bad, and the edgy. *School Library Journal* 51, no. 7 (July): 34–36.

Beers, Kylene, and Teri Lesesne. 2001. *Books for you: An annotated booklist for senior high.* 14th ed. Urbana, IL: National Council of Teachers of English.

Best Books for Young Adults. Young Adult Library Services Association. http://www.ala.org/yalsa/booklists/bbya (accessed March 21, 2008).

Best Books for Young Adults Policies and Procedures. Young Adult Library Services Association. http://www.ala.org/ala/yalsa/booklistsawards/bestbooksya/policiesprocedures.cfm (accessed June 21, 2008).

Bodart, Joni R. 2002. *Radical reads: 202 young adult novels on the edge.* Lanham, MD: Scarecrow.

Booklist: Spotlight on Graphic Novels 101, no. 14 (March 15, 2005).

Booklist: Spotlight on Graphic Novels 103, no. 14 (March 15, 2007).

Borne, C., and K. Ferst. 2004. Zines for teens. In *Thinking outside the book: Alternatives for today's teen library collection,* ed. C. Allen Nichols (pp. 1–20). Westport, CT: Libraries Unlimited.

Brehm-Heeger, Paula. 2007. *Serving urban teens.* Westport, CT: Libraries Unlimited.

Brenner, Robin E. 2007. *Understanding manga and anime.* Westport, CT: Libraries Unlimited.

Bridges, Jan. 2004. Making your teen poetry contest a winner. *VOYA* 27 (April): 24–25.

Bromann, Jennifer. 1999. The toughest audience on earth. *School Library Journal* 45, no. 10 (October): 60–63.

Bronson, Andrea. 2007. Teens' favorite authors face book bans. *Women's eNews.* Available at: http://www.womensenews.org/article.cfm/dyn/aid/3357 (accessed February 3, 2008).

Brown, Jean, and Elaine C. Stephens, eds. 2003. *Your reading: An annotated booklist for middle school and junior high.* Urbana, IL: National Council of Teachers of English.

Campbell, Patty. 2006. The lit of chick lit. *The Horn Book Magazine* 82, no. 4 (July/August): 487–491.

Carey, James O. 2003. Michael Eisenberg and Robert Berkowitz's Big6™ information problem-solving model. *School Library Media Activities Monthly* 19 (January): 24–25, 28.

Carlsen, G. Robert. 1980. *Books and the teenage reader: A guide for teachers, librarians and parents.* New York: Harper.

Cart, Michael. 2005. New things under the sun. *Booklist* 101 (January 1 & 15B): 838.

Carter, Betty. 1991. *Best books for young adults: The selections, the history, the romance.* Chicago: American Library Association.

Carter, Betty. 1992. Who is Margaret Edwards and What is this award being given in her honor? *The ALAN Review* 19, no. 3 (Spring): 45–48.

Carter, Betty. 2001. The outsiders. *Voices from the Middle* 9 (December): 54–56.

Carter, Betty, and Richard F. Abrahamson. 1990. *Nonfiction for young adults from delight to wisdom.* Phoenix, AZ: Oryx.

Charles, Jane. V. 2005. Get real! Booktalking nonfiction for Teen Read Week 2005. *Young Adult Library Services* 4, no. 1 (Fall): 12–16.

Chelton, Mary K., ed. 2000. *Excellence in library services to young adults.* Chicago: American Library Association.

The Children's Literature Web Guide. Phoenix Award. http://www.ucalgary.ca/~dkbrown/phoenix.html (accessed July 28, 2007).

Cianciolo, Patricia J. 1972. *Illustrations in children's books.* [n.p.]: W. C. Brown.

The CILIP Carnegie & Kate Greenaway Children's Book Awards. Carnegie Medal. http://www.carnegiegreenaway.org.uk (accessed July 28, 2007).

Coatney, Sharon. 2008. Keeping current: Standards for the 21st-century learner. *School Library Media Activities Monthly* 24, no. 6 (February): 56–58.

Coretta Scott King Book Awards for Authors and Illustrators. American Library Association. http://www.ala.org/ala/emiert/corettascottkingbookaward/corettascott/cfm (accessed September 27, 2007).

The Costa Book Awards. Book of the Year. http://www.costabookawards.com (accessed March 13, 2008).

Cox, Ruth. 2002. *Tantalizing tidbits for teens: Quick booktalks for the busy high school library media specialist.* Columbus, OH: Linworth.

Crane, Jean M. 2005. Art/reading/language arts: Biographies and caricatures with young adults. *School Library Media Activities Monthly* 21, no. 6 (February): 11–13.

De Marco, Joseph. 1997. Vampire literature: Something young adults can really sink their teeth into. *Emergency Librarian* 24, no. 5 (May/June): 26–28.

Dewey, Melvil. 2004. *Abridged Dewey Decimal Classification and Relative Index, Edition 14* Dublin, OH: OCLC.

Dickinson, Gail. 2007. Tough choices: The question . . . What should I do if my principal orders me to remove an unchallenged book? *Knowledge Quest* 36, no. 2 (November/December): 70–71.

Donelson, Aileen P., & Kenneth L. Nilsen. 2005. *Literature for today's young adults.* 7th ed. Boston: Allyn and Bacon.

Dorrell, Larry, and Ed Carroll. 1981. Spider-Man at the library. *School Library Journal* 27, no. 10 (August): 17–19.

Doyle, Robert P. 2007. *2007 banned books resource guide.* Chicago: American Library Association.

Dresang, Eliza, Melissa Gross, and Leslie Edmonds Holt. 2006. *Dynamic youth services through outcome-based planning and evaluation.* Chicago: American Library Association.

Dunning, Arthur S. 1959. Definition of the role of the junior novel based on analyses of thirty selected novels. PhD diss., Tallahassee: Florida State University.

Edwards, Margaret A. 1994 (reprint). *The fair garden and the swarm of beasts: The library and the young adult.* Chicago: American Library Association.

Eisenberg, Michael, and Robert E. Berkowitz. 1997. The Big Six & electronic resources: A natural fit. *Book Report* 16 (September-October): 15, 22.

Follos, Allison M. G. 2006. *Reviving reading: School library programming, author visits and books that rock!* Westport, CT: Libraries Unlimited.

Follos, Alison M. G. 2007. Change the literacy depression in your school: Read teens a story! *Library Media Connection* 25, no. 7 (April/May): 20–22.

Garden, Nancy. 1996. Annie on trial: How it feels to be the author of a challenged book. *Voice of Youth Advocates* 19 (June): 79–82, 84.

Gill, Sam D. 1999. Young adult literature for young adult males. *ALAN Review* 26, no. 2 (Winter): 61–63.

Gillespie, John T., and Corinne J. Naden. 2006. *Classic teenplots.* Westport, CT: Libraries Unlimited.

Goldsmith, Francisca. 2005. *Graphic novels now: Building, managing, and marketing a dynamic collection.* Chicago: American Library Association.

Gorman, Michele. 2003. Graphic novels and the curriculum connection. *Library Media Connection* 22, no. 3: 20.

Grillo, Thomas. 2005. Reaching teens: Back to the future. *NEA Today* 23, no. 5: 26–28.

Hall, Susan. 2007. *Using picture storybooks to teach literary devices: Recommended books for children and young adults.* Westport, CT: Libraries Unlimited.

Hart, Melissa. 2004. Attract teens with an edgy plot. *Writer* 117, no. 10 (October): 39–43.

Havighurst, Richard. 1971. *Developmental tasks and education.* New York: David McKay.

Herald, Diana Tixier. 2003. *Teen genreflecting: A guide to reading interests.* Westport, CT: Libraries Unlimited.

Hinton, Susan. 1967. Teen-agers are for real. *New York Times Book Review* (August 27): 26–29.

Holman, C. Hugh, and William Harmon. 1992. *A handbook to literature.* 6th ed. New York Company: McMillan.

Honnold, RoseMary. 2006. *The teen reader's advisor.* New York: Neal-Schuman.

Johnson, Doug. 2007. Don't defend that book. *Library Media Connection* 26 (August/September): 98.

Jones, Patrick, Michele Gorman, and Tricia Suellentrop. 2004. *Connecting young adults and libraries.* 3rd ed. New York: Neal-Schuman.

Jones, Patrick, Maureen L. Hartman, and Patricia Taylor. 2006. *Connecting with reluctant teen readers: Tips, titles, and tools.* New York: Neal-Schuman.

Jones, Patrick, Patricia Taylor, and Kirsten Edwards. 2003. *A core collection for young adults.* New York: Neal-Schuman.

Kan, Katherine L. 2006. *Sizzling summer reading programs for young adults.* 2nd ed. Chicago: American Library Association.

Keane, Nancy J. 2006. *The big book of teen reading lists: 100 great, ready-to-use book lists for educators, librarians, parents, and teens.* Westport, CT: Libraries Unlimited.

Kelsey, Marie. 2007. Are we lucky for the First Amendment? A brief history of students' right to read. *Knowledge Quest* 36, no.2 (November/December): 26–29.

Koelling, Holly, ed. 2007. *Best Books for Young Adults.* 3rd ed. Chicago: American Library Association.

Krashen, Stephen D. 2004. *The power of reading: Insights from the research.* 2nd ed. Westport, CT: Libraries Unlimited.

Kravitz, Nancy. 2002. *Censorship and the school library media center.* Westport, CT: Libraries Unlimited.

Kunzel, Bonnie, and Constance Hardesty. 2006. *The teen-centered book club: Readers into leaders.* Westport, CT: Libraries Unlimited.

Lamb, Annette, and Larry Johnson. 2007. Podcasting in the school library, Part 2: Creating powerful podcasts with your students. *Teacher Librarian* 34, no. 4 (April): 61–64.

Landt, Susan M. 2006. Multicultural literature and young adolescents: A kaleidoscope of opportunity. *Journal of Adolescent & Adult Literacy* 49 (May): 690–697.

Langemack, Chapple. 2007. *The author event primer.* Westport, CT: Libraries Unlimited.

Le Guin, Ursula K. *Plausibility in fantasy to Alexei Mutovkin: An open letter.* The Official Web Site of Ursula K. Le Guin. http://www.ursulakleguin.com/PlausibilityinFantasy.html (accessed July 12, 2008).

Lehman, Carolyn. 2006. Hero, victim, or monster? *School Library Journal* 52, no. 10: 36–37.

Lehr, Susan, ed. 1995. *Battling dragons: Issues and controversy in children's literature.* Portsmouth, NH: Heinemann.

Lesesne, Teri, and Rosemary Chance. 2002. *Hit list for young adults 2: Frequently challenged books.* Chicago: American Library Association.

Lesesne, Teri. 2003. *Making the match: The right book for the right reader at the right time, grades 4–12.* Portland, ME: Stenhouse.

Leslie, Roger, and Patricia Potter Wilson. 2001. *Igniting the spark: Library programs that inspire high school patrons.* Westport, CT: Libraries Unlimited.

Locke, Don C. 1998. *Increasing multicultural understanding: A comprehensive model* 2nd ed. Thousand Oaks, CA: Sage Publications.

Loertscher, David V. 1998. *Reinvent your school's library in the age of technology: A guide for principals and superintendents.* San Jose, CA: Hi Willow Research and Publishing.

Luedtke, Amy, Sarajo Wentling, and Jody Wurt. 2006. The brood of Frankenstein: Great literature? Maybe not, but teens love horror. *School Library Journal* 52, no. 7 (July): 34–36.

Lyga, Allyson A. W. 2004. *Graphic novels in your media center: A definitive guide.* Westport, CT: Libraries Unlimited.

Mahood, Kristine. 2006. *A passion for print: Promoting reading and books to teens.* Westport, CT: Libraries Unlimited.

Makowski, Silk. 1998. *Serious about series: Evaluations and annotations of teen fiction in paperback series.* Lanham, MD: Scarecrow.

Margaret A. Edwards Award. Young Adult Library Services Association. http://www.ala.org/yalsa/edwards (accessed March 21, 2008).

Margaret A. Edwards Award Policies and Procedures. Young Adult Library Services Association. http://www.ala.org/ala/yalsa/booklistsawards/maepolicy/policiesprocedures.cfm (accessed July 1, 2008).

McCloud, Scott. 1994 (reprint). *Understanding comics: The invisible art.* New York: HarperPerennial.

McCloud, Scott. 2006. *Making comics: Storytelling secrets of comics, manga and graphic novels.* New York: Harper.

McClure, Amy. 1995. Censorship of children's books. In *Battling Dragons: Issues and Controversy in Children's Literature,* ed. Susan Lehr. Portsmouth, NH: Heinemann.

Meigs, Cornelia et al. 1969. *A critical history of children's literature: A survey of children's books in English.* Rev. ed. New York: Macmillan.

Meyer, Stephenie. The Official Web Site of Stephenie Meyer. http://www.stepheniemeyer.com (accessed July 12, 2007).

Meyer, Stephenie. Interview on Amazon.com, *Twilight.* http://www.amazon.com (accessed July 14, 2007).

Michael L. Printz Award. Young Adult Library Services Association. http://www.ala.org/yalsa/printz (accessed March 21, 2008).

Mildred L. Batchelder Award. Association of Library Services to Children. http://www.ala.org/ala/alsc/awardsscholarship/literaryawds/batchelderaward/batchelderaward/cfm (accessed March 19, 2008).

Miller, Keith, and Allison Parker. 2007. Interview with Walter Dean Myers. *Journal of Adolescent & Adult Literacy* 50, no. 8: 688–689.

Monson, Dianne L., and Sam Sebesta. 1991. Reading preferences. In James Flood et al. (eds.), *Handbook of research on teaching the English language arts* (pp. 664–673). New York: Macmillan.

National Council of Teachers of English. *Statement on censorship and professional guidelines.* http://www.ncte.org/print.asp?id=107613&node=604 (accessed January 24, 2008).

Nichols, Mary Anne. 2002. *Merchandising library materials to young adults.* Westport, CT: Libraries Unlimited.

Nilsen, Aileen Pace, and Kenneth L. Donelson. 2000. *Literature for today's young adults.* 6th ed. New York: Longman.

Nixon, Joan Lowery. 1991. Writing mysteries young adults want to read. *Writer* 104, no. 7 (July): 18–20.

O'Dell, Katie. 2002. *Library materials and services for teen girls*. Westport, CT: Libraries Unlimited.

Odyssey Award for Excellence in Audiobook Production. Young Adult Library Services Association and the Association for Library Services to Children. http://www.ala.org/ala/yalsa/booklistawards/odyssey/odyssey.cfm (accessed June 28, 2008).

Odyssey Award for Excellence in Audiobook Production Policies and Procedures. Young Adult Library Services Association and the Association for Library Services to Children. http://www.ala.org/ala/yalsa/booklistawards/odyssey/policies.cfm (accessed June 28, 2008).

Office for Intellectual Freedom. American Library Association. http:www.ala.org/alaorg/oif (accessed January 4, 2008).

Office for Intellectual Freedom of the American Library Association. 1992. *Intellectual freedom manual*. 4th ed. Chicago: American Library Association.

Office for Intellectual Freedom of the American Library Association. 2006. *Intellectual freedom manual*. 7th ed. Chicago: American Library Association.

Orbis Pictus Award for Outstanding Nonfiction for Children. National Council of Teachers of English. http://www.ncte.org/elem/awards/orbispictus/106877.htm?source=gs (accessed March 29, 2008).

Ott, Valerie A. 2006. *Teen programs with punch: A month-by-month guide*. Westport, CT: Libraries Unlimited.

Outstanding Books for the College Bound. Young Adult Library Services Association. http://www.ala.org/yalsa/booklists/obcb (accessed March 21, 2008).

Outstanding Books for the College Bound Introduction. Young Adult Library Services Association. http://www.ala.org/ala/yalsa/booklistsawards/outstandingbooks/introduction/cfm (accessed July 1, 2008).

Peck, Richard. 1986. The genteel unshelving of a book. *School Library Journal* 32 (May): 37–39.

Plunkett-Powell, Karen. 1993. *The Nancy Drew scrapbook: 60 years of America's favorite teenage sleuth*. New York: St. Martin's.

Polanka, Sue. 2008. Off the shelf: Is print reference dead? *Booklist* 104, no. 9/10 (January 1 & 15), 127.

Popular Paperbacks for Young Adults. Young Adults Library Services Association. http://www.ala.org/yalsa/booklists/poppaper (accessed March 21, 2008).

Price, Anne, ed. 2005. *Middle and junior high core collection: A selection guide*. 9th ed. Bronx, NY: H. W. Wilson.

Pura Belpré Award. Association of Library Services to Children. http://www.ala.org/ala/alsc/awardsscholarships/literaryawds/belpremedal/belprmedal.cfm (accessed October 26, 2007).

Quick Picks for Reluctant Young Adult Readers. Young Adult Library Services Association. http://www.ala.org/yalsa/booklists/quickpicks (accessed June 28, 2008).

Quick Picks for Reluctant Young Adult Readers Policies and Procedures. Young Adult Library Services Association. http://www.ala.org/ala/yalsa/booklistawards/quickpicks/quickpicksreluctantyoungadult.cfm (accessed July 1, 2008).

Robert F. Sibert Informational Book Medal. Association of Library Services to Children. http://www.ala.org/ala/alsc/awardsscholarships/literaryawds/sibertmedal/sibert_medal.cfm (accessed August 11, 2007).

Rochman, Hazel. 1987. *Tales of love and terror: Booktalking the classics, old and new*. Chicago: American Library association.

Rochman, Hazel. 1993. *Against borders: Promoting books for a multicultural world*. Chicago: American Library Association.

Rothschild, D. Aviva. 1995. *Graphic novels: A bibliographic guide to book-length comics*. Englewood, CO: Libraries Unlimited.

Roy, Loriene. 2007. Office for Intellectual Freedom Blog. http://blogs.ala.org/oif.php?m=200712 (accessed December 4, 2007).

Scales, Pat. 2002. The pigman and he. *School Library Journal* 48, no. 6 (June): 52–54.

Schall, Lucy. 2007. *Booktalks and beyond: Promoting great genre reads to teens*. Westport, CT: Libraries Unlimited.

Scieszka, John, ed. 2005. *Guys write for guys read*. New York: Viking.

Scieszka, Jon. Guys read. http://www.guysread.com (accessed August 16, 2007).

Sidney Taylor Book Awards. The Association of Jewish Libraries. http://www.SidneyTaylorBookAward.org (accessed November 21, 2007).

Smith, Michael, and Jeffrey D. Wilhelm. 2002. *"Reading don't fix no Chevys": Literacy in the lives of young men*. Portsmouth, NH: Heinemann.

Stone, Tanya Lee. 2006. Now and forever: The power of sex in young adult literature. *VOYA* (February): 463–465.

Strauss, Gary. 2004. Nancy Drew dusts off "musty appeal" for new readers. *USA Today*. http"//unx1.shsu.edu:2048/login?url=http://search.ebscohost.com.unx1.shsu.edu:2048/login.aspx?direct=true&db=a9h&AN=JOE238193757304&loginpage=Login.asp&site=ehost-live&scope=site (accessed April 28, 2007).

Sullivan, Edward T. 2002. *Reaching reluctant young adult readers*. Lanham, MD: Scarecrow.

"This small world: A glimpse of many cultures." YALSA's Popular Paperbacks for Young Adults. http://www.ala.org/yalsa/booklists/poppaper (accessed June 23, 2008).

Thomason, Nevada. 1983. *Survey reveals truths about young adult readers*. http://web.ecohost.com.unx1.shsu.edu:2048/ehost/detail?vid=3&his=15&sid=2537df57-87d9-42a0-b1fr-a6fbec1e5848%40sessionmgr7 (accessed April 28, 2007).

Todd, Mark, and Esther Pearl Watson. 2006. *Whatcha mean, what's a zine? The art of making zines and mini-comics*. Boston: Houghton Mifflin.

Tomás Rivera Mexican American Children's Book Award. http://www.educationtxstate.edu/subpages/tomasrivera (accessed October 26, 2007).

Trelease, Jim. 2006. *The read-aloud handbook*. 6th ed. New York: Penguin.

Vaillancourt, Renee J. 2000. *Bare bones young adult services: Tips for public library generalists*. Chicago: American Library Association.

Watson, Bruce. 1991. Tom Swift, Nancy Drew and pals all had the same dad. *Smithsonian* 22 (October): 50–60.

Weiner, Stephen. 2003. *Faster than a speeding bullet: The rise of the graphic novel*. New York: Nantier Beall Minoustchine.

Welch, Rollie James. 2007. *The guy-friendly teen library*. Westport, CT: Libraries Unlimited.

Whelan, Debra Lau. 2006. Out and ignored. *School Library Journal* 52, no. 1 (January): 46–50.

Wolfson, Gene. 2008. Using audiobooks to meet the needs of adolescent readers. *American secondary education* 36, no. 2 (Spring): 105–114.

Young Adults' Choices. International Reading Association. http://www.reading.org/resources/tools/choices_young_adults.html (accessed March 21, 2008).

Young Adults' Choices for 2006. *Journal of Adolescent and Adult Literacy* 50, no. 3 (November): 223–230.

Young Adults' Choices for 2007. *Journal of Adolescent and Adult Literacy* 51, no. 3 (November): 265–272.

Reference List of Young Adult Books

Note: Included in this list of young adult books are a few children's books and a few adult books cited in the text. Publisher information is not given for books published before 1900.

Aaseng, Nathan. 1992. *Navajo code talkers.* New York: Walker.

Adams, Douglas. 1995. *The hitchhiker's guide to the galaxy.* New York: Del Rey.

Adams, Richard. [1974] 2005. *Watership down.* New York: Scribner.

Adoff, Arnold. 1990. *Sports pages.* New York: HarperTrophy.

Adoff, Arnold. 1995. *Slow dance heart break blues.* New York: Lothrop, Lee and Shepard.

Adoff, Arnold. 2000. *The basket counts.* Illus. Michael Weaver. New York: Simon & Schuster.

Al-Windawi, Thura. 2004. *Thura's diary: My life in wartime Iraq.* New York: Viking.

Alcott, Louisa May. 1868. *Little women.*

Aldrich, Thomas Bailey. 1870. *The story of a bad boy.*

Alexander, Lloyd. 2006a. *The black cauldron.* New York: Holt.

Alexander, Lloyd. 2006b. *The book of three.* New York: Holt.

Alexander, Lloyd. 2006c. *The castle of Llyr.* New York: Holt.

Alexander, Lloyd. 2006d. *The high king.* New York: Holt.

Alexander, Lloyd. 2006e. *Taran wanderer.* New York: Holt.

Alexie, Sherman. 2007. *The absolutely true diary of a part-time Indian.* Illus. Ellen Forney. New York: Little, Brown.

Alger, Horatio, Jr. 1868. *Ragged Dick; or, street life in New York.*

Almond, David. 2000. *Kit's wilderness.* New York: Delacorte.

Alvarez, Julia. 2002. *Before we were free.* New York: Random House.

Anderson, Laurie Halse. 1999. *Speak.* New York: Farrar, Straus and Giroux.

Anderson, M. T. 2002. *Feed.* Cambridge, MA: Candlewick.

Angelou, Maya. 1969. *I know why the caged bird sings.* New York: Bantam.

Anonymous. 2005. *Go ask Alice.* New York: Simon Pulse.

Appelt, Kathi. 2000. *Kissing Tennessee and other stories from the Stardust Dance.* San Diego, CA: Harcourt.

Appelt, Kathi. 2002. *Poems from homeroom: A writer's place to start.* New York: Holt.

Asimov, Isaac. [1942] 2004. *Foundation.* New York: Spectra.

Atkin, S. Beth. 1993. *Voices from the fields: Children of migrant farmworkers tell their stories.* New York: Little, Brown.

Atkins, Catherine. 1999. *When Jeff comes home.* New York: Puffin.

Atwater-Rhodes, Amelia. 1999. *In the forest of the night.* New York: Delacorte.

Atwater-Rhodes, Amelia. 2000. *Demon in my view.* New York: Delacorte.

Avi. 2008. *Wolf-rider.* New York: Simon Pulse.

Bagdasarian, Adam. 2000. *Forgotten fire.* New York: Dorling Kindersley.

Baker, Kyle. 2004. *Plastic Man! On the lam.* New York: DC Comics.

Barron, T. A. 2007a. *The fires of Merlin.* New York: Philomel.

Barron, T. A. 2007b. *The lost years of Merlin.* New York: Philomel.

Barron, T. A. 2007c. *The mirror of Merlin.* New York: Philomel.

Barron, T. A. 2007d. *The seven songs of Merlin.* New York: Philomel.

Barron, T. A. 2007e. *The wings of Merlin.* New York: Philomel.

Bartoletti, Susan Campbell. 2001. *Black potatoes: The story of the great Irish famine, 1845–1850.* Boston: Houghton Mifflin.

Bartoletti, Susan Campbell. 2005. *Hitler youth: Growing up in Hitler's shadow.* New York: Scholastic.

Bauer, Joan. 2005. *Squashed.* New York: Puffin.

Bauer, Marion Dane, ed. 1995. *Am I blue? Coming out from the silence.* New York: HarperTrophy.

Bausum, Ann. 2004. *With courage and cloth: Winning the fight for a woman's right to vote.* Washington, DC: National Geographic.

Bausum, Ann. 2006. *Freedom riders: John Lewis and Jim Zwerg on the front lines of the civil rights movement.* Washington, DC: National Geographic.

Begay, Shonto. 1995. *Navajo: Visions and voices across the mesa.* New York: Scholastic.

Bird, Isobel. 2001. *So mote it be.* New York: HarperCollins.

Block, Francesca Lia. 2004. *Weetzie Bat.* New York: HarperCollins.

Bloor, Edward. 1997. *Tangerine.* San Diego, CA: Harcourt.

Blume, Judy, ed. 1999. *Places I never meant to be: Original stories by censored authors.* New York: Simon and Schuster.

Blume, Judy. 2007. *Forever.* New York: Simon Pulse.

Bode, Janet. 1989. *New kids in town: Oral histories of immigrant teens.* New York: Scholastic.

Bode, Janet. 1990. *The voices of rape: Healing the hurt.* New York: Dell.

Bolden, Tonya. 2001. *Rock of ages: A tribute to the black church.* New York: Knopf.

Bondoux, Anne-Laure. 2006. *The killer's tears.* New York: Delacorte.

Booth, Coe. 2006. *Tyrell.* New York: Scholastic.

Bowers, Laura. 2007. *Beauty shop for rent.* Orlando, FL: Harcourt.

Bradbury, Ray. [1946] 1997. *The martian chronicles.* New York: HarperCollins.

Bradbury, Ray. [1953] 1987. *Fahrenheit 451.* New York: Ballantine.

Brashares, Ann. 2001. *The sisterhood of the traveling pants.* New York: Delacorte.

Bruchac, Joseph. 2003. *Pocahontas.* New York: Silver Whistle.

Bunyan, John. 1678. *Pilgrim's progress.*

Burgess, Melvin. 2006. *Doing it.* New York: Holt.

Burleigh, Robert. 1997. *Hoops.* Illus. Stephen T. Johnson. San Diego, CA: Harcourt Brace.

Byant, Jen. 2006. *Pieces of Georgia.* New York: Knopf.

Cabot, Meg. 2000. *Princess diaries.* New York: HarperCollins.

Campbell, Eric. 1995. *The place of lions.* San Diego, CA: Harcourt.

Canales, Viola. 2006. *Tequila worm.* New York: Random House.

Card, Orson Scott. 1977. *Ender's game.* New York: Tom Doherty.

Carey, Janet Lee. 2007. *Dragon's keep.* Orlando, FL: Harcourt.

Carlson, Lori M., ed. *Cool salsa: Bilingual poems on growing up Latino in the United States.* New York: Holt.

Cart, Michael, ed. 2001. *Love & sex: Ten stories of truth.* New York: Simon and Schuster.

Cary, Kate. 2005. *Bloodline.* NY: Razorbill.

Chambers, Aidan. 2002. *Postcards from no man's land.* New York: Dutton.

Chbosky, Stephen. 1999. *The perks of being a wallflower.* New York: MTV.

Chevalier, Tracy. *Girl with a pearl earring.* New York: Plume.

Christopher, John. 1967. *The white mountains.* New York: Simon and Schuster.

Chryssicas, Mary Kaye. 2007. *Breathe: Yoga for teens.* New York: DK.

Clarke, Arthur C. [1968] 2000. *2001: A space odyssey.* New York: Roc.

Clement-Moore, Rosemary. 2008. *Prom dates from hell.* New York: Delacorte.

Clements, Bruce. 1990. *Tom loves Anna loves Tom.* New York: Farrar, Straus and Giroux.

Cofer, Judith Ortiz. 1995. *An island like you: Stories of the barrio.* New York: Orchard.

Cohn, Rachel, and David Levithan. 2006. *Nick and Nora's playlist.* New York: Knopf.

Cooper, Susan. 2007a. *The dark is rising.* New York: Aladdin.

Cooper, Susan. 2007b. *Greenwitch.* New York: Aladdin.

Cooper, Susan. 2007c. *The Grey King.* New York: Aladdin.

Cooper, Susan. 2007d. *Over sea, under stone.* New York: Aladdin.

Cooper, Susan. 2007e. *Silver on the trees.* New York: Aladdin.

Cormier, Robert. 1985. *The chocolate war.* New York: Knopf.

Cottonwood, Joe. 1995. *Quake!* New York: Scholastic.

Covey, Sean. 1998. *The 7 habits of highly effective teens.* New York: Fireside.

Coville, Bruce. 1997. *Oddly enough.* New York: Simon Pulse.

Coville, Bruce. 2000. *Odder than ever.* San Diego, CA: Harcourt.

Crutcher, Chris. 1983. *Running loose.* New York: HarperTeen.

Crutcher, Chris. 1989. *Athletic shorts.* New York: Greenwillow.

Crutcher, Chris. 1986. *Stotan!* New York: Bantam.

Crutcher, Chris. 1987. *The crazy horse electric game.* New York: Bantam.

Crutcher, Chris. 1989. *Chinese handcuffs.* New York: Bantam.

Crutcher, Chris. 1993. *Staying fat for Sarah Byrnes.* New York: Bantam.

Crutcher, Chris. 1995. *Ironman.* New York: Bantam Doubleday Dell.

Crutcher, Chris. 2001. *Whale talk.* New York: HarperCollins.

Crutcher, Chris. 2003. *King of the mild frontier: An ill-advised autobiography.* New York: Greenwillow.

Crutcher, Chris. 2005. *Sledding hill.* New York: Greenwillow.

Curtis, Christopher Paul. 1995. *The Watsons go to Birmingham—1963.* New York: Delacorte.

Curtis, Christopher Paul. 1999. *Bud, not Buddy.* New York: Delacorte.

Curtis, Christopher Paul. 2004. *Bucking the Sarge.* New York: Random House.

Curtis, Christopher Paul. 2007. *Elijah of Buxton.* New York: Scholastic.

Cushman, Karen. 1994. *Catherine called Birdy.* Boston: Houghton Mifflin.

Daly, Maureen. [1942] 2002. *Seventeenth summer.* New York: Simon and Schuster.

Daugherty, James H. 1949. *Daniel Boone.* New York: Viking.

Deem, James M. 2005. *Bodies from the ash: Life and death in ancient Pompeii.* Boston: Houghton Mifflin.

Defoe, Daniel. 1719. *The life and surprising adventures of Robinson Crusoe of York, mariner.*

De Mari, Silvana. 2006. *The last dragon.* New York: Miramax.

De Trevino, Elizabeth Borten. [1966] 1987. *I, Juan de Pareja.* New York: Farrar, Straus and Giroux.

Dessen, Sarah. 2006. *That summer.* New York: Viking.

Deuker, Carl. 2000. *Night hoops.* Boston: Houghton Mifflin.

DeVillers, Julia. 2004. *How my private, personal journal became a bestseller.* New York: Penguin.

Dickinson, Peter. 1988. *Eva.* New York: Dell.

Draper, Sharon. 1994. *Tears of a tiger.* New York: Simon and Schuster.

Draper, Sharon. 1997. *Forged by fire.* New York: Simon and Schuster.

Draper, Sharon. 1999. *Romiette and Julio.* New York: Simon and Schuster.

Draper, Sharon. 2001. *Darkness before dawn.* New York: Simon and Schuster.

Draper, Sharon. 2003. *The battle of Jericho.* New York: Simon and Schuster.

Draper, Sharon. 2006. *Copper sun.* New York: Simon and Schuster.

Draper, Sharon. 2007a. *Fire from the rock.* New York: Dutton.

Draper, Sharon. 2007b. *November blues.* New York: Atheneum.

Drechsler, Debbie. 2001. *The summer of love.* Montreal, Quebec: Drawn & Quarterly.

Duder, Tessa. 1999. *In lane three, Alex Archer.* New York: Starfire.

Duffy, Carol Ann. 1996. *Stopping for death: Poems of death and loss.* Illus. Trisha Rafferty. New York: Holt.

Duncan, Lois. 1978. *Killing Mr. Griffin.* New York: Dell.

Duncan, Lois. 1992. *Who killed my daughter?* New York: Delacorte.

Duncan, Lois. 1997. *Gallows Hill.* New York: Delacorte.

Duncan, Lois. 1999. *I know what you did last summer.* New York: Laurel Leaf.

Edelman, Bernard, ed. 1985. *Dear America: Letters home from Vietnam.* New York: Simon and Schuster.

Eisner, Will. 1978. *Contract with God.* New York: Norton.

Eisner, Will. 2003. *Fagin the Jew.* New York: Doubleday.

Farmer, Nancy. 2002. *The house of scorpion.* New York: Atheneum.

Fiedler, Lisa. 2006. *Romeo's ex: Rosaline's story.* New York: Holt.

Fielding, Helen. 1999. *Bridget Jones's diary.* New York: Penguin.

Flake, Sharon G. 1998. *The skin I'm in.* New York: Hyperion.

Flake, Sharon G. 2001. *Money hungry.* New York: Hyperion.

Flake, Sharon G. 2003. *Begging for change.* New York: Jump at the Sun.

Flake, Sharon G. 2004. *Who am I without him? Short stories about girls and the boys in their lives.* New York: Jump at the Sun.

Flake, Sharon G. 2005. *Bang.* New York: Jump at the Sun.

Fletcher, Ralph. 1996. *Buried alive: The elements of love.* New York: Atheneum.

Flinn, Alex. 2004. *Nothing to lose.* New York: HarperTeen.

Flinn, Alex. 2007. *Beastly.* New York: HarperCollins.

Forbes, Esther. [1943] 1980. *Johnny Tremain.* New York: Yearling.

Franco, Betsy, ed. 2001. *Things I have to tell you: Poems and writing by teenage girls.* Cambridge, MA: Candlewick.

Frank, Anne. [1947] 1997. *The diary of a young girl.* New York: Viking.

Freedman, Russell. 1988. *Lincoln: A photobiography.* New York: Clarion.

Freedman, Russell. 1992. *Indian chiefs.* New York: Holiday.

Freedman, Russell. 1993. *Eleanor Roosevelt: A life of discovery.* New York: Clarion.

Freedman, Russell. 2006. *Freedom walkers: The story of the Montgomery bus boycott.* New York: Holiday.

Freymann-Weyr, Garrett. 2003. *My heartbeat.* New York: Puffin.

Fritz, Jean. 1998. *The great little Madison.* New York: Putnam.

Funke, Cornelia. 2004. *Dragon rider.* Anthea Bell, trans. New York: Scholastic.

Furlong, Monica. 1987. *Wise child.* New York: Random House.

Furlong, Monica. 1990. *Juniper.* New York: Random House.

Furlong, Monica. 2004. *Colman.* New York: Random House.

Gallo, Donald R., ed. 1992. *Short circuits: Thirteen shocking stories by outstanding writers for young adults.* New York: Delacorte.

Gallo, Donald R., ed. 1993. *Join in: Multiethnic short stories by outstanding writers for young adults.* New York: Delacorte.

Gallo, Donald R., ed. 1999. *Time capsule: Short stories about teenagers throughout the twentieth century.* New York: Delacorte.

Galloway, Priscilla. 1995. *Truly grim tales.* New York: Delacorte.

Gantos, Jack. 2002. *Hole in my life.* New York: Farrar, Straus and Giroux.

Garden, Nancy. 1982. *Annie on my mind.* New York: Farrar, Straus and Giroux.

Garden, Nancy. 1999. *The year they burned the book.* New York: Farrar, Straus and Giroux.

Garden, Nancy. 2006. *Endgame.* Orlando, FL: Harcourt.

Garland, Sherry. 1994. *I never knew your name.* Illus. Sheldon Greenberg. New York: Ticknor and Fields.

George, Jean Craighead. [1959] 1997. *My side of the mountain.* New York: Puffin.

Geras, Adele. 1990. *The tower room.* San Diego, CA: Harcourt.

Giles, Gail. 2006. *What happened to Cass McBride?* New York: Little, Brown.

Gilmore, Kate. 1999. *The exchange student.* Boston: Houghton Mifflin.

Glenn, Mel. 1982. *Class dismissed!* New York: Clarion.

Glenn, Mel. 1996. *Who killed Mr. Chippendale? A mystery in poems.* New York: Dutton.

Glenn, Mel. 2000. *Split image: A story in poems.* New York: HarperCollins.

Glover, Savion, and Bruce Weber. 2000. *Savion: My life in tap.* New York: Morrow.

Goldberg, Myra. 2001. *Bee season.* New York: Anchor.

Golding, William. [1954] 1999. *Lord of the flies.* New York: Penguin.

Goodall, Jane. 2001. *The chimpanzees I love: Saving their world and ours.* New York: Scholastic.

Gordon, Ruth, ed. 1995. *Pierced by a ray of sun: Poems about the times we feel alone.* New York: HarperCollins.

Gorog, Judith. 1996. *When nobody's home: Fifteen baby-sitting tales of terror.* New York: Scholastic.

Grandits, John. 2007. *Blue lipstick: Concrete poems.* New York: Clarion.

Green, John. 2005. *Looking for Alaska.* New York: Dutton.

Greenberg, Jan, and Sandra Jordan. 2001. *Vincent Van Gogh: Portrait of an artist.* New York: Delacorte.

Greenberg, Jan, and Sandra Jordan. 2004. *Andy Warhol: Prince of pop.* New York: Delacorte.

Greene, Bette. [1973] 2006. *Summer of my German soldier.* New York: Puffin.

Grimes, Nikki. 2003. *Bronx masquerade.* New York: Puffin.

Gruen, Sara. 2006. *Water for elephants.* Chapel Hill, NC: Algonquin.

Guiley, Rosemary Ellen. 2007. *The encyclopedia of ghosts and spirits.* 3rd ed. New York: Facts On File.

Gutman, Bill. 1998. *Tiger Woods: Golf's shining young star.* Millbrook Press.

Haddix, Margaret Peterson. 2005. *Double identity.* New York: Simon and Schuster.

Hamanaka, Sheila. 1999. *Treasures of Japan.* New York: HarperCollins.

Hamilton, Virginia. [1974] 2006. *M. C. Higgins, the great.* New York: Aladdin.

Hamilton, Virginia. 1995. *Her stories: African American folktales, fairy tales, and true tales.* Illus. Leo and Diane Dillon. New York: Scholastic.

Harris, Robie. 1994. *It's perfectly normal: Changing bodies, growing up, sex & sexual health.* Illus. Michael Emberley. Cambridge, MA: Candlewick.

Harrison, Lisi. 2004. *The clique.* New York: Little, Brown.

Harrison, Michael. 1999. *Facing the dark.* New York: Holiday House.

Hartinger, Brent. 2004. *Geography club.* New York: HarperTeen.

Haugen, David M., ed. 2008. *Africa.* New York: Greenwillow.

Hautman. 2004. *Sweetblood.* New York: Simon Pulse.

Heinlein, Robert. [1960] 1991. *Stranger in a strange land.* New York: Ace.

Hentoff, Nat. 1983. *The day they came to arrest the book.* New York: Laurel Leaf.

Herrera, Juan Felipé. 2005. *Downtown boy.* New York: Scholastic.

Hess, Nina. 2007. *A practical guide to monsters.* Renton, WA: Mirrorstone.

High, Linda Oatman. 2006. *Sister Slam and the poetic motormouth road trip.* New York: Bloomsbury.

Higuri, You. 2005. *Cantarella.* Vol. 1. [n.p.]: Go! Media Entertainment.

Hinton, S. E. 1980. *Tex.* New York: Laurel Leaf.

Hinton, S. E. [1967] 1995. *The outsiders.* New York: Puffin.

Hobbs, Will. 1999. *The maze.* New York: HarperTrophy.

Hobbs, Will. 2004a. *The big wander.* New York: Aladdin.

Hobbs, Will. 2004b. *Far north.* New York: HarperTrophy.

Hobbs, Will. 2006. *Crossing the wire.* New York: HarperCollins.

Holland, Isabel. 1987. *The man without a face.* New York: HarperTeen.

Holm, Jennifer L., and Matthew Holm. 2005. *Babymouse: Our hero.* New York: Random House.

Holub, Josef. 2005. *An innocent soldier.* New York: Scholastic.

Hoobler, Dorothy, and Thomas Hoobler. 1999. *The ghost in the Tokaido Inn.* New York: Philomel.

Hoose, Phillip. 2004. *The race to save the Lord God bird.* New York: Farrar, Straus and Giroux.

Horowitz, Anthony. 2004. *Stormbreaker.* New York: Puffin.

Hosler, Jay. 2000. *Clan Apis.* Columbus, OH: Active Synapse.

Houston, Jeanne Wakatsuki, and James D. Houston. 1973. *Farewell to Manzanar.* Boston, MA: Houghton Mifflin.

Hudson, Jan. 1984. *Sweetgrass.* New York: Scholastic.

Hughes, Langston. 2007. *The dream keeper and other poems.* Illus. Brian Pinkney. New York: Knopf.

Hughes, Monica. 1980. *Keeper of the Isis light.* New York: Scholastic.

Hurwin, Davida Wills. 1997. *A time for dancing.* New York: Puffin.

Huxley, Aldous. [1932] 2006. *Brave new world.* New York: HarperPerennial.

Hyman, Trina Schart. 1977. *The sleeping beauty.* New York: Little, Brown.

Janeczko, Paul, ed. 1983. *Poetspeak: In their work, about their work.* New York: Macmillan.

Janeczko, Paul, ed. 1993. *Looking for your name: A collection of contemporary poems.* New York: Orchard.

Janeczko, Paul, ed. 1987. *Going over to your place: Poems for each other.* New York: Bradbury.

Janeczko, Paul. 2004. *Blushing: Expressions of love in poems & letters.* New York: Scholastic.

Jiménez, Francisco. 1997. *Circuit: Stories from the life of a migrant child.* Albuquerque: University of New Mexico Press.

Jiménez, Francisco. 2001. *Breaking through.* Boston: Houghton Mifflin.

Johansen, Bruce E., and Barry M. Pritzker, eds. 2007. *Encyclopedia of American Indian history.* 4 vols. Santa Barbara, CA: ABC-CLIO.

Johnson, Angela. 1994. *Toning the sweep.* New York: Scholastic.

Johnson, Angela. 1998. *The other side: Shorter poems.* New York: Orchard.

Johnson, Angela. 2000. *Heaven.* New York: Simon Pulse.

Johnson, Angela. 2003. *The first part last.* New York: Simon and Schuster.

Johnson, Dave. 2000. *Movin': Teen poets take voice.* New York: Orchard.

Jones, Diana Wynne. 1986. *Howl's moving castle.* New York: Greenwillow.

Jones, Diana Wynne. 2001a. *Castle in the air.* New York: Eos.

Jones, Diana Wynne. 2001b. *Dark lord of Dirkholm.* New York: HarperTeen.

Jones, Diana Wynne. 2001c. *Year of the griffin.* New York: HarperTeen.

Jurmain, Suzanne. 2005. *The true and dramatic story of Prudence Crandall and her students.* Boston: Houghton Mifflin.

Kadohata, Cynthia. 2004. *Kira-Kira.* New York: Atheneum.

Kadohata, Cynthia. 2006. *Weedflower.* New York: Atheneum.

Katz, Jon. 2000. *Geeks: How two lost boys rode the Internet out of Idaho.* New York: Villard.

Keene, Carolyn. 1930. *The secret of the old clock.* New York: Grosset & Dunlap.

Kerr, M. E. 1973. *If I love you, am I trapped forever?* New York: HarperCollins.

Kerr, M. E. 1983. *Me me me me me: Not a novel.* New York: HarperCollins.

Kerr, M. E. 1990. *Gentlehands.* New York: HarperTeen.

Kerr, M. E. 1995. *Deliver us from Evie.* New York: HarperTeen.

Kerr, M. E. 2007a. *Dinky Hocker shoots smack!* New York: HarperTeen.

Kerr, M. E. 2007b. *Someone like Summer.* New York: HarperTeen.

Keyes, Daniel. [1966] 2005. *Flowers for Algernon.* New York: Harvest.

Kibuishi, Kazu, ed. 2005. *Flight.* Vol. 1. New York: Image Comics.

Kidd, R. 2007. *Monkey town.* New York: Simon Pulse.

Klass, David. 2006. *Firestorm: Book one of the Caretaker trilogy.* New York: Farrar, Straus and Giroux.

Klause, Annette Curtis. 1992. *The silver kiss.* New York: Laurel Leaf.

Klause, Annette Curtis. 1997. *Blood and chocolate.* New York: Delacorte.

Krakauer, Jon. 1997. *Into thin air: A personal account of the Mount Everest disaster.* New York: Doubleday.

Lasky, Kathryn. 1994. *Memoirs of a bookbat.* San Diego, CA: Harcourt.

Latham, Jean Lee. [1956] 2003. *Carry on, Mr. Bowditch.* Boston: Houghton Mifflin.

Le Guin, Ursula K. [1969] 1987. *The left hand of darkness.* New York: Ace.

Le Guin, Ursula K. 2001a. *Tehanu.* New York: Simon Pulse.

Le Guin, Ursula K. 2001b. *The tombs of Atuan.* New York: Simon Pulse.

Le Guin, Ursula K. 2004a. *The farthest shore.* New York: Pocket.

Le Guin, Ursula K. 2004b. *Wizard of Earthsea.* New York: Spectra.

Le Guin, Ursula K. 2006a. *Gifts.* Orlando, FL: Harcourt.

Le Guin, Ursula K. 2006b. *Voices.* Orlando, FL: Harcourt.

Le Guin, Ursula K. 2007. *Powers.* Orlando, FL: Harcourt.

Lee, Harper. [1960] 2002. *To kill a mockingbird.* New York: Harper Perennial.

Lester, Julius. 1995. *Othello.* New York: Scholastic.

Lewis, C. S. [1938] 2003. *Out of the silent planet.* New York: Scribner.

Lewis, C. S. 2005. *The lion, the witch and the wardrobe.* New York: HarperCollins.

L'Engle, Madeleine. [1962] 2007. *A wrinkle in time.* New York: Square Fish.

Lipsyte, Robert. [1967] 1987. *The contender.* New York: HarperTeen.

Lipsyte, Robert. 1991. *The brave.* New York: HarperCollins.

Lipsyte, Robert. 1993. *The chief.* New York: HarperCollins.

Lipsyte, Robert. 2003. *Warrior angel.* New York: HarperCollins.

Lobel, Anita. 1998. *No pretty pictures: A child of war.* New York: Greenwillow.

Lockhart, E. 2006. *Fly on the wall.* New York: Delacorte.

Lorbiecki, Marybeth. 1996. *Just one flick of a finger.* Illus. David Diaz. New York: Dial.

Lowry, Lois. 1993. *The giver.* Boston: Houghton Mifflin.

Lowry, Lois. 2000. *Looking back: A book of memories.* New York: Delacorte.

Lutz, Lisa. 2007. *The Spellman files.* New York: Simon and Schuster.

Lyga, Barry. 2006. *The astonishing adventures of fanboy and goth girl.* Boston: Houghton Mifflin.

Lyga, Barry. 2007. *Boy toy.* Boston: Houghton Mifflin.

Lynch, Chris. 1996. *Slot machine.* New York: HarperTeen.

Lynch, Chris. 2007. *Inexcusable.* New York: Simon Pulse.

Macaulay, David. 1973. *Cathedral: The story of its construction.* Boston: Houghton Mifflin.

Macaulay, David. 1976. *Underground.* Boston: Houghton Mifflin.

Macaulay, David. 1977. *Castle.* Boston: Houghton Mifflin.

Macaulay, David. 1982. *Pyramid.* Boston: Houghton Mifflin.

Macaulay, David. 1983. *City: A story of Roman planning and construction.* Boston: Houghton Mifflin.

Macaulay, David. 1989. *Mill.* Boston: Houghton Mifflin.

Macaulay, David. 1995. *Ship.* Boston: Houghton Mifflin.

MacGregor, Rob. 1995. *Prophecy rock.* New York: Simon & Schuster.

Mackler, Carolyn. 2000. *Love and other four-letter words.* New York: Laurel Leaf.

Mackler, Carolyn. 2003. *The earth, my butt, and other big round things.* Cambridge, MA: Candlewick.

Mackler, Carolyn. 2006. *Vegan virgin valentine.* Cambridge, MA: Candlewick.

Marcus, Leonard S., ed. 2000. *Authortalk: Conversations with Judy Blume, Bruce Brooks, Karen Cushman, Russell Freedman, Lee Bennett Hopkins, James Howe, Johanna Hurwitz, E. L. Konigsburg, Lois Lowry, Ann M. Martin, Nicholasa Mohr, Gary Paulsen, Jon Scieszka, Seymour Simon and Laurence Yep.* New York: Simon and Schuster.

Mason, Jeff, ed. 2002. *9–11 emergency relief.* Gainsville, FL: Alternative Comics.

Mazer, Harry, ed. 1997. *Twelve shots: Outstanding stories about guns.* New York: Delacorte.

McCaffrey, Anne. 1961. *The ship who sang.* New York: Del Rey.

McCaffrey, Anne. 1999a. *Dragonflight.* Minneapolis, MN: Tandem.

McCaffrey, Anne. 1999b. *Dragonquest.* Minneapolis, MN: Tandem.

McCaffrey, Anne. 1999c. *White dragon.* Minneapolis, MN: Tandem.

McCaffrey, Anne. 2003a. *Dragondrums.* New York: Aladdin.

McCaffrey, Anne. 2003b. *Dragonsinger.* New York: Aladdin.

McCaffrey, Anne. 2003c. *Dragonsong.* New York: Aladdin.

McCaughrean, Geraldine. 2006. *Cyrano.* Orlando, FL: Harcourt.

McCaughrean, Geraldine. 2007. *The white darkness.* New York: HarperCollins.

McCormick, Patricia. 2006. *Sold.* New York: Hyperion.

McCullough, Frances, ed. 1984. *Love is like the lion's tooth: An anthology of love poems.* New York: HarperCollins.

McDonald, Janet. 2001. *Spellbound.* New York: Farrar Straus Giroux.

McKinley, Robin. [1978] 2005. *Beauty: A retelling of beauty and the beast.* New York: Eos.

McKinley, Robin. 1982. *The blue sword.* New York: Greenwillow.

McKinley, Robin. 1998. *Rose daughter.* New York: Ace.

McKinley, Robin. 2002. *Spindle's end.* New York: Puffin.

McKissack, Patricia C., and Frederick L. 2003. *Days of jubilee: The end of slavery in the United States.* New York: Scholastic.

McWhorter, Diane. 2004. *A dream of freedom: The civil rights movement from 1954 to 1968.* New York: Scholastic.

Medley, Linda. 2006. *Castle waiting.* Seattle, WA: Fantagraphics Books.

Meigs, Cornelia. 1934. *Invincible Louisa: The story of the author of "Little Women."* New York: Little, Brown.

Meltzer, Milton. 1976. *Never to forget: The Jews of the Holocaust.* New York: HarperCollins.

Meltzer, Milton. 1997. *Langston Hughes.* Brookfield, CT: Millbrook.

Meyer, Carolyn. 1992. *Where the broken heart still beats: The story of Cynthia Ann Parker.* New York: Harcourt.

Meyer, Carolyn. 1993. *White lilacs.* San Diego, CA: Harcourt.

Meyer, Carolyn. 1994. *Rio Grande stories.* San Diego, CA: Harcourt.

Meyer, Carolyn. 1995. *Drummers of Jericho.* New York: Gulliver.

Meyer, Carolyn. 2006. *Loving Will Shakespeare.* Orlando, FL: Harcourt.

Meyer, Stephenie. 2005. *Twilight.* New York: Little, Brown.

Meyer, Stephenie. 2006. *New moon.* New York: Little, Brown.

Meyer, Stephenie. 2007. *Eclipse.* New York: Little, Brown.

Meyer, Stephanie. 2008. "10 second interview: A few words with Stephanie Meyer." Amazon.com. http://amazon.com/Twilight-Saga-Book-1/dp/0316015849/ref=pd_bbs_sr_1?ie=UTF8&s=book&qid=12144228908sr=1-1.

Middleton, John, and Joseph C. Miller, eds. 2007. *Encyclopedia of Africa.* Farmington Hills, MI: Gale.

Montgomery, L. M. [1908] 2004. *Anne of Green Gables.* New York: Sterling.

Montgomery, Sy. 2004. *The tarantula scientist.* Photos by Nic Bishop. Boston: Houghton Mifflin.

Montgomery, Sy. 2006. *Quest for the tree kangaroo: An expedition to the cloud forest of New Guinea.* Photos by Nic Bishop. Boston: Houghton Mifflin.

Mora, Pat. 2000. *My own true name: New and selected poems for young adults.* Houston, TX: Arte Publico.

Moriarty, Jaclyn. 2004. *The year of secret assignments.* New York: Scholastic.

Morrison, Lillian. 1965. *Sprints & distances: Sports in poetry and the poetry in sport.* New York: Thomas Y. Crowell.

Morrison, Lillian. 1995. *Slam dunk.* New York: Hyperion.

Morrison, Toni. 1993. *The bluest eye.* New York: Knopf.

Morrison, Toni. 2004. *Beloved.* New York: Vintage.

Moses, Sheila. 2004. *The legend of Buddy Bush.* New York: Simon & Schuster.

Mourlevat, Jean-Claude. 2006. *The pull of the ocean.* New York: Delacorte.

Murdock, Catherine Gilbert. 2006. *Dairy queen.* Boston: Houghton Mifflin.

Murphy, Jim. 2003. *An American plague: The true and terrifying story of the yellow fever epidemic of 1793.* New York: Clarion.

Myers, Walter Dean. 1983. *Hoops.* New York: Laurel Leaf.

Myers, Walter Dean. 1987. *Motown and Didi.* New York: Laurel Leaf.

Myers, Walter Dean. 1995. *Scorpions.* New York: Amistad.

Myers, Walter Dean. 1988. *Fallen angels.* New York: Scholastic.

Myers, Walter Dean. 1999. *Monster.* New York: HarperCollins.

Myers, Walter Dean. 2000. *145th street: Short stories.* New York: Delacorte.

Myers, Walter Dean. 2001a. *Bad boy: A memoir.* New York: HarperCollins.

Myers, Walter Dean. 2001b. *The greatest: Muhammed Ali.* New York: Scholastic.

Myers, Walter Dean. 2002. *Patrol: An American soldier in Vietnam.* Illus. Ann Grifalconi. New York: HarperCollins.

Myers, Walter Dean. 2004a. *Here in Harlem: Poems in many voices.* New York: Holiday.

Myers, Walter Dean. 2004b. *Shooter.* New York: Amistad.

Myers, Walter Dean. 2005. *Autobiography of my dead brother.* New York: Harper-Tempest.

Myers, Walter Dean. 2007. *What they found: Love on 145th street.* New York: Random House.

Myers, Walter Dean. 2008. *Sunrise over Fallujah.* New York: Scholastic.

Na, An. 2001. *A step from heaven.* Asheville, NC: Front Street.

Namioka, Lensey. 1994. *April and the dragon lady.* San Diego, CA: Harcourt.

Namioka, Lensey. 1999. *Ties that bind, ties that break.* New York: Delacorte.

Napoli, Donna Jo. 1996. *Zel.* New York: Dutton.

Napoli, Donna Jo. 2000. *Beast.* New York: Atheneum.

Neimark, Anne E. 1998. *Myth maker: J. R. R. Tolkien.* Illus. Brad Weinman. New York: Beech Tree.

Nelson, Marilyn. 2001. *Carver: A life in poems.* Asheville, SC: Front Street.

Nemeth, Sally. 2006. *The heights, the depths, and everything in between.* New York: Knopf.

Newman, Leslea. 2005. *Jailbait.* New York: Delacorte.

Nix, Garth. 1996. *Sabriel.* New York: HarperCollins.

Nix, Garth. 1997. *Shade's children.* New York: HarperCollins.

Nix, Garth. 2001. *Lirael.* New York: HarperCollins.

Nix, Garth. 2003. *Abhorsen.* New York: HarperCollins.

Nixon, Joan Lowry. 1991. *Whispers from the dead.* New York: Laurel Leaf.

Nixon, Joan Lowry. 1998. *The gaunting.* New York: Delacorte.

Nixon, Joan Lowry. 1999. *Who are you?* New York: Delacorte.

Nixon, Joan Lowry. 2004. *The kidnapping of Christina Lattimore.* Orlando, FL: Harcourt.

Nolan, Han. 2006. *Summer of kings.* Orlando, FL: Harcourt.

Nye, Jody Lynn, and Anne McCaffrey. 1997. *The dragonlover's guide to Pern.* 2nd ed. Illus. Todd Cameron Hamilton, maps and illustrations by James Clouse. New York: Del Rey.

Nye, Naomi Shihab. 1997. *Habibi.* New York: Simon & Schuster.

Nye, Naomi Shihab. 2002. *19 varieties of gazelle.* New York: Greenwillow.

O'Dell, Scott. [1961] 1971. *Island of the blue dolphins.* New York: Yearling.

Oppel, Kenneth. 2004. *Airborn.* New York: HarperCollins.

Osa, Nancy. 2003. *Cuba 15.* New York: Delacorte.

Paint Me Like I Am: Teen Poems from Writerscorps. 2003. New York: HarperTempest.

Paolini, Christopher. 2003. *Eragon.* New York: Knopf.

Paolini, Christopher. 2005. *Eldest.* New York: Knopf.

Paterson, Katherine. 1980. *Jacob have I loved.* New York: Harper Teen.

Paterson, Katherine. 1991. *Lyddie.* New York: Lodestar.

Patterson, Lillie. 1969. *Martin Luther King, Jr.: Man of peace.* Illus. Victor Mays. Champaign, IL: Garrard.

Paulsen, Gary. 1991. *The river.* New York: Yearling.

Paulsen, Gary. 1994. *Father water, mother woods: Essays on fishing and hunting in the north woods.* New York: Delacorte.

Paulsen, Gary. 1996. *Brian's winter.* New York: Laurel Leaf.

Paulsen, Gary. 1997. *Sarny: A life remembered.* New York: Delacorte.

Paulsen, Gary. 1998. *My life in dog years.* New York: Delacorte.

Paulsen, Gary. 1999. *Brian's return.* New York: Delacorte.

Paulsen, Gary. 2000. *The beet fields.* New York: Delacorte.

Paulsen, Gary. 2007. *Harris and me.* Orlando, FL: Harcourt.

Paulsen, Gary. 2006. *Hatchet.* New York: Aladdin.

Peck, Richard. 1986. *Remembering the good times.* New York: Laurel Leaf.

Peck, Richard. 1991. *Anonymously yours: A memoir.* New York: Messner.

Peck, Richard. 1995a. *The last safe place on earth.* New York: Delacorte.

Peck, Richard. 1995b. *Lost in cyberspace.* New York: Dial.

Peck, Richard. 1998. *A long way from Chicago.* New York: Dial.

Peck, Richard. 2000. *A year down yonder.* New York: Dial.

Peck, Richard. 2004. *The teacher's funeral.* New York: Dial.

Peck, Richard. 2006. *Here lies the librarian.* New York: Dial.

Peck, Richard. 2007. *Wings of heroes.* New York: Dial.

Pennebaker, Ruth. 1997. *Don't think twice.* New York: Holt.

Peters, Julie Anne. 2006. *Luna.* New York: Little, Brown.

Pettit, Jayne. 1996. *Maya Angelou: Journey of the heart.* New York: Lodestar/Dutton.

Pfeffer, Susan Beth. 2006. *Life as we knew it.* Orlando, FL: Harcourt.

Philbrick, Rodman. 2001. *Freak the mighty.* New York: Scholastic.

Philbrick, Rodman. 2002. *The last book in the universe.* New York: Scholastic.

Pierce, Tamora, and Josepha Sherman, eds. 2005. *Young warriors: Stories of strength.* New York: Random House.

Pike, Christopher. 2004. *Alosha.* New York: Tom Doherty.

Pines, T., ed. 1991. *Thirteen: 13 tales of horror by 13 masters of horror.* New York: Scholastic.

Pinkney, Andrea Davis. 2000. *Let it shine: Stories of black women freedom fighters.* Illus. Stephen Alcorn. San Diego, CA: Gulliver/Harcourt.

Plain, Nancy. 1994. *Mary Cassatt: An artist's life.* New York: Dillon.

Plummer, Louise. 1995. *The unlikely romance of Kate Bjorkman.* New York: Delacorte.

Plum-Ucci, Carol. 2000. *The body of Christopher Creed.* San Diego, CA: Harcourt.

Polacco, Patricia. 1994. *Pink and say.* New York: Philomel.

Pollard, Michael. 2001. *Johann Gutenberg: Master of modern printing.* New York: Blackbirch.

Potok, Chaim. [1967] 1987. *The chosen.* New York: Fawcett.

Pratchett, Terry. 2003. *The amazing Maurice and his educated rodents.* New York: HarperTeen.

Pratchett, Terry. 2004. *Wee free men.* New York: HarperTeen.

Pratchett, Terry. 2005. *A hat full of sky.* New York: Harper Trophy.

Pratchett, Terry. 2006. *Wintersmith.* New York: HarperCollins.

Pressler, Mirjam. 2001. *Anne Frank: A hidden life.* New York: Puffin.

Pullman, Philip. 1985. *The ruby in the smoke.* New York: Knopf.

Pullman, Philip. 1989. *The shadow in the north.* New York: Laurel Leaf.

Pullman, Philip. 1992. *The tiger in the well.* New York: Laurel Leaf.

Pullman, Philip. 1995. *The golden compass.* New York: Knopf.

Pullman, Philip. 1997. *The subtle knife.* New York: Knopf.

Pullman, Philip. 2000. *The amber spyglass.* New York: Knopf.

Pyle, Howard. 1883. *The merry adventures of Robin Hood.*

Rabb, Margo. 2007. *Cures for heartbreak.* New York: Delacorte.

Rees, Douglas. 2003. *Vampire High.* New York: Laurel Leaf.

Reinagle, Damon J. 1995. *Draw medieval fantasies: A step by step guide.* Cincinnati, OH: F&W Publications.

Reinhardt, Dana. 2007. *A brief chapter in my impossible life.* New York: Wendy Lamb.

Rennison, Louise. 1999. *Angus, thongs and full-frontal snogging.* New York: HarperCollins.

Rennison, Louise. 2002. *On the bright side, I'm now the girlfriend of a sex god.* New York: HarperTeen.

Rennison, Louise. 2003. *Knocked out by my nunga-nungas.* New York: HarperTeen.

Rennison, Louise. 2005. *Away laughing on a fast camel.* New York: HarperTeen.

Rice, Anne. 1993a. *Interview with the vampire.* New York: Ballantine.

Rice, Anne. 1993b. *The vampire Lestat.* New York: Ballantine.

Riekehof, Lottie L. 1987. *The joy of signing: The illustrated guide for mastering sign language and the manual alphabet.* Springfield, MO: Gospel Publishing House.

Riley, Sam G. 2007. *African Americans in the media today: An encyclopedia.* 2 vols. Westport, CT: Greenwood.

Rinaldi, Anne. 1992. *A break with Charity: A story about the Salem witch trials.* San Diego, CA: Harcourt.

Rinaldi, Anne. 1993. *Wolf by the ears.* New York: Scholastic.

Ritter, John. 2000. *Choosing up sides.* New York: Putnam.

Rodriguez, Deborah. 2007. *Kabul beauty school: An American woman goes behind the veil.* New York: Random House.

Rosenberg, Liz, ed. 1998. *Earth-shattering poems.* New York: Holt.

Rosenberg, Liz, ed. 2000. *Light-gathering poems.* New York: Holt

Rowling, J. K. 1997. *Harry Potter and the sorcerer's stone.* New York: Levine/ Scholastic.

Rowling, J. K. 1999a. *Harry Potter and the chamber of secrets.* New York: Levine/ Scholastic.

Rowling, J. K. 1999b. *Harry Potter and the prisoner of Azkaban.* New York: Levine/ Scholastic.

Rowling, J. K. 2000. *Harry Potter and the goblet of fire.* New York: Levine/Scholastic.

Rowling, J. K. 2003. *Harry Potter and the order of the phoenix.* New York: Levine/ Scholastic.

Rowing, J. K. 2005. *Harry Potter and the half-blood prince.* New York: Levine/ Scholastic.

Rowling, J. K. 2007. *Harry Potter and the deathly hallows.* New York: Levine/ Scholastic.

Ryan, Pam Muñoz. 2000. *Esperanza rising.* New York: Scholastic.

Ryan, Pam Muñoz. 2004. *Becoming Naomi León.* New York: Scholastic.

Ryan, Sara. 2003. *Empress of the world.* New York: Puffin.

Sachar, Louis. 2003. *Holes.* New York: Yearling.

Salinger, J. D. [1951] 2001. *The catcher in the rye.* Boston: Back Bay.

Salisbury, Graham. 1994. *Under the blood-red sun.* New York: Delacorte.

Salisbury, Graham. 2005. *Eyes of the emperor.* New York: Random House.

Salisbury, Graham. 2006. *House of the red fish.* New York: Random House.

Sanchez, Alex. 2003. *Rainbow boys.* New York: Simon Pulse.

Sanchez, Alex. 2006. *So hard to say.* New York: Simon Pulse.

Satrapi, Marjane. 2003. *Persepolis: The story of a childhood.* New York: Pantheon.

Schlosser, Eric, and Charles Wilson. 2006. *Chew on this: Everything you don't want to know about fast food.* Boston: Houghton Mifflin.

Schmidt, Gary. 2004. *Lizzie Bright and the Buckminster boy.* Boston: Houghton Mifflin.

Schmidt, Gary. 2007. *The Wednesday wars.* Boston: Houghton Mifflin.

Schreiber, Ellen. 2005. *Vampire kisses.* New York: HarperTeen.

Scieszka, Jon. 1996. *The true story of the 3 little pigs by A. Wolf.* Illus. Lane Smith. New York: Puffin.

Scieszka, John, ed. 2005. *Guys write for guys read.* New York: Viking.

Scieszka, Jon, and Lane Smith. 1992. *The stinky cheese man and other fairly stupid tales.* New York: Viking.

Scieszka, Jon, and Lane Smith. 1995. *Math curse.* New York: Viking.

Scott, Michael. 2007. *The alchemyst: The secrets of the immortal Nicholas Flamel.* New York: Delacorte.

Selznick, Brian. 2007. *The invention of Hugo Cabret.* New York: Scholastic.

Shakespeare, William. 2007. *Romeo and Juliet.* Illus. Sonia Leong. New York: Amulet.

Shan, Darren. 2000. *Cirque du freak: A living nightmare.* New York: Little, Brown.

Sheldon, Dyan. 2005. *Confessions of a teenage drama queen.* New York: Candlewick.

Shelley, Mary. 1818. *Frankenstein.*

Shuker, Nancy. 2001. *Maya Angelou: America's poetic voice.* New York: Blackbirch.

Shusterman, Neal. 2006. *The Schwa was here.* New York: Puffin.

Siegel, Siena Cherson. 2006. *To dance: A ballerina's graphic novel.* Illus. Mark Siegel. New York: Simon and Schuster.

Singer, Marilyn, ed. 2004. *Face relations: 11 Stories about seeing beyond color.* New York: Simon and Schuster.

Sis, Peter. 1998. *Tibet: Through the red box.* New York: Farrar, Straus, Giroux.

Sis, Peter. 2007. *The wall: Growing up behind the iron curtain.* New York: Farrar, Straus, Giroux.

Skelton, Matthew. 2006. *Endymion spring.* New York: Delacorte.

Sleator, William. [1974] 1991. *House of stairs.* New York: Puffin.

Sleator, William. 1995a. *Interstellar pig.* New York: Puffin.

Sleator, William. 1995b. *Singularity.* New York: Puffin.

Sleator, William. 1999. *The duplicate.* New York: Puffin.

Sleator, William. 1995. *Oddballs.* New York: Puffin.

Sleator, William. 1996. *The night the heads came.* New York: Dutton.

Sleator, William. 1998. *The boy who reversed himself.* New York: Puffin.

Sleator, William. 1999. *The beasties.* New York: Puffin.

Sleator, William. 2000. *The boxes.* New York: Puffin.

Sleator, William. 2002. *Marco's millions.* New York: Puffin.

Sleator, William. 2004. *Parasite pig.* New York: Puffin.

Sleator, William. 2005. *The boy who couldn't die.* New York: Abrams.

Sleator, William. 2005. *Green futures of Tycho.* New York: Starscape.

Smith, Cynthia Leitich. 2001. *Rain is not my Indian name.* New York: HarperCollins.

Smith, Jeff. 1993. *Bone.* Los Gatos, CA: Cartoon Books.

Smith, Roland. 2007. *Peak.* Orlando, FL: Harcourt.

Smith, Roland. 2007. *Elephant run.* New York: Hyperion.

Sones, Sonya. 1999. *Stop pretending.* New York: HarperCollins.

Sones, Sonya. 2000. *What my mother doesn't know.* New York: Simon and Schuster.

Sonnenblick, Jordan. 2006. *Notes from the midnight driver.* New York: Scholastic.

Soto, Gary. 1990. *Baseball in April and other stories.* San Diego, CA: Harcourt.

Soto, Gary. [1990] 2006. *A fire in my hands.* New York: Scholastic.

Soto, Gary. 1993. *Local news.* San Diego, CA: Harcourt.

Soto, Gary. 1998. *Petty crimes.* San Diego, CA: Harcourt.

Soto, Gary. 2003a. *The afterlife.* Orlando, FL: Harcourt.

Soto, Gary. 2003b. *Pacific crossing.* Orlando, FL: Harcourt.

Soto, Gary. 2004. *Chato and the party animals.* New York: Puffin.

Soto, Gary. 2005a. *Help wanted.* Orlando, FL: Harcourt.

Soto, Gary. 2005b. *Neighborhood odes.* Orlando, FL: Harcourt.

Soto, Gary. 2006a. *Accidental love.* Orlando, FL: Harcourt.

Soto, Gary. 2006b. *Jesse.* Orlando, FL: Harcourt.

Spiegelman, Art. [1973] 1986. *Maus I: A survivor's tale; My father bleeds history.* New York: Random House.

Spiegelman, Art. 1992. *Maus II: A survivor's tale; And here my troubles began.* New York: Pantheon.

Spiegelman, Art. 2003. *In the shadow of no towers.* Orlando, FL: Harcourt.

Spinelli, Jerry. [1982] 2000. *Space station seventh grade.* New York: Little, Brown.

Spinelli, Jerry. [1984] 2000. *Who put that hair in my toothbrush?* New York: Little Brown.

Spinelli, Jerry. [1986] 2000. *Jason and Marceline.* New York: Little, Brown.

Spinelli, Jerry. 1998. *Knots in my yo-yo string: The autobiography of a kid.* New York: Knopf.

Spinelli, Jerry. 1999. *Maniac Magee.* New York: Little, Brown.

Spinelli, Jerry. 2000. *Stargirl.* New York: Knopf.

Spinelli, Jerry. 2003. *Milkweed.* New York: Knopf.

Spinelli, Jerry. 2007. *Love, Stargirl.* New York: Knopf.

Stanley, Diane. 2002. *Saladin: Noble prince of Islam.* New York: HarperCollins.

Staples, Suzanne Fisher. 1989. *Shabanu: Daughter-of-the-wind.* New York: Knopf.

Steinbeck, John. [1965] 2002. *Of mice and men.* New York: Penguin.

Stephens, Anne. 1860. *Malaeksa: Indian wife of a white hunter.*

Stevenson, Robert Louis. 1883. *Treasure Island.*

Stevenson, Robert Louis. 1886. *Kidnapped.*

Stewart, Sean, and Jordan Weisan. 2006. *Cathy's book: If found call 650-266-8233.* Philadelphia, PA: Running Press.

Stewart, Whitney. 1996. *The 14th Dalai Lama: Spiritual leader of Tibet.* Minneapolis. Lerner.

Stoker, Bram. 1897. *Dracula.*

Stone, Tanya Lee. 2006. *Bad boys can be good for a girl.* New York: Random House.

Strasser, Todd. 2002. *Give a boy a gun.* New York: Simon Pulse.

Strasser, Todd. 2005. *Can't get there from here.* New York: Simon Pulse.

Stratemeyer. 1898. *Under Dewey at Manila; or, The war fortunes of a castaway.*

Swanson, Julie A. 2004. *Going for the record.* New York: Eerdmans.

Swift, Jonathan. 1726. *Gulliver's travels.*

Takaya, Natsuki. 2004. *Fruits basket.* Vol. 1. Los Angeles: Tokyopop.

Talbot, Brian. 1995. *The tale of one bad rat.* Milwaukie, OR: Dark Horse.

Tan, Shaun. 2006. *The arrival.* New York: Scholastic.

Taylor, Mildred. [1976] 2004. *Roll of thunder, hear my cry.* New York: Puffin, 2004.

Taylor, Mildred. 1991. *Let the circle be unbroken.* New York: Puffin.

Taylor, Mildred. 1992. *The road to Memphis.* New York: Puffin.

Taylor, Mildred. 2001. *The land.* New York: Dial.

Taylor, Sydney. [1951] 1989. *All-of-a-kind family.* New York: Banton Doubleday Dell.

Taylor, Theodore. [1969] 2003. The cay. New York: Laurel Leaf.

Temple, Frances. 1995. *The Ramsay scallop.* New York: HarperTrophy.

Tharp, Jim. 2006. *Knights of the hill country.* New York: Knopf.

Thimmesh, Catherine. 2006. *Team moon: How 400,000 people landed Apollo 11 on the moon.* Boston: Houghton Mifflin.

Todd, Mark, and Esther Pearl Watson. 2006. *Whatcha mean, what's a zine? The art of making zines and mini-comics.* Boston: Houghton Mifflin.

Tolkien, J. R. R. [1937] 2007. *The Hobbit, or there and back again.* Boston: Houghton Mifflin.

Tolkien, J. R. R. [1954] 2002. *The fellowship of the ring: Being the first part of The Lord of the Rings.* Boston: Houghton Mifflin.

Tolkien, J. R. R. [1954] 2002. *The two towers: Being the second part of The Lord of the Rings.* Boston: Houghton Mifflin.

Tolkien, J. R. R. [1955] 2002. *The return of the king: Being the third part of The Lord of the Rings.* Boston: Houghton Mifflin.

Townsend, Sue. 2003. *The secret diary of Adrian Mole, aged 13¾.* New York: HarperTrophy.

Tunis, John R. 1942. *All-American.* New York: Harcourt Brace.

Turner, Ann. 1991. *Rosemary's witch.* New York: HarperCollins.

Twain, Mark. 1876. *The adventures of Tom Sawyer.*

Twain, Mark. 1884. *The adventures of Huckleberry Finn.*

Van Allsburg, Chris. 1984. *The mysteries of Harris Burdick.* Boston: Houghton Mifflin.

Van Loon, Hendrik Willem. [1921] 1967. *The story of mankind.* New York: Liveright.

Vaughan, Brian K. 2006. *Pride of Baghdad.* Illus. Niko Henrichon. New York: DC Comics.

Velde, Vivian Vande. 1995. *Companions of the night.* Orlando, FL: Harcourt/Magic Carpet Books.

Velde, Vivian Vande. 1997. *Curses, Inc. and other stories.* San Diego, CA: Harcourt.

Velde, Vivian Vande. 2001. *Being dead.* San Diego, CA: Harcourt.

Velde, Vivian Vande. 2005. *Witch dreams.* Tarrytown, NY: Marshall Cavendish.

Verne, Jules. 1870. *Twenty thousand leagues under the sea.*

Verne, Jules. 1874. *Journey to the center of the earth.*

Voigt, Cynthia. 1994. *When she hollers.* New York: Scholastic.

Volponi, Paul. 2006. *Rooftop.* New York: Viking.

Vreeland, Susan. 2002. *The passion of Artemisia.* New York: Penguin.

Walker, Kate. 2001. *Peter.* Boston: Houghton Mifflin.

Warner, Susan. 1840. *Wide, wide world.*

Warren, Andrea. 2001. *Surviving Hitler: A boy in the Nazi death camps.* New York: HarperCollins.

Watson, Esther Pearl, and Mark Todd, eds. 2000. *The pain tree and other teenage angst-ridden poetry.* Boston: Houghton Mifflin.

Wayland, April Halprin. 2002. *Girl coming in for a landing: A novel in poems.* Illus. Elaine Clayton. New York: Knopf.

Weeks, Sarah. 2005. *So B. it: A novel.* New York: HarperCollins.

Weis, Margaret. 2003. *Mistress of dragons.* New York: Tom Doherty.

Weis, Margaret. 2004. *The dragon's son.* New York: Tom Doherty.

Weis, Margaret. 2005. *Master of dragons.* New York: Tom Doherty.

Wells, H. G. 1895. *The time machine.*

Wells, H. G. 1898. *War of the worlds.*

Werlin, Nancy. 2000. *The killer's cousin.* New York: Laurel Leaf.

Werlin, Nancy. 2004. *Double helix.* New York: Dial.

Westerfield, Scott. 2006. *Peeps.* New York: Razorbill.

Whelan, Gloria. 2000. *Homeless bird.* New York: HarperCollins.

Wiesel, Elie. 2006. *Night.* Rev. ed. New York: Hill and Wang/Farrar Straus and Giroux.

Wild, Margaret. 2007. *Woolvs in the sitee.* Illus. Anne Spudvilas. Asheville, NC: Front Street.

Willard, Nancy. 1982. *A visit to William Blake's Inn: Poems for the innocent and experienced travelers.* New York: Voyager.

Willard, Nancy, ed. 1998. *Step lightly: Poems for the journey.* San Diego, CA: Harcourt.

Williams-Garcia, Rita. 1988. *Blue tights.* New York: Puffin.

Williams-Garcia, Rita. 1995. *Like sisters on the homefront.* New York: Dutton.

Williams-Garcia, Rita. 1998. *Fast talk on a slow track.* New York: Puffin.

Williams-Garcia, Rita. 2001. *Every time a rainbow dies.* New York: HarperCollins.

Williams-Garcia, Rita. 2004. *No laughter here.* New York: HarperCollins.

Windsor, Patricia. 1993. *The Christmas killer.* New York: Scholastic, Inc.

Winick, Judd. 2000. *Pedro and me: Friendship, loss, and what I learned.* New York: Holt.

Wittlinger, Ellen. 2001. *Hard love.* New York: Simon Pulse.

Wittlinger, Ellen. 2007a. *Parrotfish.* New York: Simon and Schuster.

Wittlinger, Ellen. 2007b. *Sandpiper.* New York: Simon Pulse.

Wolff, Euwer Virginia. 1993. *Make lemonade.* New York: Holt.

Woods, Brenda. 2004. *Emako Blue.* New York: Putnam.

Woodson, Jacqueline. 1995. *From the notebooks of Melanin Sun.* New York: Scholastic.

Woodson, Jacqueline. 1998. *If you come softly.* New York: Penguin.

Woodson, Jacqueline. 2002. *Our Gracie aunt.* Illus. Jon J. Muth. New York: Hyperion.

Woodson, Jacqueline. 2002. *Hush.* New York: Penguin.

Woodson, Jacqueline. 2006a. *I hadn't meant to tell you this.* New York: Puffin.

Woodson, Jacqueline. 2006b. *Lena.* New York: Puffin.

Woodson, Jacqueline. 2006c. *Miracle's boys.* New York: Puffin.

Wrede, Patricia. 1996. *Book of enchantments.* San Diego, CA: Harcourt.

Wrede, Patricia. 2003a. *Calling on dragons.* Orlando, FL: Harcourt/Magic Carpet Books.

Wrede, Patricia. 2003b. *Dealing with dragons.* Orlando, FL: Harcourt/Magic Carpet Books.

Wrede, Patricia. 2003c. *Searching for dragons.* Orlando, FL: Harcourt/Magic Carpet Books.

Wrede, Patricia. 2003d. *Talking to dragons.* Orlando, FL: Harcourt/Magic Carpet Books.

Wright, Richard. [1940] 2005. *Native son.* New York: HarperPerennial.

Wyss, Johann. 1812. *Swiss family Robinson.*

Yang, Gene Luen. 2006. *American born Chinese.* New York: First Second.

Yates, Elizabeth. [1951] 1989. *Amos Fortune, free man.* New York: Puffin.

Yep, Laurence. [1975] 2002. *Dragonwings: Golden mountain chronicles: 1903.* New York: HarperTrophy.

Yolen, Jane. [1982] 2005. *Dragon's blood.* New York: Magic Carpet.

Yolen, Jane. [1984] 2005. *Heart's blood.* New York: Magic Carpet.

Yolen, Jane. [1987] 2005. *A sending of dragons.* New York: Magic Carpet.

Yolen, Jane. 1994. *Here there be unicorns.* Illus. David Wilgus. San Diego, CA: Harcourt.

Yolen, Jane. 1995. *Here there be witches.* Illus. David Wilgus. San Diego, CA: Harcourt.

Yolen, Jane. 2002. *Briar Rose.* New York: Tor Teen.

Yolen, Jane, and Martin H. Greenberg. 1991. *Vampires: A collection of original stories.* San Diego, CA: Harcourt.

Yonge, Charlotte. 1856. *The daisy chain.*

Young, Ed. 1997. *Voices of the heart.* New York: Scholastic.

Zeises, Lara M. 2005. *Contents under pressure.* New York: Laurel Leaf.

Ziegesar, Cecily von. 2000. *Slam.* New York: Alloy.

Zindel, Paul. [1968] 2005. *The pigman.* New York: HarperTeen.

Zindel, Paul. [1969] 2005. *My darling, my hamburger.* New York: HarperTeen.

Zindel, Paul. [1971] 2005. *The effects of gamma rays on man-in-the-moon marigolds.* New York: HarperTeen.

Zindel, Paul. [1976] 1993. *Pardon me, you're stepping on my eyeball!* New York: Starfire.

Zindel, Paul. [1984] 2005. *The pigman's legacy.* New York: HarperTeen.

Zindel, Paul. 1993. *The pigman and me.* New York: Starfire.

Zindel, Paul. 1994. *Loch.* New York: HarperCollins.

Zindel, Paul. 1996. *Doom stone.* New York: Hyperion.

Zindel, Paul. 1999. *Raptor.* New York: Hyperion.

Zindel, Paul. 2000. *Rats.* New York: Hyperion.

Zindel, Paul. 2000. *Gadget.* New York: HarperCollins.

Zusak, Markus. 2006. *The book thief.* New York: Alfred A. Knopf.

Index

About the Author

ROSEMARY CHANCE teaches children's and young adult literature at Sam Houston State University in the Department of Library Science. She has been a public school teacher, a school library media specialist, and a coordinator of media services. She holds a BA in English from Texas A&M at Kingsville, an MLS from Sam Houston State University, and an MLIS and a PhD in library science from Texas Woman's University. It has been her privilege to serve on the 2005 John Newbery Award Committee, the 2001 Michael L. Printz Award Committee, and as chair of the 2003 Margaret A. Edwards Award Committee.

Recent Titles in Library and Information Science Text Series